by the same author:

MICHAEL FIELD'S COOKING SCHOOL   [1965]

Michael Field's Culinary Classics and Improvisations

MICHAEL FIELD'S
CULINARY CLASSICS
and
IMPROVISATIONS

Illustrations by

MOZELLE THOMPSON

ALFRED · A · KNOPF

New York

THIS IS A BORZOI BOOK *Published by Alfred A. Knopf, Inc.*

A portion of the Poultry section appeared in slightly different form under
the title "Turkey: Main Dish and More" in McCall's, December 1965.

Several of the recipes in the Lamb, Poultry, and Fish and Shellfish
sections appeared in McCall's, October 1967.

Manufactured in the United States of America

To Frances and Jonathan, again

Contents

Introduction   *Culinary Classics and Improvisations* is the result of a long and continuing interest in an important, and yet often neglected, area of American cooking: the transformation of leftover, cooked food from one form to another. While working on this book and investigating the cuisines of the past, I found—as I had expected I would—a wealth of dishes which literally demanded previously cooked food as a base. Never considered "leftover" dishes by their creators in the sense in which we disparagingly use the term today, they were culinary creations of great charm and originality, many of them, in fact, masterpieces.

The list of their names and origins is as tantalizing as it is endless: French *mirotons*, Polish *bigos*, Greek *moussakas*, Italian *cannelloni*, Russian *pirogs*, and scores of dishes from China, Spain, Turkey, Hungary, Persia, Armenia, and other faraway places. What the exact profiles of the original dishes were we will never know, generation after generation of cooks having modified techniques, and changed, added, or subtracted ingredients. But their general characteristics, whatever the variations played upon them, remain the same; Middle Eastern *moussakas* are still made with eggplant and minced cooked lamb or beef, and the Polish *bigos* with sauerkraut and cooked pork. And if these delicious dishes never turn out twice the same way, it is simply because they are usually improvised with the material the cook happens to have on hand.

I have approached these improvisations more formally, and needless to say, my recipes are precise, freely improvised though they are, and the results predictable. In time, of course, you may create your own improvisations—perhaps you already do. Because of this (and to underline, in effect, my own convictions) I have prefaced each chapter with theoretical, technical, and practical explanations for the best ways to re-serve, reheat, and recook specific foods.

But as inventive and skillful as you may be, there are two factors necessary for the success of these or any other improvisations. The first is that the previously cooked food be, ideally, of the highest quality; hence the use of the culinary classic as my point of departure. The classic recipes for meats, fowl, and fish, in the various forms I present them, are designed to give you the best traditional version of a representative dish of its kind. The second, and indispensable, factor is to have available the necessary amount of the previously cooked food with which to make the improvisation. How much of each classic (and most of them easily serve from six to eight people) is reserved for future dishes must be determined by you, the cook. You may decide, in fact, to make a classic for use *only* in the improvisations. If, however, the classic is planned for an occasion and you expect it might be entirely consumed, it would be wise then to cook one and a half times the amount—or even twice as much of it—thus deliberately providing yourself with enough cooked food for any number of subsequent improvisations. And by glancing through the improvisations following each classic (where the number of servings for every recipe is indicated) you can, if you wish, plan and cook ahead of time a sufficient amount of food to suit your daily or even weekly needs.

I intend this book to provide a new and adventurous approach to creative cooking based on sound culinary principles. If it in any way expands your culinary horizons, sets your sights higher and makes you more daring, I will have achieved in large measure what I set out to do.

Michael Field's Culinary Classics and Improvisations

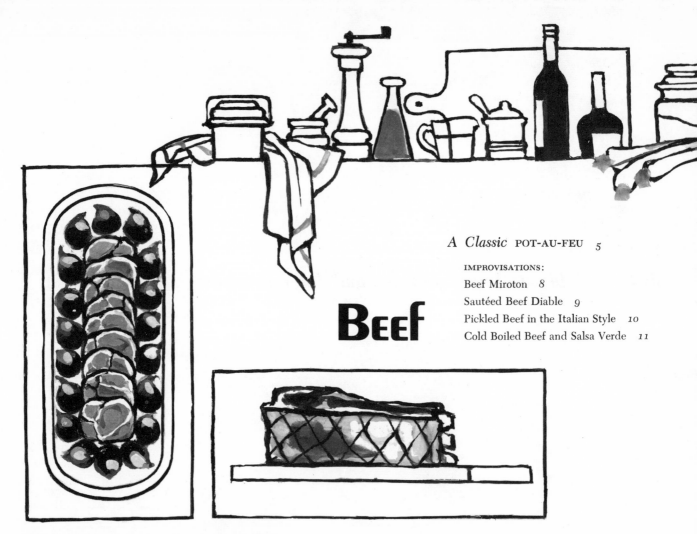

Beef

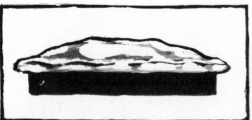

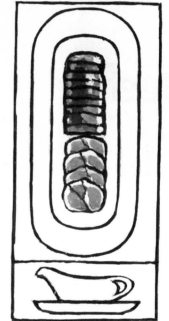

Beef

Beef When most Americans speak of meat they usually mean beef. And surely, if we have any food of which we can really be proud, it is our beef. Few grazing areas in the world produce beef with so closely grained a texture or so definite and characteristic a taste.

But expertise in raising cattle has little to do with cooking beef. Although, for the most part, we do indeed cook our superb steaks, pot roasts, and hamburgers straightforwardly and effectively, when we try to cook beef more imaginatively, the results leave much to be desired. Older cuisines offer a greater variety of subtly different beef dishes, and it is from them that much of the following material derives.

Four classical and traditional ways of cooking beef are here explored in detail: boiling, braising, roasting, and pot-roasting. Each process not only uses different cuts of beef but produces significantly different textural results. These in turn profoundly affect the methods by which these meats may be reheated or recooked.

It will be observed, no doubt, by the experienced cook, and learned, it is hoped, by the novice, that rare roast beef and rare braised fillet of beef are accorded considerably different treatment in their improvised recipes than beef which has been boiled or pot-roasted. And with good reason. Rare beef, unless it is ground or chopped, must be reheated with the utmost care whether it is sauced or not. Too much heat too quickly applied will cause the undercooked meat fibers to contract immediately, and the result, if it is edible at all, will be dry and tasteless and, more often than not, tough as well.

Boiled and pot-roasted meat, on the other hand, can be subjected to more extensive recooking. Because in both instances the initial method of cooking has assured the beef a constant supply of moist heat breaking down its tissues gently to a softer, more pliable consistency, it can even be reheated in its original form without any loss of quality. For some tastes, the reheated beef seems even better the second day, but this, of course, is questionable.

Be that as it may, boiled and pot-roasted beef can for these reasons be used interchangeably in many of the beef recipes although the blander boiled beef will necessarily require more seasoning if it is to be used in place of the better flavored pot roast.

▶ ◀

A Classic Pot-au-Feu

5-pound piece of boneless beef: *rump, cross rib, bottom round, brisket, or chuck*

2 cloves garlic, *cut into ⅛-inch slivers*

4–5 pounds beef marrow bones and 1 veal knuckle, *all sawed into 3-inch pieces*

3 quarts fresh beef stock, if available; otherwise, canned beef bouillon and canned chicken stock in equal proportions

2 tablespoons butter

4 medium yellow onions

2 large carrots, *scraped and cut into 4-inch chunks*

1 large tomato, *coarsely chopped*

A bouquet consisting of 6 parsley sprigs, 4 celery tops with leaves, 1 large bay leaf, and 1 leek (white part only), *tied together with string*

1 teaspoon thyme

12 whole black peppercorns

Salt

VEGETABLE
GARNISH

6 medium carrots, *scraped and cut into 2-inch olive shapes or cylinders*

4 medium white turnips, *peeled and quartered, or trimmed into olive shapes*

3 parsnips, *peeled and quartered*

6–8 medium leeks, if available (white parts only), *tied into a bundle*

2-pound green cabbage, *cored and quartered* (optional)

6–8 medium potatoes

The best cut of beef for a *pot-au-feu* is one which will survive 2 or 3 hours of slow cooking without shredding or falling apart. The cuts suggested here are listed in order of preference, but each has a perceptibly different texture when cooked; therefore, it is a matter of deciding, after trying the various cuts, which one you like best.

Have the meat tied securely so that it will hold its shape while cooking. With the point of a small sharp knife, make 5 or 6 incisions in the meat and into each insert a sliver of garlic; the flavor of the garlic won't be as pervasive as you might think and it will give the beef a bit more character after it is cooked.

Place the beef and bones in a soup kettle large enough to hold them comfortably and pour in 3 quarts of cold stock. If there isn't enough liquid to cover the meat and bones by about 4 inches, add more stock, or supplement it, if you must, with cold water. Bring the stock to a boil. Meanwhile, in a small heavy frying pan, melt the butter, then add the whole onions and carrot chunks. Cook the vegetables over medium heat, turning them frequently until they are as brown as you can get them without burning them. When the stock begins to boil, remove all the foam and scum from the surface with a large spoon or skimmer, and turn the heat down to the barest simmer. Skim again, then add the browned onions and carrots, the tomato, the bouquet, thyme, peppercorns, and salt to taste. Half cover the pot and simmer as slowly as possible (the surface of the stock should barely quiver) for about 2½ hours, skimming whenever necessary. The meat should be almost, but not quite done at the end of this time, but it is impossible to be precise about this; some cuts may take from ½ to 1 hour longer. However, if a fork inserted into the beef meets a slight but decided resistance, you are on safe ground. Remove the meat and bones from the pot. With a small fork or the point of a knife, scoop out the marrow from the bones before throwing them away. Save the marrow for later.

Now strain the stock through a fine sieve, or better still, through a fine sieve lined with a double thickness of cheesecloth. Let the stock rest a minute or so, then carefully skim off most, but not all of the surface fat. Scrub the pot thoroughly before pouring the stock back into it.

Add the meat and the vegetable garnish of carrots, turnips, parsnips, and the bundle of leeks. Bring the stock to a boil, then cook, uncovered, over moderate heat for 20 minutes or so, until the vegetables are tender but not falling apart. By then the meat should also be cooked through; but if you have miscalculated and it is still tough, remove the vegetables and cook the meat a little longer. Then return the vegetables to the pot to heat through. If you plan to use the cabbage, blanch it first by plunging it into a kettle of boiling salted water and letting it boil vigorously, uncovered, for about 8 minutes. Drain and add it to the *pot-au-feu* about 5 minutes or so before the other vegetables are done. The potatoes, on the other hand, should be boiled separately until done, then drained thoroughly and dried gently in a towel.

Present the *pot-au-feu* as two courses: first the soup to which you have added the cut-up marrow, a little cooked rice or *pasta,* and a sprinkling of finely chopped parsley; then a platter of the meat, sliced and surrounded with its garniture of vegetables over which you have poured a little melted butter. Serve with hot French bread, *salsa verde* (p. 11), or horseradish sauce (p. 19); or simply with a dish of coarse salt and a variety of mustards and pickles.

▶ This classic *pot-au-feu* reheats perfectly. It may therefore be made hours ahead, although the vegetable garnish, if you plan to use it, will be at its best if you cook it just before serving.

▶ Remaining vegetables from the *pot-au-feu* may be cut into matchlike strips, then heated in the broth. Sprinkled with a little finely chopped parsley and served hot, the result is an improvised consommé julienne. If there is any of the original cooked cabbage left, chop it finely, season it with salt and pepper, and spread it in small mounds on thin slices of toasted French or Italian bread. Dust a little Parmesan cheese on each mound, top with a bit of butter, and brown under the broiler for a few seconds. Serve separately with the soup or float a round in each soup plate.

▶ The *pot-au-feu* can be made the base of any soup or sauce calling for brown stock. If you have no immediate use for the extra broth, cool it, uncovered, then refrigerate in a tightly covered jar or bowl. Every four days bring it to a boil, let it cool, uncovered, then cover and refrigerate as before. More easily, of course, you can freeze it.

▶ The cold braised beef vinaigrette improvisation on page 37 can be made almost as successfully with cold boiled beef from this *pot-au-feu,* although it will lack the robustness of the braised beef's flavor.

Beef Miroton

Serves 4

8 tablespoons butter, *4 for sautéing and 4 melted for topping*

1 cup onions, *finely chopped*

2 tablespoons red wine vinegar

2 tablespoons flour

1 teaspoon thyme

1 teaspoon tomato paste

1½ **cups stock from the** *pot-au-feu* or an equivalent amount of canned beef bouillon, undiluted

A bouquet consisting of 2 sprigs parsley, 1 celery top with leaves, and 1 small bay leaf, *tied together with string*

Salt

Freshly ground black pepper

2 cups cooked potatoes (freshly boiled if possible), *sliced about ¼ inch thick*

8–12 slices boiled beef, *free of all fat and gristle and cut about ¼ inch thick*

½ cup dry bread crumbs

2 tablespoons parsley, *finely chopped*

Choose for this recipe a baking dish attractive enough to bring to the table—an oval copper or enamel one 8 or 9 inches long and about 1½ inches deep would be ideal.

Make the sauce first: over moderate heat melt in a small heavy frying pan 4 tablespoons of the butter (the other 4 should be left to melt slowly in a separate pan for later use). When the foam subsides, add the chopped onions and cook, stirring frequently, until they color lightly. Pour in 2 tablespoons of vinegar and boil briskly until the vinegar completely cooks away. Turn off the heat. Add 2 level tablespoons of flour and mix into the onions thoroughly until no trace of the flour remains. Stir in the thyme and tomato paste. With a whisk beat into this *roux* 1½ cups of stock (hot or cold) and, stirring constantly, bring it to a boil. When the sauce is smooth and thick, lower the heat, add the bouquet, some salt and freshly ground pepper, and cover the pan. Simmer slowly for about 20 minutes, stirring every now and then. If the sauce seems to be getting unmanageably thick, add a little more stock or, if you must, water. Meanwhile arrange the potato slices on a flat plate and pour 2 tablespoons of the warm melted butter over them. Let them steep in the butter until the sauce is finished. Preheat the oven to 450 degrees.

Spread a thin layer of sauce on the bottom of the baking dish and lay the slices of meat in it, letting each piece overlap slightly. Spoon the remaining sauce over the meat. Place the buttered potato slices around the meat so that they form an attractive overlapping border. Scatter the bread crumbs over the meat and moisten them with the remaining 2 tablespoons of melted butter.*

Bake in the upper third of the oven for about 10 or 15 minutes, or until the sauce begins to bubble and the bread crumbs lightly brown. Just before serving, slide under a hot broiler to brown the potatoes. Sprinkle lightly with parsley and serve directly from the dish.

* *Note:* This beef *miroton* may be prepared up to the point of its final baking, then covered with plastic wrap and refrigerated or kept in a cool place until you are ready to heat it. A *miroton* can also be improvised with slices of braised veal instead of beef.

Sautéed Beef Diable

Serves 4

MARINADE

2 tablespoons red wine vinegar	Freshly ground black pepper
½ teaspoon dry mustard	½ cup olive oil
½ teaspoon salt	2 cloves garlic, *sliced*

8–12 slices boiled beef, *about ¼ inch thick*	1½ cups fine, dry bread crumbs
3 eggs (yolks only)	3 tablespoons vegetable oil
¾ cup prepared mustard, preferably the Dijon type	2 tablespoons butter
	2 tablespoons parsley, *finely chopped*
½ cup flour	1 lemon, *quartered or cut into rounds*

In a small bowl mix the wine vinegar with the dry mustard, salt, and a few grindings of black pepper. With a wire whisk slowly beat in the olive oil and add the sliced garlic. Pour half of this marinade into a shallow glass or enamel baking dish, lay the meat slices in it in one layer, then spoon over them the remaining marinade. Let the meat steep for about 1 hour (or longer, if you like) at room temperature.

At least 1 hour or so before you plan to sauté the beef, remove the slices from the marinade and pat each one dry with paper toweling. In a small bowl stir the egg yolks briefly, then beat into them, 1 tablespoon at a time, the prepared mustard. The mixture will be fairly thick; thin it to the consistency of heavy cream by beating in as much of the marinade you think it needs.

Spread the bread crumbs on a long sheet of waxed paper. With a pastry brush paint each slice of meat heavily with the mustard mixture, then lay it on the crumbs. With the flat of a knife or a spatula pat the crumbs onto both sides of the meat slices until they are solidly coated, then place them side by side on a platter lined with waxed paper. Cover them with a second sheet and refrigerate for at least ½ hour before sautéing.

To sauté, first heat the 3 tablespoons of oil and the 2 tablespoons of butter in a large heavy frying pan. When the foam subsides, add the meat. Don't crowd the pan or you will dislodge the crumb coating. Sauté the meat rather briskly, but watch carefully for any signs of burning. When the crumbs are a golden-brown on one side, turn the slices over with a large spatula, adding more butter and oil to the pan if it seems dry. Brown the other side and deposit each slice of meat as it is finished on a heated platter; keep the meat warm in a 250-degree oven if, for any reason, dinner must wait.

Serve sprinkled lightly with finely chopped parsley and accompanied with slices or wedges of lemon.

Pickled Beef in the Italian Style

Serves 4–6

1 cup onions, *thinly sliced*
½ cup carrots, *thinly sliced*
¼ cup celery, *thinly sliced*
4 cloves garlic, *whole or thinly sliced*
½ cup white wine vinegar
¼ cup olive oil
⅓ cup dry white wine
2 cups stock from the *pot-au-feu*, *thoroughly degreased,* or an equivalent amount of fresh or canned chicken stock, *thoroughly degreased*

Lemon, *4 thin slices*
A bouquet consisting of 4 sprigs parsley and 1 large bay leaf, *tied together with string*
8 whole black peppercorns
½ teaspoon thyme
1 teaspoon salt
8–12 slices cold boiled beef, *about ¼ inch thick and trimmed of all fat and gristle*
2 tablespoons fresh chives, *finely cut,* or 2 tablespoons fresh parsley, *finely chopped*

ACCOMPANI-
MENTS
(OPTIONAL)

Pickled mushrooms
Artichoke hearts in oil
Black olives (preferably Mediterranean)

Fennel, *cut into spears*
Ripe tomatoes, *peeled and sliced*
French or Italian bread, *hot*

In a small enamel or stainless-steel saucepan combine the sliced onions, carrots, celery, green pepper, and garlic. Add the wine vinegar and bring it to a boil, stirring constantly with a wooden spoon until the wine almost completely evaporates. Be careful not to let the vegetables burn. Add the olive oil, white wine, stock, lemon slices, bouquet, peppercorns, thyme, and salt. Bring the liquid to a boil, then turn down the heat, half cover the pan, and simmer the marinade for about 20 minutes, or until the vegetables are tender but not too soft. Taste for salt at this point; to be most effective, the marinade should be highly seasoned.

Lay the meat slices side by side in a flameproof enamel or glass baking dish and pour in the hot marinade, spooning the vegetables evenly over the top of the meat. Over moderate heat, bring the marinade almost but not quite to the boil, then turn the heat down and let the meat simmer slowly for about 5 minutes. Cool to room temperature, cover securely with plastic wrap or waxed paper, and refrigerate. Let the meat marinate for at least a day before serving, though for some tastes even 3 or 4 days is not too long. In any case, the meat gains in flavor as it stands. If you have used the stock from the *pot-au-feu*, the marinade will, in all likelihood, stiffen into jelly when it is cold. Serve it with the meat, with or without the marinating vegetables, as you prefer. But be sure to sprinkle the meat at the last moment with the fresh chives or parsley. Suitable and colorful accompaniments might consist of pickled mushrooms, artichoke hearts in oil, black olives, spears of fresh fennel, slices of ripe tomatoes (peeled), and the like. Hot Italian or French bread is certainly a must with this.

Cold Boiled Beef and Salsa Verde

Serves 4

8–12 slices cold boiled beef, *about ¼ inch thick and trimmed of all fat and gristle*

SALSA VERDE

2 tablespoons shallots or scallions, *finely chopped*
1 teaspoon garlic, *finely chopped*
4 flat anchovies, *drained and finely chopped*
2 tablespoons capers, *drained, washed, dried, and finely chopped*

3 tablespoons parsley, *finely chopped*
3 tablespoons lemon juice, *strained*
4 tablespoons olive oil
Salt
Freshly ground black pepper

The secret of this extraordinary sauce is to chop all its ingredients as finely as possible. No particular flavor should predominate, as would most assuredly be the case were the shallots or scallions, garlic, anchovies, or parsley too coarsely minced. The finished sauce should have almost the appearance and texture of a purée.

Combine the shallots or scallions, garlic, anchovies, and capers and moisten them with the lemon juice and olive oil. Mix gently, then season quite highly with freshly ground black pepper and somewhat more discreetly with salt, remembering that anchovies can be quite salty.

Remove the beef from the refrigerator at least an hour before serving; it will have more flavor at room temperature. Serve the sauce separately.

A Classic Braised Fillet of Beef ▶◀

5 tablespoons butter, 3 *for sautéing vegetables and 2 for browning fillet*
1 cup onions, *finely chopped*
½ cup carrots, *finely chopped*
½ cup celery, *finely chopped*
1 small leek (white part only), *finely chopped*
3 tablespoons vegetable oil
3½–4 pounds fillet of beef
2½ cups fresh brown stock or 1½ cups canned beef bouillon and 1 cup canned chicken stock

1 cup dry Madeira
A bouquet consisting of 4 sprigs parsley and 1 large bay leaf, *tied together with string*
½ teaspoon thyme
Salt
Freshly ground black pepper
2 teaspoons arrowroot dissolved in 2 tablespoons Madeira (optional)

So that your fillet of beef will baste itself internally as it cooks, have it larded with 3 or 4 strips of larding pork. If the butcher can't or won't do this for you, ask him to bard it instead—that is, have the fillet wrapped in a thin sheet of pork, veal, or beef fat. Whether the fillet is larded or barded, it should be tied securely at 1-inch intervals to help keep its shape as it cooks.

Preheat the oven to 350 degrees. In a heavy casserole just large enough to hold the fillet comfortably, melt 3 tablespoons of the butter. When the foam subsides, add the chopped onions, carrots, celery, and leek, and cook over low heat, stirring occasionally, until the vegetables are soft and ever so lightly colored. This should take about 10 minutes. Meanwhile, heat 3 tablespoons of vegetable oil and the remaining 2 tablespoons of butter in a large, heavy frying pan.

When the fat is almost smoking, add the fillet and brown it rapidly on all sides, then transfer it to the bed of vegetables in the casserole. Pour in the Madeira and stock, and add more stock if necessary; the liquid should come about a third of the way up the sides of the meat. Finally, add the bouquet and the thyme and, after sprinkling the meat with salt and pepper, insert a meat thermometer in the exact center of the fillet. Be sure that the point of the thermometer comes to rest halfway through the meat. Bring the stock to a boil on top of the stove, then drape a sheet of foil or double thickness of waxed paper loosely over the meat and cover the casserole tightly. Place it in the lower third of the oven, where it should cook slowly for 35 to 40 minutes. Baste the fillet every 10 minutes and check the thermometer after 30 minutes. When it reads 137 degrees the meat will be rare; 140, medium rare—under no circumstances allow the fillet to cook beyond that. Remove the casserole from the oven and carefully transfer the fillet to a heated platter. Cut away the strings. The beef will be considerably easier to carve if you let it rest for about 8 minutes while you prepare the sauce.

Tip the casserole and with a large spoon skim the braising sauce of as much of its surface fat as you can. Then quickly bring the sauce to a boil on top of the stove, and let it continue to boil until it has reduced to about a third of its original volume. If you feel after tasting the sauce that its flavor is sufficiently intense before that point, remove the casserole from the heat sooner. Taste again for seasoning and thicken the sauce, if you like, by adding 2 teaspoons of arrowroot dissolved in 2 tablespoons of Madeira and bringing it almost but not quite to a boil. Pour the sauce, strained or not as you prefer, into a sauceboat, and serve with the fillet, sliced about ½ inch thick.

▶ For this classic braised fillet of beef a meat thermometer is almost obligatory, but unfortunately few domestic types can be trusted. If at the end of 45 minutes you cannot obtain a reading on the thermometer, remove the meat from the oven at once. The likelihood is that the fillet may be a little more well done than you would have preferred it, but at least not so overdone as to make it inedible.

▶ The improvisations on the classic braised fillet of beef and roast beef recipes can be used interchangeably, although it is important to recognize that the texture of the fillet is considerably softer than that of the roast beef. And any leftover steak, should you have some on hand, may be used as a substitute for either of them, remembering that the cooked steak will be the firmest textured of the three.
▶ Mix cubes of boiled or braised beef into a freshly made potato salad (p. 112, omitting the corned beef) dressed with French dressing, thinly sliced scallions, and chopped fresh herbs—basil, dill, or parsley.

IMPROVISATIONS

Fillet of Beef Stroganoff

Serves 4

6 tablespoons butter, *3 for the roux and 3 for sautéing the shallots or scallions, garlic, and mushrooms*

2 tablespoons flour

1 teaspoon tomato paste

1½ cups stock: either **unthickened leftover Madeira sauce from the fillet** combined with fresh or canned beef stock, or all fresh or canned beef bouillon

3 tablespoons shallots or scallions, *finely chopped*

½ teaspoon garlic, *finely chopped*

½ pound mushrooms, *thinly sliced*

½ teaspoon lemon juice

½–¾ cup sour cream

3 tablespoons fresh dill, *finely chopped*

16–20 thin strips cold braised fillet of beef, *1 by 2 inches each*

Salt

⅛ teaspoon cayenne

1 tablespoon parsley, *finely chopped* (optional)

The basic sauce for this dish may be made hours ahead and simply reheated with a finishing touch or two added just before serving.

Slowly melt 3 tablespoons of the butter in a large frying pan without letting it brown. Off the heat stir in 2 level tablespoons of flour and return the pan to the heat. Then, stirring almost constantly, brown the flour lightly, taking particular care not to let it burn. When this *roux* is delicately colored, mix into it the tomato paste and pour into the pan, all at once, the 1½ cups of hot or cold stock. Bring slowly to a boil over moderate heat, beating all the while with a wire whisk, until the sauce is very thick and smooth. Turn the heat down to the barest simmer and let the sauce cook slowly while you prepare the mushrooms.

Heat the remaining 3 tablespoons of butter in a medium-sized frying pan; when the foam subsides, stir in the chopped shallots or scallions and garlic. Cook slowly for a few minutes until the shallots are soft and translucent, then add the sliced mushrooms. Sprinkle them with the lemon juice, raise the heat and cook briskly, stirring, until the mushrooms are barely cooked through, a matter of 3 or 4 minutes at the most. With a rubber spatula scrape the entire contents of the pan into the stroganoff sauce, and stir in 2 tablespoons of the chopped dill. Simmer the sauce for about 5 minutes, then put it aside until you are ready to serve the completed dish.

At that point, heat the sauce again. As soon as it reaches the boiling point, turn the heat down to the barest simmer. Add the strips of beef and turn them over in the hot sauce until they are heated through, but under no circumstances let them cook in the sauce. Then, with a wire whisk or small wooden spoon, stir into the simmering sauce ½ cup of the sour cream, mixing it in about 1 tablespoon at a time. If the sauce seems excessively thick, thin it with a few more tablespoons of sour cream or, if you prefer, with a little stock. Add the cayenne. Taste for salt, then transfer the beef stroganoff to a heated serving dish. Sprinkle the top with a little more chopped dill or parsley and serve with buttered noodles or rice.

Fillet of Beef Bourguignon

Serves 4

½ pound salt pork (mildly cured, if possible), *cut into ¼-inch dice*

12 small white onions, about 1 inch in diameter, *peeled*

Salt

Freshly ground black pepper

1½ cups dry red wine (a French Burgundy or an American Pinot Noir)

2 tablespoons shallots or scallions, *finely chopped*

½ teaspoon garlic, *finely chopped*

1 small carrot, *finely chopped (about 1 tablespoon)*

2 tablespoons flour

1 teaspoon tomato paste

1½ cups stock: either **unthickened leftover**

Madeira sauce from the fillet combined with fresh or canned beef stock, or all fresh or canned beef bouillon

½ teaspoon thyme

A bouquet consisting of 3 sprigs parsley, 1 celery top with leaves, and 1 bay leaf, *tied together with string*

4 tablespoons butter, *2 for sautéing mushrooms and 2 softened for the sauce*

½ pound mushrooms, *whole if small, quartered or sliced otherwise*

¼ teaspoon lemon juice

16–20 strips cold braised fillet of beef, *1 by 2 inches*

2 tablespoons parsley, *finely chopped*

This *bourguignon* sauce and its garniture of onions and mushrooms may be made hours ahead and simply reheated with the fillet of beef just before serving.

Make the onion garniture first. Preheat the oven to 350 degrees. Render the diced salt pork by frying it in a heavy frying pan until the bits become brown and crisp; then scoop them up with a slotted spoon and put them aside until later in a small bowl lined with paper toweling to absorb any excess fat. Heat the rendered fat in the frying pan until it almost smokes. Drop in the peeled small white onions and shake the pan with a back-and-forth motion so that the onions roll around in the fat and brown on all sides. Don't work too hard at this; it is almost impossible to brown them evenly. Remove the onions with a slotted spoon and arrange them in a small baking dish in one layer. Pour into the dish 5 or 6 tablespoons of the pork fat, sprinkle the onions lightly with salt and pepper, and bake them in the center of the oven for about 30 minutes, or until they are tender but not falling apart. Turn the onions over from time to time, and when you test them for tenderness use the point of a small sharp knife rather than a fork. When they are done, remove them to a dish lined with paper toweling.

Begin the sauce by bringing the 1½ cups of wine to a boil in an enamel pan and letting it boil briskly, uncovered, until the wine has reduced to 1 cup. Meanwhile, remove all but 3 tablespoons of pork fat from the frying pan. (If by some mischance there isn't enough of the original rendered fat left in the pan, add some butter.) Over moderate heat slowly cook the chopped shallots or scallions, garlic, and carrots in the fat. When the vegetables have colored lightly, take the pan from the heat and stir in 2 level tablespoons of flour. Return the pan to the heat again and, stirring almost constantly, cook the *roux* only long enough to brown the flour lightly. Be careful not to let it burn. Stir in the tomato paste and then pour into the pan the reduced wine and the stock. Bring the sauce to a boil, beating all the while with a wire whisk; when it is quite smooth and thick, reduce the heat to the barest simmer. Add the thyme and the bouquet. Season the sauce lightly with salt and freshly ground black pepper and simmer with the pan half covered for about 20 minutes. If at any point the sauce seems to be getting too thick, thin it with a little stock—never, it must be added, with uncooked wine. Meanwhile prepare the mushrooms by heating 2 tablespoons of the butter in a frying pan and sautéing the mushrooms lightly for 3 or 4 minutes until they are barely cooked through. Put them aside in a small bowl.

When the sauce is finished, remove the bouquet and add the previously prepared onions and the sautéed mushrooms. Just before serving, heat the sauce to boiling, then turn the heat down to the barest simmer. Add the strips of beef and cook them only long enough to heat them through; cooking them longer may toughen them. Taste the sauce for seasoning, then gently stir in the 2 tablespoons of soft butter. Sprinkle the beef *bourguignon* with chopped parsley and serve with either boiled potatoes, noodles, or rice.

Fillet of Beef with Mushrooms and Ham en Papillote

Serves 4

6 tablespoons butter, *4 for the duxelles and 2 softened for buttering papillotes*

3 tablespoons shallots or scallions, *finely chopped*

¾ pound mushrooms, *finely chopped (about 3 cups)*

Salt

Freshly ground black pepper

¼ teaspoon lemon juice

1 tablespoon parsley, *finely chopped*

⅓ cup Madeira

¼ cup braising sauce from the original fillet or ¼ cup canned beef bouillon

4 slices cold rare fillet, *about ½ inch thick*

8 thin (⅛-inch thick) slices of boiled or smoked ham, *cut to the same size as the fillets of beef*

Any remaining Madeira sauce from the fillet or béarnaise sauce (p. 221) (optional)

First make the *duxelles,* the classic French mushroom-shallot mixture. Melt 4 tablespoons of butter in a large enamel or stainless-steel frying pan and stir in the chopped shallots or scallions. Sauté for 1 or 2 minutes, then add the mushrooms and simmer them slowly until they give off some of their juices. Let the liquid cook almost entirely away. When the mushrooms are quite dry but not brown, pour the Madeira and stock over them, raise the heat, and again—but this time briskly—cook all the liquid away, stirring constantly. Remove the pan from the heat. Season with the lemon juice, chopped parsley, and salt and pepper to taste, then spoon the finished *duxelles* into a small bowl and cool.

Lay 4 large sheets of parchment paper or aluminum foil on top of each other and cut them into heart shapes 12½ inches wide and 8½ inches long. Brush each heart with 1 teaspoon of softened butter, fold the paper lengthwise to make a crease down the center, then place a slice of ham on each of the half ovals. Spread each ham slice with a thick layer of *duxelles,* cover with a lightly salted slice of fillet, spread some more *duxelles* on the fillet, and top with a slice of ham. Enclose this edifice by folding over it the other half of the oval, then crimp the edges of the paper together as securely as you can. Put the papillotes aside until you are ready to cook them.

Preheat the oven to 450 degrees. Lightly butter or oil a baking sheet and arrange papillotes on it, one next to the other. Place the pan in the center of the oven for about 8 minutes, or just long enough to heat the fillet through without actually cooking it. Cut the papillotes open at the table and serve with a sauceboat of either Madeira sauce (from the original fillet) or béarnaise sauce (p. 221).

Note: To vary this, you might include in each papillote a thin slice of Gruyère, fontina, bel paese, or taleggio cheese. Place the cheese between the ham and the fillet, then proceed as described above.

Sliced Fillet of Beef in Madeira Aspic with a Garniture of Vegetables and Watercress

Serves 4

¼ cup cold beef or chicken stock or water

1 envelope unflavored gelatin

2 cups stock: **any remaining unthickened, strained sauce from the original fillet** plus fresh or canned beef stock, or equal parts of canned beef bouillon and chicken stock

1 small bay leaf

¼ teaspoon lemon juice

½ teaspoon tomato paste

6 whole black peppercorns

¼ teaspoon thyme

Salt

2 egg whites

3 tablespoons Madeira

8 slices rare cold fillet of beef, *about ¼ inch thick*

8–12 small white onions, *braised and cooled* (see p. 31)

12 thin rounds of carrots, *cooked and cooled*

½ package frozen artichoke hearts, *cooked and cooled*

Watercress

No matter how attractive they may look, most so-called aspics are pallid, tasteless affairs. But this one has decided character and is well worth the extra effort it takes to prepare.

Soften the envelope of gelatin in ¼ cup of stock (thoroughly degreased) or cold water. Meanwhile measure the 2 cups of stock (in either of the suggested combinations) into a deep saucepan, making absolutely certain that there isn't a particle of grease floating around in the stock. Stir in the softened gelatin, the bay leaf, lemon juice, tomato paste, peppercorns, and thyme. Season quite highly with salt, remembering that cold deadens the flavor of food and the aspic seasonings will flatten out considerably when the aspic is set. To clarify the aspic, beat the egg whites to a froth and, just before they stiffen, mix them into the stock. Stirring constantly with a wire whisk, bring this mixture to a boil over moderate heat. Cook and stir it until the liquid begins to rise in the pot and threatens to boil over; whisk once or twice more, then turn off the heat and let the froth subside. Don't disturb the pot for at least 5 minutes. Meanwhile place a fine-meshed sieve over a small but deep bowl—deep enough so that the bottom of the sieve will not touch the surface of the liquid after it has drained through. Line the sieve with a kitchen towel that has been moistened with cold water and wrung dry. Pour the hot aspic, egg white and all, into it and don't disturb the mixture until the now brilliantly clear aspic has dripped through. Remove the sieve and stir in the Madeira. Cool, in or out of the refrigerator, but don't let the aspic set. (If it does, of course you may reheat it again to return it to its liquid state.)

Select a small attractive platter with an inch or so indentation or well and chill it. Arrange the slices of fillet down the center of the platter and let each slice overlap the other. Sprinkle the meat lightly with salt. Place the onions, carrot rounds, and artichoke hearts around the meat, alternating or arranging the vegetables to suit your decorative fancy. Spoon the cold but still liquid aspic over the meat and vegetables, covering them as completely as possible. Refrigerate until set, a matter of a couple of hours at the most. Any remaining aspic may be poured into a shallow pan, chilled until set, then cut up or chopped and used as further decoration.

When the platter of aspic is set, arrange small bouquets of watercress around it and serve with a rice (p. 125) or French potato salad (p. 112) and hot French or Italian bread.

▶ ◀

A Classic Roast Beef in the English Style

6-pound roast beef: *either prime ribs, boneless sirloin, or the first cut of eye round*	1 tablespoon salt
1 teaspoon freshly ground black pepper	2 teaspoons rosemary, *crumbled*

HORSERADISH SAUCE (OPTIONAL)	2 tablespoons lemon juice or wine vinegar	Salt
	2–3 tablespoons fresh horseradish, *grated*, or 4 tablespoons bottled horseradish, *drained and squeezed dry in a towel*	½ cup heavy cream, *stiffly whipped*

Ask the butcher for a well-aged roast with at least a 1-inch-thick layer of its own fat or a ½-inch sheet of barding fat wrapped around the meat and securely tied. If you have bought a rib roast (2 ribs will come to about 6 pounds after trimming), have the short ribs removed, roast them with the beef, and use them another day in one of the improvisation recipes. If you have bought a rib roast, don't have it boned but ask the butcher to remove the chine or backbone and tie it back on.

Apart from contributing its flavor, the bone will give the meat a natural platform upon which to rest and will make for easier carving. A simple sirloin beef or eye round need only be tied in 1-inch intervals along its length so that it will better keep its shape.

For best results use a meat thermometer. Roast timings based on weight are unpredictable and depend upon factors you can't always control: the thickness of the meat, the accuracy of your oven, even how well insulated it is.

Preheat the oven to 500 degrees, remembering that most ovens take anywhere from 15 to 20 minutes to reach this temperature. Meanwhile, rub the combined salt, pepper, and rosemary into the beef. Place the roast on a rack in a shallow pan just large enough to hold it, and slide the pan into the center of the oven. Roast undisturbed for 20 minutes. Then turn the heat down to 350 degrees and continue to roast, without basting, for about 1 hour or longer, or until the thermometer reads 130 degrees. The beef will be rare when it is served.

If you prefer it more done, let the roast cook until the thermometer reads 140 degrees for medium or 150 degrees for well done (however, it should be mentioned that several of the improvisations call for *rare* beef and so it might be wise not to cook the roast too well done all the way through). These readings are predicated on the assumption that the beef will be allowed to rest for 15 minutes after it is removed from the oven. Because the meat will firm up as it stands, it will be easier to carve and, contrary to what one might expect, it will not cool as it waits but will continue to cook internally. When it is served, the meat should be exactly at the state of doneness desired. Serve it with its own juices or, if you like, with an English horseradish sauce made by mixing together 2 tablespoons of lemon juice or vinegar, the horseradish, a little salt, and ½ cup of cream, stiffly whipped.

▶ If you plan to make the roast beef *au poivre* (p. 22) or the roast beef *tartare* (p. 26), carve your classic roast beef at dinner first at one end for a bit and then at the other. Unorthodox as this may appear, it will assure your saving a really rare piece of beef (the center portion of any undercooked roast will be rarer in the center than at the ends) for the improvisations that call for this.

▶ Any small chunks of leftover beef may be cut into ½-inch cubes, speared with decorative picks, and arranged upright in a shallow dish of *salsa verde* (p. 11). And small pieces of leftover beef can be finely chopped and mixed with *salsa verde* and used as a sandwich filling, or, for that matter, as a canapé spread. Top the canapés with a rolled anchovy, stuffed olive, or strip of pimiento.

IMPROVISATIONS

Roast Beef Hash

Serves 4

5 tablespoons butter, *3 for sautéing onions and pepper and 2 for cooking hash*

6 tablespoons onions, *finely chopped*

3 tablespoons green pepper, *chopped*

2 cups cold roast beef, *free of all fat and gristle and finely chopped, not ground*

3 cups cooked baking potatoes, *freshly boiled, cooled, and coarsely chopped*

5 tablespoons beef or chicken stock, fresh or canned

Salt

Freshly ground black pepper

2 tablespoons Worcestershire sauce

1 tablespoon vegetable oil

2 tablespoons parsley, *finely chopped*

Melt 3 tablespoons of butter in a 10-inch heavy frying pan and over moderate heat cook the chopped onions and green pepper for about 5 minutes, or just long enough for them to soften without browning. Scrape them into a large mixing bowl. Add the roast beef, potatoes, stock, salt, and freshly ground black pepper to taste, and the Worcestershire sauce. Mix gently but thoroughly with your hands or with two forks. Cover the bowl and let the hash rest for a few minutes to allow the meat and potatoes to absorb the liquid and seasonings.

To cook the hash, heat in the frying pan 2 tablespoons of butter and 1 tablespoon of oil. When the fat is hot but not sizzling, add the hash, patting it down into the pan gently with a large spatula. Cook over moderate heat for about 40 minutes, shaking the pan every now and then to make sure the hash isn't sticking to the bottom. As it cooks, the hash will inevitably produce some fat; tip the pan and skim it from the sides with a small spoon or, better still, with a bulb baster. During the last 10 minutes of cooking, to remove any extra fat, lay a double thickness of paper toweling on top like a blotter, pressing it down on the hash. Repeat this blotting procedure as often as you think necessary.

To serve, have ready a large circular heated platter. If you prefer to fold the hash over omelette fashion, under no circumstances attempt this maneuver unless you are certain the hash hasn't stuck to the bottom of the pan, which, more often than not, it tends to do. A far more reliable procedure is to place the platter on top of the frying pan and turn the hash out. If, by some chance, part of the crust sticks to the pan, remove it with a spatula and patch it into place. Sprinkle the top with the chopped parsley and serve the hash either alone or with a variety of condiments, such as mustard, pickles, horseradish, and the like.

Sautéed Roast Beef au Poivre

Serves 4

4 slices very rare roast beef, *½ inch to ¾ inch thick*
Salt
2 tablespoons whole black peppercorns
8 tablespoons butter (¼ pound)
½ cup sifted flour

4 tablespoons olive oil
¼ cup cognac
½ cup beef stock, fresh or canned
2 teaspoons lemon juice
1 tablespoon chives or parsley, *minced*

Crush the black peppercorns in a mortar with a pestle or wrap them in a kitchen towel or a double piece of cheesecloth and press a rolling pin back and forth over them. However you do it, the peppercorns should be coarsely crushed when you have finished, not reduced to a powder. Salt each piece of beef lightly, then with the heel of your hand firmly press as much of the peppercorns as you can into both sides of the meat. Curiously enough, the pepper will not make the flavor of the meat as biting as you would think, only pleasantly aromatic. Cream the butter by beating it with a wooden spoon until it is soft, smooth, and light in color. Put aside about half of it and carefully and generously spread the other half over the pepper encrusted slices of beef. Refrigerate between pieces of waxed paper until ready to cook, at least 1 hour. The longer the beef mellows the more flavor it will have.

Since the sautéing of the beef must be done in the shortest possible time if it is not to toughen, it is wise to have a serving platter and plates heating in a 250-degree oven before you begin cooking. Also have the other ingredients immediately at hand so that you can carry through the whole simple operation without any interruption.

Heat the olive oil in a large heavy frying pan until it literally begins to smoke. Quickly dip the beef slices in the sifted flour, gently shake off any excess, and cook the beef no longer than a minute or two on each side. During this time, they should acquire a lightly brown crust and be thoroughly heated through. Arrange them, each slice slightly overlapping, on the heated platter, and keep them warm in the oven while you complete the sauce. Pour off most of the oil in the pan and to the remainder add the cognac. Bring this to a boil over high heat, and after it has boiled away completely add the beef stock. Boil rapidly for 1 or 2 minutes until it has reduced to about half, then remove the pan from the heat, add the lemon juice, minced chives or parsley, and the remaining creamed butter. Tip the pan back and forth until the butter melts, add a few pinches of salt, and pour the sauce over the beef. Serve at once.

Broiled Deviled Roast Beef Rib Bones

Serves 2–4

Roasted rib bones with some meat adhering to them

Short ribs, if you have roasted them with the original beef roast

1 tablespoon salt
½ teaspoon freshly ground black pepper
¼ cup red wine vinegar
} *combined*

½ cup Dijon or Düsseldorf mustard
2 cups fine bread crumbs
¼ pound butter (8 tablespoons), *melted*
Lemon quarters
Watercress

If your rib roast has been carved too close to the bone and there is no beef left, there is little point in preparing this dish. And that goes for the short ribs, too. But even a minimum amount of meat left on the bones makes broiling them worthwhile.

A few hours before you plan to cook them, arrange the bones on a rack set over a shallow roasting or jelly-roll pan. Combine the salt, pepper, and vinegar, and with a pastry brush moisten the bones and meat thoroughly. Let them stand about 10 minutes, then with the same brush spread them with the mustard. Now sprinkle the bones with the bread crumbs, making sure that every area of the bone is covered. Refrigerate for 1 hour or so, or until ready to use.

Preheat the broiler to its highest point, or if you prefer to roast the bones, preheat the oven to 500–550 degrees. Sprinkle the melted butter over the breaded bones and either bake them (for about 15 minutes) or broil them (for about 10 minutes) until a fine brown crust has formed and the meat and bones are as hot as you can get them without burning them. Serve at once with lemon quarters and watercress.

Beef with Water Chestnuts and Shredded Cabbage

Serves 4

5 tablespoons peanut oil, *2 for the sauce base and 3 for cooking the cabbage*
1 teaspoon garlic, *finely chopped*
1¾–2 cups chicken stock, fresh or canned
½ teaspoon ginger root, *finely chopped* (optional)
3 tablespoons soy sauce
2 teaspoons cornstarch
1 small can water chestnuts, *drained and thinly sliced*

2 **cups cooked roast beef,** *trimmed of all fat and cut into approximately 1½-inch chunks*
4 cups green cabbage, *finely shredded*
½ cup scallions, *finely sliced, including at least 2 inches of the green stem*
2 tablespoons parsley, *finely chopped*
Boiled rice

Combine in a 10-inch heavy frying pan 2 tablespoons of the peanut oil, the garlic, 1 cup of the chicken stock, the ginger root (optional), and soy sauce. Bring this to a boil, then let it simmer as slowly as possible with the pan half covered for about 10 minutes. Meanwhile dissolve the 2 level teaspoons of cornstarch in ¼ cup of cold chicken stock or water and stir it into the simmering sauce. Stirring almost constantly, cook the sauce for 3 minutes longer, or until it becomes clear and somewhat thickened. Add the sliced water chestnuts and the cold roast beef. Simmer the meat in the sauce only long enough—perhaps 10 minutes—to heat it through without actually cooking it. Meanwhile mix into the shredded cabbage the remaining 3 tablespoons of oil and ¾ cup of chicken stock. Bring this to a boil in a small saucepan, cover, and cook the cabbage over moderate heat for about 5 minutes. It must retain more than a hint of its original crispness. Strain it through a sieve (save and use the cooking stock for another purpose, if you like) and spread the cabbage evenly over a hot serving platter. Quickly pour over it the entire contents of the frying pan—beef, water chestnuts, and all the sauce. Sprinkle the top with the sliced scallions and chopped parsley and serve at once with a large bowl of hot, dry boiled rice.

Paupiettes of Beef in the French Style

Serves 4

8 slices rare roast beef, *at least 5 inches in diameter and cut about ¼ inch thick*

½ pound well-seasoned fresh sausage meat

2 tablespoons onions, *finely chopped*

3–4 chicken livers

3 tablespoons cognac

¾ cup bread crumbs

2 tablespoons heavy cream

1 egg, *lightly beaten*

2 tablespoons parsley, *finely chopped*

1 teaspoon lemon juice

Salt

Freshly ground black pepper

⅓ cup Dijon or Düsseldorf mustard

2 tablespoons vegetable oil

3 tablespoons butter

Lemon quarters

Trim the roast beef of all fat and gristle. Piece by piece, pound them between two sheets of waxed paper with the flat of a butcher's cleaver or wooden meat mallet until they are quite thin. Be careful not to let them tear.

Fry the sausage meat, starting it in a cold frying pan set over moderate heat. Break the meat up with a fork as it begins to cook. When the meat is quite brown, drain it of all its fat by straining it through a sieve set over a small bowl. Reserving the sausage in a mixing bowl, return 2 tablespoons of the pork fat to the frying pan, and over moderate heat cook the chopped onions for about 4 minutes. Scrape them into the bowl with the sausage and add 2 more tablespoons of fat to the pan. Heat this almost to smoking, add the chicken livers and fry them for about 3 minutes, or until they are quite brown on the outside but still pink within. Remove the pan from the heat and flame the livers with the cognac. This is best done by heating the cognac in a small pan or ladle, setting it alight with a match and pouring it over the livers. Shake the pan back and forth until the flame dies out. Chop the livers coarsely and add them, with all the pan drippings, to the sausage and onion mixture. Soak 4 tablespoons of bread crumbs in 2 tablespoons of cream and add to the bowl, as well as a lightly beaten egg. With a large fork mix the stuffing gently but thoroughly together. Add the chopped parsley, lemon juice, and salt, and freshly ground black pepper to taste.

Divide the stuffing among the 8 slices of beef and roll them up, tucking in the ends to form neat little cylinders. With a pastry brush thoroughly paint each *paupiette* with the mustard, then roll them in the remaining bread crumbs, making sure they are heavily and completely coated. Refrigerate for at least 1 hour before cooking.

To cook, heat the oil and butter in a large heavy frying pan until the foam subsides. Add the *paupiettes* and fry them over as intense heat as possible without letting them burn. Turn them with tongs in the hot fat as they cook, and within 4 or 5 minutes they should have a fine brown crust and be completely heated through. Try not to overcook them or the beef may toughen. Serve at once with lemon quarters.

Roast Beef Tartare

Serves 4	**2 cups *very rare* roast beef**	1 tablespoon parsley, *finely chopped*
	2 eggs (yolks only)	2 tablespoons capers, *drained, washed, and dried*
	⅓ cup scallions or white onions, *finely chopped*	
	½ teaspoon garlic, *finely chopped*	1 teaspoon lemon juice
	1 tablespoon Worcestershire sauce	1½ teaspoons salt
	⅛ teaspoon Tabasco	Freshly ground black pepper

GARNISH	4 eggs (yolks only)	Capers, *washed and dried*
(OPTIONAL)	½ cup scallions or white onions, *finely chopped*	Lemon wedges
	Parsley, *finely chopped*	Watercress
	8–12 rolled anchovies	Hot buttered toast or black bread

For those who like the flavor of the classic steak *tartare* but object to the texture of raw beef, this version with the beef ever so slightly cooked makes a fine alternative. Naturally, the original roast beef must have been cooked only to the rare state, if the dish is to be truly successful.

Trim the beef of every bit of its fat and sinews. Cut away, too, the outer, well-cooked portions of the beef and put them aside for another purpose. Only the red center of the roasted beef should be used. With the sharpest of knives dice the beef as finely as you can without mashing it. And don't, under any circumstances, be tempted to grind it: the meat will simply disintegrate.

In a small mixing bowl, gently mix together the meat, egg yolks, scallions or white onions, garlic, Worcestershire sauce, Tabasco, parsley, capers, lemon juice, salt, and pepper. Taste for seasoning and form the beef into 4 plump rounds. These may now be served on individual plates with a small dusting of chopped parsley or, more elaborately, with an egg yolk nestling in the center of each patty. Part or all of the optional garniture may be passed around in small dishes and bottles of Worcestershire sauce, Tabasco, and mustard should be available for those who prefer their beef highly seasoned. Hot buttered toast or black bread and cold beer make fine accompaniments.

A Salad of Celery Root and Roast Beef in Mustard Mayonnaise

Serves 4

1½ pounds celery root (also called celeriac), *peeled, washed, dried, and cut into julienne strips about ⅛ inch thick and 1 inch long (approximately 2 cups)*

1–1½ **cups cold rare roast beef,** *trimmed of all fat and gristle and cut into julienne strips about ¼ inch wide and 1 inch long*

1 cup freshly made mayonnaise (p. 218) or prepared commercial mayonnaise

2 teaspoons Dijon or Düsseldorf mustard

½ teaspoon English dry mustard

1 teaspoon lemon juice

4–6 tablespoons heavy cream

Salt

Cayenne

Romaine or Boston lettuce

1 egg, *hard-cooked and coarsely chopped*

1 tablespoon parsley, *finely chopped*

The success of this salad will depend on how well you have seasoned your mayonnaise. Freshly made mayonnaise is, of course, to be preferred, but a good, unsweetened commercial variety will do if it must. In either case, mix the mustards (more than the amounts specified, if you like) and lemon juice into the mayonnaise, then thin it by beating in the heavy cream a tablespoon at a time until the sauce is fluid enough to run lazily off a spoon when it is lifted out of the bowl. Taste for seasoning and add as much salt and cayenne as you think it needs.

In a large mixing bowl combine the julienned celery root, roast beef, and mayonnaise, and gently mix them together with a large spoon until the celery root and beef are well coated. Let it rest, covered with plastic wrap, for at least 1 hour before serving. Stir it every now and then. It can be refrigerated if you wish, but the salad will have far more flavor if it is served at room temperature.

When ready to serve, spoon the celery root and beef mixture onto crisp lettuce arranged in a large glass salad bowl. Sprinkle the top with the coarsely chopped egg and dust lightly with chopped parsley.

Cold Roast Beef au Poivre with Fresh Figs or Melon

Serves 4–6

4–8 slices rare roast beef, *trimmed of all fat and cut about ½ inch thick*
Salt
2 tablespoons black peppercorns

8 ripe fresh figs or eight ½-inch-thick slices of ripe honeydew, cantaloupe, Persian, or casaba melon, *peeled*

Prepare the roast beef slices precisely as described in the recipe on page 22 for sautéed roast beef *au poivre,* omitting the butter and flour, and of course, the cooking process.

Let the beef absorb the pepper flavor for 1 hour or even longer. Then serve the meat on a platter surrounded by the figs or chilled melon slices.

Roast Beef Vinaigrette with French Potato Salad

Serves 4–6

The roast beef is prepared exactly as for cold braised beef vinaigrette (p. 37). The recipe for the French potato salad is given on page 112.

▶ ◀

A Classic Yankee Pot Roast

Serves 6

5 pounds of rump, bottom round, or chuck: *not less than 5 inches around and encased in a ¼-inch layer of fat*
1 clove garlic, *cut into four or five ⅛-inch slivers*
½ pound fresh pork fat, *rendered,* or 3 tablespoons vegetable oil and 2 tablespoons butter
3 tablespoons butter
1½ cups onions, *coarsely chopped*

1 cup carrots, *coarsely chopped*
1 large tomato, *cut into quarters*
A bouquet of 5 sprigs parsley, 1 leek (white part only), 3 celery tops with leaves, and 1 large bay leaf, *tied together with string*
½ teaspoon thyme
1 teaspoon salt
Freshly ground black pepper

No matter which cut of beef you choose, be sure to ask the butcher to encase it in a thin layer of barding fat and tie it securely in 4 or 5 places along its length, so that it will keep its shape while cooking. With the point of a sharp knife make 4 or 5 incisions in the meat and into each insert a sliver of garlic. Preheat the oven to 350 degrees.

Heat the rendered pork fat or oil-butter in a large heavy frying pan until it literally begins to smoke. Add the meat, and over moderate heat brown it on all sides. This should take about 15 minutes. Meanwhile, in a heavy casserole or Dutch oven just about large enough to hold the meat, heat 3 tablespoons of butter and cook the chopped onions and carrots, stirring from time to time, until they color lightly.

When the meat is a dark mahogany brown, remove it from the frying pan and place it on top of the vegetables in the casserole. Add the cut-up tomato, bouquet, and thyme, and sprinkle the meat with the salt and some freshly ground black pepper. Heat the casserole on top of the stove until you hear it sizzle, then drape the meat loosely with a piece of aluminum foil, cover the casserole tightly, and place it in the lower third of the preheated oven.

After about 1 hour of cooking, turn the meat over. The meat and vegetables by this time will have given off a great deal of liquid; if it seems to be bubbling too rapidly, turn the oven down to 325 or even 300 degrees. Continue to cook until the beef is completely tender and can easily be pierced with a fork—for most cuts, this should take from 2½ to 3 hours. However, after the second hour it might be well to test the meat periodically to make certain it doesn't overcook.

When the meat is done, remove it from the casserole and strain the cooking juices and their vegetables through a sieve set in a mixing bowl. Press down hard on the vegetables with the back of a large spoon to extract all their liquid before throwing them away. Let the gravy rest 1 or 2 minutes, then skim most of the fat from the surface, reserving it for later use. Taste for seasoning and return the gravy to the casserole with the meat to be heated through again just before you serve it. The gravy may be thickened with arrowroot or flour, if you wish, although it will have considerably more flavor if it is served as is. Moreover, any remaining unthickened gravy can be used to enhance the numerous improvisations that follow.

▶ Should you have no immediate use for the braising liquid left from your Yankee pot roast (or, in fact, from any other classic meat dish in this book) or the drippings remaining on a platter after carving a roast beef or a roast leg of lamb, save it, even if it consists of only a few thimblesful. A spoonful or more of this highly concentrated *jus*—as the French call it—can be used to flavor any improvised beef dish, either by making it part of the stock called for or adding it in small amounts on your own.

odds
and
ENds

▶ Any beef remaining from this classic pot roast or the other beef recipes may be used with good effect in place of the veal suggested for the *fricadelles* of veal improvisation on page 62.

▶ It should be noted that the *moussaka* on page 45 can be made almost if not quite as successfully with beef remaining from this Yankee pot roast instead of with the more characteristic lamb.

IMPROVISATIONS

Pot Roast Pie with Braised White Onions and Mushrooms

Serves 6

PASTRY

1¼ cups flour

6 tablespoons butter, *chilled and cut into ½-inch pieces*

1 egg, *lightly beaten*

FILLING

12 small white onions, *about 1 inch in diameter*

¼ pound salt pork, *cut into ¼-inch dice*

½ pound mushrooms (about 2½ cups), *thinly sliced*

3 tablespoons fat skimmed from the pot roast or 3 tablespoons butter

2½ cups stock: unthickened pot roast gravy and canned beef bouillon, *combined;* or 1½ cups canned beef bouillon and ¾ cup canned chicken stock, *combined*

3 tablespoons flour

Salt

Freshly ground black pepper

¼ teaspoon lemon juice

2–2½ cups cold pot roast, *cut into 1½-inch cubes*

½ package frozen peas, *thoroughly defrosted and drained,* or 1 cup peas, *freshly cooked*

1 tablespoon parsley, *finely chopped*

For successful pastry, prepare the dough at least 4 hours before you plan to use it, or even the night before. Place in a mixing bowl the chilled butter, flour, and salt, and rub them through the thumb and forefingers of both hands until the fat and flour are well combined. Don't allow the mixture to become oily, although if it does it won't be a disaster. Add the lightly beaten egg and, with two dinner knives, mix the flour and egg together until all the moistened flour particles adhere to each other. Quickly form the dough into a compact ball, dust it lightly with a handful of flour, and refrigerate, wrapped in waxed paper, until ready to roll out.

Start the filling by braising the onions first: slowly heat the diced salt pork in a large heavy frying pan, raise the heat as the pork begins to give off its fat and, stirring constantly, cook until the pork bits have crisped and turned a golden brown. Remove them with a slotted spoon and put them aside. Add the peeled onions to the hot fat in the pan and cook them until they brown lightly. Cover the pan, and over fairly low heat cook the onions for about 30 minutes, or until they can easily be pierced with the point of a knife. Remove them from the fat with a slotted spoon and put them aside with the pork bits. Pour off all but 3 tablespoons of fat from the frying pan and cook the sliced mushrooms for about 2 or 3 minutes, turning them in the hot fat constantly. Remove the mushrooms from the fat and put them aside with the onions.

In a small saucepan melt 3 tablespoons of pot roast fat, if you have saved it when skimming it from the braising liquid; otherwise use butter. Off the heat, stir in 3 level tablespoons of flour and mix until smooth. Add to this, all at once, the 2½ cups of stock and stir with a whisk for a minute or two. Return the pan to the heat and cook, stirring constantly with a whisk, until the sauce is thick and smooth. Season with salt and freshly ground pepper to taste and the lemon juice. Preheat the oven to 475 degrees.

Pour the finished sauce into a 1-quart, 2-inch-high circular baking dish. Add the cut-up pot roast, the braised onions, browned pork bits, mushrooms (all thoroughly drained), green peas, and the chopped parsley. Quickly roll out the pastry (which you have allowed to soften a bit after removing it from the refrigerator) and when it is about ¼ inch thick and 1 or 2 inches larger in diameter than the baking dish, carefully lift it on your rolling pin and fit it over the dish. Secure the pastry to the dish by tucking the extra dough under its rim and crimping the edge of the circle with your fingers if you want a decorative effect. With a small knife make two 1-inch slits in the crust to allow the steam to escape and then bake the pie in the center of the oven for 15 minutes, then reduce the heat to 350 degrees and bake for 10 to 15 minutes more. Serve at once.

Pirog of Beef

Serves 8

PASTRY

¼ pound sweet butter, *chilled and cut into ½-inch pieces*

3 tablespoons lard or vegetable shortening, *chilled*

2 cups flour

½ teaspoon salt

⅓ cup ice water

FILLING

7 tablespoons butter, *3 for sautéing onions and garlic, 1 for buttering cooky sheet, and 3 melted for accompaniment*

½ cup onions, *finely chopped*

½ teaspoon garlic, *finely chopped*

1 tablespoon flour

½ **cup unthickened pot roast gravy** or ½ cup beef stock, fresh or canned

2 **cups cooked pot roast**, *finely chopped*

2 tablespoons dill, *finely chopped*

1 teaspoon salt

Freshly ground black pepper

2 teaspoons red wine vinegar

2 eggs, *hard-cooked and coarsely chopped*

2 cups cooked rice (about ⅔ cup raw rice cooked) or cooked buckwheat groats, *cold*

1 egg (yolk only) ⎱ *combined*
2 tablespoons heavy cream ⎰

Sour cream (optional)

In a large mixing bowl combine the cut-up sweet butter, the lard or shortening, flour, and salt. Quickly rub through the thumb and forefingers of both hands until fat and flour are well mixed and most of the lumps have disappeared. Don't allow the mixture to become oily, but small bits of unassimilated fat here and there won't affect the final result. Pour the ice water over the flour all at once. Toss together with both hands until all the flour particles are moistened sufficiently to adhere to each other. Quickly and lightly press the dough together into a compact ball and dust it lightly with a small handful of flour. Wrap in waxed paper and chill for 2 hours or longer.

Prepare the filling by sautéing the chopped onions and garlic in 3 tablespoons of the butter for about 5 minutes, stirring occasionally, until they are soft but not brown. Remove the pan from the heat and add the tablespoon of flour. Mix together thoroughly, then pour in the stock. Stir with a wire whisk for a moment or two and return the pan to the heat. Still stirring, cook the mixture until it thickens, at which point turn down the heat and let it simmer a minute or two. Stir in the chopped beef, 1 tablespoon of the dill, and the salt, black pepper, and vinegar, then scrape the entire contents of the pan into a mixing bowl and let it cool.

Remove the pastry from the refrigerator at least 15 minutes before you plan to roll it out. Meanwhile butter a heavy cooky sheet and preheat the oven to 425 degrees. Roll the pastry on a floured board into a rectangle 11 by 16 inches and about ⅛ inch thick. You will undoubtedly have more dough than you need, but the extra amount will give you sufficient leeway should you have any difficulty rolling the dough into the desired shape.

Working as fast as you can (the pastry, because it is a short one, softens easily) spread 1 cup of the cooked rice or groats on the rectangle, leaving a space about 4 inches all around it. Sprinkle a little dill, salt, and pepper on the rice and then spread over it some of the chopped egg and all the meat mixture. Cover the meat with the remaining chopped egg, dill, some salt and pepper, and the remaining cup of rice or groats. With a spatula pat the sides and top of the construction gently into shape. With a small knife cut 1-inch triangles from the short ends of the pastry, then lift the long ends up and over the filling, pinching the flaps of the pastry together to seal it. Moisten the triangular ends of the pastry with a little cold water and bring them up over the *pirog* like the flaps of an envelope, pressing them firmly into the dough to seal them. With the largest spatula you own (use two, if they are small) ease the *pirog* gently over onto the buttered cooky sheet so that the long seam is concealed. Cut two 1-inch slits on top of the *pirog* to allow the steam to escape and brush the entire surface of the pastry with the egg-yolk–cream mixture.

Bake the *pirog* in the center of the oven for 10 minutes, then turn the heat down to 350 degrees and continue to bake for about another 50 minutes, or until the *pirog* is a golden brown and the pastry thoroughly cooked. Before serving, pour 1½ tablespoons of hot melted butter into each of the two slits you made earlier, and cut the *pirog* into approximately 1-inch slices. Small bowls of melter butter and/or sour cream make fine accompaniments for this savory, traditional Russian dish.

Bigos

Polish Hunter's Stew

The recipe for this dish is exactly the same as the one for *bigos* on page 76. Substitute 1½ cups of cold pot roast for the pork, or—as they often do in Poland—use a combination of cooked pot roast and cooked pork, if you have both on hand.

Cannelloni with Beef and Spinach Filling

Serves 4–6

PASTA DOUGH (or make the *crêpe* batter on page 134)	1½ cups flour 1 whole egg 1 egg white	1 tablespoon olive oil 1 tablespoon water 1 teaspoon salt	
FILLING	2 tablespoons olive oil 4 tablespoons onions, *finely chopped* 1 teaspoon garlic, *finely chopped* 1 package frozen chopped spinach, *defrosted,* or ½ pound fresh spinach, *cooked* **1 cup cooked pot roast,** *finely chopped*	2 tablespoons heavy cream 5 tablespoons Parmesan cheese, *grated* 2 eggs, *lightly beaten* ½ teaspoon salt Freshly ground black pepper ½ teaspoon oregano	
CREAM SAUCE	3 tablespoons butter 3 tablespoons flour 1 cup light cream	½ teaspoon salt ⅛ teaspoon cayenne	
TOMATO SAUCE	3 tablespoons olive oil ½ cup onions, *finely chopped* 8-ounce can Italian plum tomatoes 3 tablespoons tomato paste	1 teaspoon dried basil 1 teaspoon sugar ½ teaspoon salt Freshly ground black pepper	
	2 tablespoons Parmesan cheese, *grated*	Butter	

For the *pasta* dough, combine in a mixing bowl the flour, the whole egg and the egg white, the oil, water, and salt, adding a little more water if necessary to make the flour particles adhere to each other. Form the dough into a ball, then, on a floured surface, knead it for about 10 minutes until it is smooth, elastic, and shiny. Let it rest for 10 minutes or so. Divide the dough into three parts and roll each part out on a lightly floured board until it is as thin as you can possibly make it; in fact, it should be almost translucent. Sprinkle the sheets lightly with flour and let them dry for about 10 minutes. Trim the edges and, with a sharp knife, cut the *pasta* into rectangles approximately 3 by 4 inches. Drop these into boiling salted water and cook them vigorously for about 5 minutes or until they are tender but still slightly resistant to the bite— *al dente,* as the Italians call it. Remove the rectangles (which will have expanded somewhat) from the pot and drop them into cold water to stop their cooking. Dry them by laying them side by side on paper toweling. If preparing the *pasta* from scratch seems too much of a chore (and it *is* worth it) use the *crêpe* batter instead, making it precisely as described on page 134. It is surprisingly effective in this recipe.

For the filling, cook the chopped onions and garlic in the olive oil for about 4 minutes, until they are soft but not brown. Meanwhile, squeeze the defrosted or freshly cooked spinach through the fingers to extract all its liquid, then with a sharp knife chop it as fine as you can. Add the spinach to the onions, raise the heat and, stirring almost constantly, cook it until it begins to stick lightly to the pan. With a spatula, scrape the mixture into a mixing bowl. Add the meat, cream, Parmesan cheese, eggs, salt, pepper, and oregano; then mix together thoroughly and taste for seasoning. Place a tablespoon or so of this filling on either a square of cooked *pasta* or a *crêpe* and roll it up without tucking in the ends. Continue in this fashion, adjusting the amounts of filling to the number of *cannelloni* or *crêpes* you plan to make. Before arranging them in a baking dish, make the two sauces.

Melt 3 tablespoons of butter in a small saucepan, then, off the heat, stir in 3 level table-spoons of flour. Mix until smooth, then add, all at once, the cupful of cream. Mix with a whisk for a moment or two, then return the pan to the heat and cook, stirring constantly, until the sauce thickens. Season with salt and cayenne and simmer for a moment or two before putting it aside.

The tomato sauce is just as easily made although it takes somewhat longer. Cook the chopped onions in 3 tablespoons of olive oil for about 5 minutes, until they are soft and lightly colored. Add the can of tomatoes and the tomato paste, the basil, sugar, salt, and pepper. Bring to a boil, then reduce the heat to as low as possible and simmer the sauce anywhere from 40 minutes to 1 hour. When it is finished, rub it through a sieve, forcing the tomato pulp through with the back of a large spoon.

Choose a large shallow baking pan that will just about hold the number of *cannelloni* you intend to cook. Spread a thin layer of cream sauce on the bottom of the pan. Lay the *cannelloni* on this, side by side, and mask each one with a tablespoon or so of the tomato sauce, then spread the remaining cream sauce over them all. Sprinkle with the Parmesan cheese and dot with small pieces of butter. The *cannelloni* can be baked at once or put aside, covered with plastic wrap, and refrigerated until you decide to cook them.

Preheat the oven to 375 degrees. Bake the uncovered *cannelloni* for about 20 minutes, or until they begin to bubble. Slide them quickly under a hot broiler to brown the top and serve at once.

Pâté of Pot Roast

Serves 6 to 8 as a cocktail spread

1 cup cold pot roast, *trimmed of all fat and gristle and coarsely chopped*
6 anchovy fillets, *drained, washed, and dried*
½–¾ cup cold pot roast gravy, *unthickened,* or an equivalent amount of canned beef or chicken stock

¼ pound sweet butter, *softened*
1 teaspoon onion, *finely grated*
¾ teaspoon lemon juice
½ teaspoon salt
Freshly ground black pepper

Combine in the jar of an electric blender* the pot roast, anchovies, and ½ cup of gravy or stock. Purée at high speed, stopping the machine from time to time to scrape down the sides with a rubber spatula, adding more liquid when necessary to produce a smooth, fairly fluid purée. Use a little more than the suggested amount of liquid should the blender clog. Although this is not absolutely essential, rub the purée through a sieve with the back of a large spoon to achieve as smooth a paste as possible.

Cream the butter in a mixing bowl by beating it with a spoon for a few minutes until it is smooth and light in color. A spoonful at a time, mix the butter into the meat purée, and continue to beat the mixture until the butter and meat are completely combined. Add the grated onion, the lemon juice, the salt (more if you think it needs it), and a few grindings of black pepper. Spoon the *pâté* into a small crock—earthenware, if possible—cover tightly, and refrigerate for at least 4 hours, or until the *pâté* is firm. Serve on hot buttered toast or French or black bread with cocktails or beer.

* *Note:* To make the *pâté* by hand, chop the pot roast and anchovies as finely as you can, then with a mortar and pestle pound them vigorously until they are reduced to a paste. Rub the paste through a fine sieve with the back of a large spoon and proceed with the recipe as described above.

Cold Braised Beef Vinaigrette

Serves 4–6

3 tablespoons red wine vinegar
1 teaspoon salt
Freshly ground black pepper
1 teaspoon Dijon or English dry mustard
9 tablespoons olive oil
2 tablespoons capers, *drained, washed, dried, and coarsely chopped*

½ teaspoon garlic, *finely chopped*
2–3 tablespoons parsley, *finely chopped*
½ cup onions, *thinly sliced*
6–8 **slices cold, well-trimmed pot roast,** *cut into symmetrical pieces about ¼ inch thick;* or 2½– 3 **cups cold pot roast,** *cut into 1½- or 2-inch cubes*

This salad is best made at least 2 or 3 hours before you plan to serve it; its success depends on the length of time the beef is marinated.

Combine in a small mixing bowl the vinegar, salt, a few grindings of black pepper, and the mustard, and mix them thoroughly to dissolve them. Beat in the olive oil and add the capers, garlic, and 2 tablespoons of the parsley.

Spread the slices or cubes of beef in a shallow baking dish large enough to hold the meat in one layer. Scatter over them the sliced onions and pour in the dressing. Make sure that all the onions and all parts of the meat are moistened thoroughly. Marinate at room temperature until ready to serve.

Serve the meat on a platter with the onion rings scattered over it and sprinkled with a little more chopped parsley. You may accompany the salad, if you like, with a garnish of sliced tomatoes, cold vegetables, hard-cooked eggs, moistened with any remaining dressing. A cold potato salad and hot French bread make fine additions.

A *Classic* BRAISED SHOULDER OF LAMB
WITH WHITE BEANS *41*

Lamb

A *Classic* ROAST LEG OF LAMB IN THE
FRENCH STYLE *48*

Lamb

Of all the meat in general use throughout the United States today lamb has the most individual and insistent character, and its special flavor is always recognizable however it is prepared. If for some tastes this is one of its lesser attractions, for others the flavor of lamb, properly cooked, has a greater appeal than beef. And, evidently, more and more Americans are beginning to think so, for we are consuming lamb now in larger quantities than ever before in our history.

Like our beef, American lamb is often of superb quality, but we seem never to do more with it than roast the legs, grill the chops, and stew the rest. That there are other ways to cook lamb is clear when we observe French and Middle Eastern cooks, for whom the cooking of lamb reflects traditions that go back centuries. And there is almost an infinity of dishes from which to choose. Most of the recipes for the lamb dishes described in the following pages are derived from the superior inventions of these extraordinary cooks.

As they long ago learned, and as many of us know, lamb lends itself particularly well to reheating and recooking, depending, of course, on how it was cooked originally. Although the pristine flavor of roast lamb cannot be recaptured by reheating as can that of braised lamb, roast lamb can be submitted to simple or elaborate recooking processes without becoming tough or stringy like other roast meats. For this reason, in the recipes that follow roast and braised lamb are interchangeable, except where rare meat is called for and then it is necessary to use the rarer parts of a roast lamb. It should be remembered, however, that braised meat always has more flavor reheated than roast meat; therefore, when the meats are substituted for each other the seasonings should be readjusted.

A Classic Braised Shoulder of Lamb with White Beans

7-pound shoulder of lamb, *boned and tied* (*about 5 pounds after boning*)

2 cloves garlic, *cut into slivers*

¼ pound fresh pork fat, *diced and rendered,* or 4 tablespoons vegetable oil

4 tablespoons butter

3 medium onions, *thinly sliced*

3 large carrots, *cut into 1-inch chunks*

3 stalks celery, *cut into 1-inch pieces*

2 cups beef stock, fresh or canned

1 cup dry white wine

1 teaspoon thyme

2 medium tomatoes, *peeled, seeded, and coarsely chopped,* or a 1 pound 3 ounce can solid-pack tomatoes, *strained and coarsely chopped*

A bouquet consisting of 4 sprigs parsley, 1 large leek (white part only), and 1 bay leaf, *tied together with string*

Salt

Freshly ground black pepper

1 pound pea beans, marrow peas, or Great Northern beans, *cooked* (directions in recipe)

2 tablespoons parsley, *finely chopped*

With a small knife make deep incisions along the length of the lamb and in each one insert a sliver of garlic. In a large heavy frying pan heat—almost to the smoking point—the rendered pork fat or vegetable oil. Add the shoulder of lamb and, over moderate heat, brown it on all sides, allowing about 20 minutes to do the job well.

Preheat the oven to 325 degrees. Choose a large flameproof casserole just about big enough to hold the lamb shoulder comfortably, and in it melt the 4 tablespoons of butter. Add the sliced onions, carrots, and celery pieces. Stir from time to time and cook the vegetables over moderate heat for about 15 minutes, or until they soften and color lightly.

Remove the browned lamb from the frying pan and place it fat side up on the vegetables in the casserole. Add the stock, wine, thyme, tomatoes, and the bouquet, and sprinkle the lamb generously with salt and freshly ground pepper. Drape a sheet of aluminum foil loosely over the meat, cover the casserole, and bring it to a boil on the top of the stove. Immediately transfer the casserole to the lower third of the oven and let the lamb braise for about 3 hours. Basting is unnecessary.

Cook the beans in one of two ways. Either soak them overnight covered with cold water, or use a short cut: an hour before you plan to cook them, put the beans in a large pot and cover them with cold water and bring the water to a boil; turn off the heat at once and let the beans soak in the hot water for about 1 hour. Then bring the water to the boiling point again, turn down the heat to barely simmering, and cook the beans, uncovered (and as slowly as possible if you don't want them to burst), for about 1¼ hours, or until they are tender but not falling apart. Drain the beans thoroughly and put them aside.

Before serving the lamb, remove it from the casserole and strain the braising juices into a bowl through a large sieve, pressing down hard on the vegetables with a spoon before throwing them away. Skim almost all the fat from the surface of the sauce, return the lamb to the casserole, and pour the sauce over it. Add the beans, then reheat meat, beans, and sauce on top of the stove just before serving.

Slice the lamb carefully with a long sharp knife, and lay the slices, slightly overlapping, down the center of a heated platter. Arrange the beans on either side of the meat. Moisten the lamb slices and the beans with a few tablespoons of the hot braising sauce, sprinkle with the chopped parsley, and serve. Pour the remaining sauce into a heated sauceboat and pass it separately.

▶ This classic braised shoulder of lamb can, of course, be made without the beans if you wish, but at the sacrifice of a few improvisations. In that event, serve the lamb with noodles, rice, or potatoes.

▶ Don't be tempted to use the blender to purée the beans for the bean soup and lamb improvisations that follow. Admittedly, it would make the task much easier, but the slightly grainy texture which gives the soup its special character would be lost. Except for sauces like the tunafish one in *vitello tonnato* and the *pâté* improvisations scattered throughout the book, the blender, for puréeing purposes at least, should be used with discretion.

iMPROViSATiONS

Shepherd's Pie with Braised Lamb in the French Style

Serves 6

1½ pounds baking potatoes, *peeled and cut into quarters (about 3½–4 cups)*

8 tablespoons butter, *4 softened for the purée-ing, 3 for sautéing, and 1 softened for dotting top of pie*

⅓–½ cup heavy cream

Salt
Freshly ground black pepper
⅓ cup onions, *finely chopped*
¼ teaspoon garlic, *finely chopped*
3 tablespoons flour
1½ cups braising liquid from the braised lamb,
or an equivalent amount of fresh or canned
beef stock, or a combination of them both

1 teaspoon tomato paste
1 tablespoon red wine vinegar
2 cups (packed down) braised lamb, *chopped*
and trimmed of all fat and gristle
1 tablespoon parsley, *finely chopped*
¼ cup Parmesan cheese, *freshly grated, mixed*
with 2 tablespoons dry bread crumbs

Cook the quartered potatoes in salted boiling water to cover until they are tender but not falling apart. Drain them at once, return them to the pan, and shake them over low heat until they are dry and mealy. Force the potatoes through a ricer and beat into them, either by hand or with an electric mixer, 4 tablespoons of softened butter and then the cream, a few tablespoons at a time. Use as much cream as you need to make the purée smooth, but make sure it remains thick enough to hold its shape in a spoon. Season the potatoes with salt and freshly ground black pepper.

While the potatoes are cooking, melt 3 tablespoons of butter in a large heavy frying pan. When the foam subsides, add the finely chopped onions. Cook over moderate heat for about 8 minutes, stirring frequently, until the onions are soft, transparent, and lightly colored. Then stir in the garlic and cook a moment longer. Off the heat add 3 level tablespoons of flour and stir until smooth. Pour in 1½ cups of braising liquid or stock. Beat vigorously with a whisk to partially dissolve the flour, then cook over moderate heat, whisking constantly, until the sauce becomes smooth and very thick. Add the tomato paste and vinegar, and simmer for 1 or 2 minutes before stirring in the chopped lamb. Mix the lamb and sauce together thoroughly and cook for 2 minutes, or until the meat absorbs some of the sauce. Taste for seasoning.

Preheat the oven to 400 degrees. Butter an 8-cup soufflé or deep baking dish attractive enough to bring to the table. Spread about a cupful of the warm whipped potatoes on the bottom, smoothing it with a spatula. Carefully spoon the lamb mixture over the top. Sprinkle the meat with a tablespoon of chopped parsley. Now spread the remaining potatoes over the layer of meat, again smoothing it into place with a spatula. Dust the top evenly with the Parmesan-crumb mixture and dot all over with a tablespoon of butter.

Bake in the center of the hot oven for about 20 minutes, or until the top of the pie is lightly browned. Slide under the broiler for a few seconds to give the crust a little more color and serve at once.

Note: Shepherd's pie, which can be the dreariest dish in the whole repertoire of leftover cookery, is presented in the above improvisation in a fresh guise. And the word "fresh" is used advisedly. Don't use leftover mashed potatoes even if you have them on hand, but whip potatoes from scratch with butter and plenty of heavy cream. And *chop*, don't grind, cold meat for the filling. Topped with good Parmesan cheese, bread crumbs, and butter, then gratinéed, shepherd's pie in this version is a hearty and honest dish.

As an added refinement to the pie, extra puréed potatoes may be piped decoratively through a pastry bag fitted with a star tube. Also, the buttered baking dish in which the pie is to be cooked may be coated liberally with a combination of grated cheese and bread crumbs before it is filled.

Other cold meats may of course be substituted for the braised lamb, notably the Yankee pot roast (p. 28), the roast beef (p. 19), or the leg of lamb (p. 48). The beef from the *pot-au-feu* (p. 5) will do well enough if it must, but it is really too bland in flavor to cope with the masses of puréed potatoes enveloping it.

Bean Soup and Lamb

Serves 4–6

3 cups cooked beans—if **possible, the beans originally cooked with the braised lamb** or freshly cooked beans

4–4¼ cups chicken stock, fresh or canned; **include, as part of this amount, any braising liquid left from the lamb**

¾ **cup braised lamb,** *cut into ½-inch dice*

Salt

Freshly ground black pepper

2 tablespoons parsley, *finely chopped*

Combine in a 2- or 3-quart saucepan the beans and 3 cups of the stock. Bring it to a boil, then, with the pan half covered, simmer on the lowest possible heat for about 20 minutes. With the back of a large spoon, purée the beans through a fine sieve (*not* with a blender) set over a mixing bowl. And if the purée still seems coarse, rub it through once more. Return the purée to the saucepan and heat again, beating gently with a wire whisk to smooth it. Add the remaining cup of stock and a little more if the soup still seems too thick. Taste and add as much salt and pepper as you think it needs. Just before serving, stir in the diced lamb and heat it through. Sprinkle a dusting of chopped parsley on each serving.

Moussaka

Serves 4–6

2 eggplants, weighing about 1 pound each, *cut into ½-inch slices,* or one 2-pound eggplant

Salt

½–¾ cup olive oil, *for sautéing the shallots or scallions and garlic, the onions, the potatoes, and the eggplant slices*

¼ cup shallots or scallions, *finely chopped*

1½ teaspoons garlic, *finely chopped*

3 cups braised lamb, *finely chopped or ground*

2 teaspoons red wine vinegar

2 tablespoons tomato paste

3 tablespoons parsley, *finely chopped*

Freshly ground black pepper

½ cup lamb braising liquid, if available, or ½ cup beef bouillon, fresh or canned

1 egg, *lightly beaten*

1 cup onions, *thinly sliced*

4 medium potatoes, *peeled and sliced ¼ inch thick*

½ cup flour

1½ pounds fresh tomatoes, *peeled, seeded, and coarsely chopped,* or about 2 cups canned tomatoes, *thoroughly drained and coarsely chopped*

Cut the unpeeled eggplants into ½-inch slices, sprinkle the slices on both sides with salt (about 1 tablespoon altogether) and lay them side by side on a large flat platter. Place another platter or plate on top of them and let the slices stand for about 1 hour, to drain. Meanwhile prepare the other ingredients.

Heat 2 tablespoons of olive oil in a large heavy frying pan and over moderate heat sauté the shallots or scallions and garlic for about 3 minutes, or until they are soft and lightly colored. Scrape them into a large mixing bowl. Add the chopped or ground lamb, vinegar, tomato paste, parsley, ½ teaspoon salt, and ¼ teaspoon pepper, the braising liquid or bouillon, and 1 egg, lightly beaten. With a large spoon mix all the ingredients together gently but thoroughly and taste for seasoning; it will probably need more salt and pepper. Heat another 2 tablespoons of olive oil in the frying pan and quickly sauté the cup of sliced onions. When they are lightly colored, transfer them to a small bowl with a slotted spoon. Fry the potatoes in 2 tablespoons of olive oil in the same way. Let them cook over moderate heat until they are lightly brown and almost half done. Put them aside in a separate bowl.

Pat the eggplant slices dry with paper toweling and dip them lightly in flour, shaking them to remove any excess. Sauté the eggplant slices in the remaining olive oil over high heat as quickly as possible. They should be quite brown but barely cooked.*

Choose a 2-quart baking dish about 3 inches high in which to assemble, cook, and serve the *moussaka*. Preheat the oven to 375 degrees. Arrange the ingredients in the dish in the following fashion: cover the bottom with half the eggplant, then all the meat mixture, half the chopped tomatoes, all the sliced onions, the remaining tomatoes, and finally the remaining eggplant. Arrange the sliced potatoes in concentric circles on top of the eggplant, then cover the dish tightly with a sheet of aluminum foil. Place the dish in a jelly-roll pan (to catch the juices that may spill into the oven) and bake the *moussaka* for about 1 hour; remove the foil during the last 20 minutes to allow the potatoes to brown. Before serving, remove as much oil as you can from the sides and top of the dish with a bulb baster.

* *Note:* The eggplant slices for the *moussaka* should be sautéed, not for the purpose of cooking them through, but to brown them in oil as quickly as possible. If cooked at too leisurely a pace, the eggplant slices will absorb astonishing amounts of oil, which they will later release in the *moussaka* and make it excessively oily.

A Cassoulet with Braised Lamb and Sausage

Serves 4–6

½ pound fresh well-seasoned pork sausage meat, *formed into cakes about 1½–2 inches in diameter*

4 tablespoons shallots or scallions, *finely chopped*

1 tablespoon garlic, *finely chopped*

Salt

Freshly ground black pepper

4–5 cups cooked white beans from the original braised lamb, if possible, or **part from the original lamb** and part freshly cooked, or all freshly cooked

2 tablespoons parsley, *finely chopped*

2 cups cold braised lamb, *cut into approximately 1½-inch pieces**

1½ cups stock: either **wholly the braising liquid from the lamb,** or **part braising liquid** and part beef bouillon, or all beef bouillon, fresh or canned

½ cup bread crumbs, *coarsely grated*

1 tablespoon butter, *softened and cut into small pieces*

Start frying the sausage cakes in a cold frying pan set over moderate heat. Brown them on both sides, remove them from the pan, then put them aside to drain on paper toweling. Discard all but 2 tablespoons of the sausage fat from the frying pan and in it sauté the shallots or scallions and garlic over moderate heat for about 3 minutes, or until they are soft but not brown. Set them aside in a small bowl.

Choose a 6-cup flameproof casserole, preferably a deep one, in which to assemble, cook, and serve the *cassoulet*. Preheat the oven to 350 degrees. Arrange the ingredients in the casserole as follows, sprinkling each layer with a little salt and pepper: a ½-inch-or-so layer of cooked beans; a little of the shallot- or scallion-garlic mixture and some parsley; a layer of lamb, then a layer of sausage cakes, then another layer of beans, and the remainder of the shallots or scallions, garlic, and parsley. Pour in the braising liquid (which should come almost to the top of the beans), sprinkle the beans with the bread crumbs and dot them with the butter. Heat the casserole on top of the stove until the stock begins to bubble, than transfer the *cassoulet* to the center of the oven, where it should bake undisturbed for about 1¼ hours, or until the crumbs are brown and all the stock has been absorbed. Serve directly from the casserole.

* *Note:* The *cassoulet,* as made traditionally in Toulouse, Castelnaudary, and Carcassonne in France, often contains among its ingredients—in addition to the lamb and sausage—goose or duck plus pork as well. When making the above *cassoulet,* use one or all of these meats if you have them on hand. Small pieces of braised duck (p. 150) and roast pork (p. 74) would be especially suitable.

Braised Lamb and Vegetables in the Provençal Style

Serves 4

4 tablespoons olive oil
2 cups braised lamb, *cut into 1½-inch pieces*
2 teaspoons lemon juice
1 teaspoon garlic, *finely chopped*
1 teaspoon shallots or scallions, *finely chopped*
1 large green pepper, *seeded and cut into 2-inch squares*
4 medium leeks with their diameters no larger than 1 inch (white parts and an inch or so of their stems)
2 small zucchini, *cut into ¾-inch rounds*
3-inch strip of orange peel
½ teaspoon salt
Freshly ground black pepper
4 medium tomatoes, *cut into quarters*
1 tablespoon parsley, *finely chopped*

In a 10-inch heavy frying pan or shallow casserole, heat the olive oil until it almost begins to smoke. Add the lamb and brown the pieces for 2 or 3 minutes, turning them constantly in the hot oil with a spoon. Reduce the heat to moderate and mix in the lemon juice, garlic, and chopped shallots or scallions. Cook for 1 or 2 minutes longer, then add the green pepper, leeks, zucchini, orange peel, salt, and a few grindings of black pepper. Cover the pan tightly and let the vegetables and meat cook over moderate heat for about 10 minutes, or until the leeks and zucchini are tender but still slightly firm. Add the tomatoes and cook 5 minutes longer.

The charm of this dish is to have the vegetables decidedly undercooked, their fresh flavor supporting the fully cooked and browned lamb. To serve, arrange the meat and vegetables on a heated platter, pour over them the pan juices, and sprinkle with the parsley.

► ◄

A Classic Roast Leg of Lamb in the French Style

6- or 7-pound leg of lamb
2 cloves garlic, *peeled and cut into ⅛-inch slivers*
3 tablespoons vegetable oil
2 tablespoons crystal salt (*gros sel*) or table salt
2 large onions, *thinly slivered*
2 large carrots, *thinly sliced*

4 stalks celery, *cut into 1-inch pieces*
1½ cups stock: fresh beef or chicken stock, or canned chicken and beef bouillon in equal porportions
Salt
Freshly ground black pepper
½ teaspoon lemon juice

When you buy your leg of lamb, ask the butcher *not* to remove the fell, the thin parchment-like covering around the leg. Old wives' tales notwithstanding, the fell does not give the lamb an excessively "lamby" taste, but instead encases the meat in a fine crisp crust as it roasts, thus sealing in its juices. Remove the meat from the refrigerator about 2 hours before you plan to roast it.

Preheat the oven to 500 degrees. With the point of a small knife make 6 or 8 short incisions along the length of the leg and insert in each a sliver of garlic. Brush the meat thoroughly with the vegetable oil and pat it all over with crystal salt. Place the leg, fat side up, on a rack set in a shallow roasting plan just about large enough to hold the meat comfortably. Roast, uncovered and undisturbed, for 20 minutes in the center of the 500-degree oven. Then turn the heat down to 375 degrees, scatter the cut-up onions, carrots, and celery around the meat, and continue to roast without basting (and still uncovered, of course) for about 50 or 55 minutes longer.

At its best, a roast leg of lamb should be served medium-rare, and to make certain of its degree of doneness use a meat thermometer, inserted in the fleshiest part of the leg. For medium-rare lamb, remove the roast from the oven when the theremometer reads 145 degrees. Let the meat rest on a heated platter for 15 minutes: it will be much easier to carve. And because its internal heat will continue to cook it as it rests, the lamb will be at the desirable state of doneness when you are ready to serve it.

Meanwhile make the sauce. Add to the roasting pan the 1½ cups of stock and bring it to a boil on top of the stove. Let it boil briskly for about 3 or 4 minutes and scrape into the juices all the brown sediment clinging to the bottom and sides of the pan. Strain the sauce (when it has boiled down to the intensity of flavor which satisfies you) through a fine sieve set into a small saucepan, pressing down hard on the vegetables with a spoon to extract all their juices before throwing them away. Skim the sauce of most of its surface fat, add salt and freshly ground pepper to taste, and stir in the lemon juice. Reheat the sauce before serving it in a gravyboat.

► Whatever your prejudices about rare lamb, don't overcook the leg; it is at its best pink. If you insist upon well-done leg of lamb, however, then braise it—don't roast it—and follow the recipe on page 41 for the classic braised shoulder of lamb, which is almost always cooked to the well-done stage.

► This classic roast leg of lamb may be served with the lemon sauce on page 221 in place of the pan gravy suggested. Make the gravy as described, however, and save it for use in the lamb improvisations in the Madras curry recipe (p. 53), for example, as part or in place of the cup of stock required.

odds
and
ENds

► Although, ideally, the improvisations following the roast and braised lamb recipes will be at their best if you use the type of cooked lamb suggested, the roast and braised lamb can, if you wish, be used interchangeably.

► Rare pieces of roast lamb (p. 48) may be substituted for the braised lamb in the braised lamb and vegetables improvisation on page 47. The roast meat will not have quite as much flavor as the braised, but if the lamb is barely cooked and remains rare when it is served, it will provide compensations of its own.

► The dilled lamb croquettes on page 50 can be made as small as you like and served as hors d'oeuvres instead of main-course croquettes. You would probably want to cut the recipe in half, a good thing if you have only a small amount of lamb left over. Spear the deep-fried croquettes on picks so that they can be dipped into any of the sauces suggested at the end of the recipe.

IMPROVISATIONS

Dilled Lamb Croquettes

Serves 4

3 tablespoons butter

2 tablespoons onions, *finely chopped*

½ cup plus 3 level tablespoons flour, *the 3 table-spoons for the sauce and the ½ cup for coating the croquettes*

¾ cup beef stock, fresh or canned (**include in this amount any unthickened lamb juices, if possible**)

2 whole eggs plus 1 yolk, *the 2 eggs for the coating and the yolk for the croquette mixture*

2 tablespoons heavy cream

2 cups (firmly packed) roast lamb, *ground, free of all fat and gristle*

2 tablespoons fresh dill, *finely chopped*

1 tablespoon parsley, *finely chopped*

¼ teaspoon thyme

½ teaspoon salt

Freshly ground black pepper

2 teaspoons lemon juice

1½ tablespoons vegetable oil

½ cup dry bread crumbs

Deep fat for frying

Melt 3 tablespoons of butter in a small saucepan. Over moderate heat, cook the finely chopped onions in this for 4 or 5 minutes until they are soft but not colored. Then, off the heat, mix into it 3 level tablespoons of flour. Pour over it, all at once, ¾ cup of stock, and with a whisk stir until the flour partially dissolves. Return the pan to the heat and, whisking constantly, bring the sauce to a boil. It will be very thick. Simmer for 1 or 2 minutes to remove any floury taste. Meanwhile combine the egg yolk with 2 tablespoons of cream and then be sure to add 2 tablespoons of the hot sauce. Now you can beat the warmed egg mixture into the rest of the sauce in the pan and boil for 5 seconds, without fear of curdling. With a rubber spatula transfer the sauce to a large mixing bowl; add the ground lamb, dill, parsley, thyme, salt, a few grindings of black pepper, and the lemon juice and, with a large spoon, beat the mixture until it is as smooth as possible. Taste for seasoning. Spread the mixture out about ¾ of an inch thick on a platter, cover it with plastic wrap, and refrigerate it for anywhere from 4 hours to overnight.

When the lamb mixture is firm, scoop it up in large spoonfuls and form them into any croquette shape which suits your fancy: balls (3 inches or so in diameter), cork shapes, or cones. Roll them lightly in flour and shake off the excess. Dip them, one at a time, in the eggs (first lightly beaten with the vegetable oil), then roll in the bread crumbs. Make sure that the exposed surfaces of the croquettes are thoroughly covered or the filling will break through when they are deep-fried. Chill again for 1 hour or so before frying.

Fry the croquettes, 2 or 3 at a time, in deep fat to cover, heated to 375 degrees on the deep-fat thermometer. Gently turn them in the fat with a large spoon to ensure their cooking evenly. When they are a deep golden brown all over (this will take only a few minutes) transfer them to a baking dish lined with paper toweling to absorb any excess fat. The croquettes may be kept warm in a 250-degree oven for 15 minutes or so if they must wait before being served. However, they are at their best and crispest if served the moment they are done.

Serve with lemon quarters or with any of the following sauces: lemon sauce (p. 221), caper sauce (p. 63), cucumber-yoghurt sauce (p. 223).

Lamb in a Skillet with Fresh Tomatoes, Scallions, and Parsley in the Turkish Style

Serves 4

2 cups roast leg of lamb, *cut into ¾- to 1-inch pieces*
1 teaspoon garlic, *finely chopped*
Salt
½ teaspoon freshly ground black pepper
4 tablespoons olive oil
½ cup fresh tomatoes, *peeled, seeded, and cut into julienne strips 1 inch by ½ inch*

½ cup scallions, *cut into paper-thin rounds* (include some of the green stem also)
½ cup parsley (flat-leaf type, if possible), *coarsely chopped*
1 teaspoon lemon peel, *grated*
Lemon quarters

Combine in a small bowl the pieces of lamb, the chopped garlic, salt to taste, and the freshly ground pepper. Mix together thoroughly. Choose a 10-inch traditional sauté pan or any deep heavy frying pan attractive enough to bring to the table. Heat 4 tablespoons of olive oil in the pan until it almost begins to smoke. Add the seasoned lamb and, over high heat, brown the pieces quickly, turning them with a large spoon or spatula for about 8 minutes, taking care not to let them burn. Toss in the tomato strips° and, stirring continuously, cook them for about 3 minutes with the lamb; they should be barely cooked through and should retain more than a hint of their original texture and freshness.

With a spatula, push the meat and tomatoes toward the center of the pan and surround them with the scallions and parsley, arranged in a ring. Sprinkle the meat with the grated lemon peel and cover the pan tightly. Turn off the heat and let the residual heat in the pan warm the herbs through. Serve directly from the pan after about 5 minutes. Lemon quarters are the perfect accompaniment to the lamb and French or Italian bread should be served to sop up the tomato-and-herb-flavored olive oil.

° *Note:* To prepare the tomatoes, drop them into boiling water for about 10 seconds. Peel them at once and cut in quarters. Run a small sharp knife under the pulp of each quarter and cut it away, leaving the thin outer shell of the tomato. Cut the shells into julienne strips and use the tomato pulp for other purposes.

Lamb and Leek Balls

Makes 16–18
one-inch balls

7–8 medium-sized leeks (white part only), *well washed and finely chopped* (*about 2 cups*)
½ teaspoon garlic, *finely chopped*
1½ **cups cold roast leg of lamb**, *finely ground*
1 tablespoon parsley, *finely chopped*
1 tablespoon lemon juice
½ teaspoon salt
Freshly ground black pepper

2 whole eggs plus 3 egg yolks, *the whole eggs for the coating and the egg yolks for the lamb and leek mixture*
2–4 tablespoons heavy cream
½ cup flour
1½ tablespoons vegetable oil
1 cup bread crumbs
Deep fat for frying

Blanch the chopped leeks by covering them with boiling water in a small saucepan and letting them boil vigorously for about 8 minutes. Drain and run cold water over them to stop their cooking. Squeeze the leeks dry, either with your fingers or by firmly pressing them down in a sieve with the back of a spoon.

In a large mixing bowl combine the leeks, garlic, lamb, parsley, lemon juice, salt, a few grindings of black pepper, and the 3 egg yolks. Beat with a large spoon until the mixture is smooth, then moisten with 2 tablespoons of cream. If it seems too dry, add 1 or 2 more tablespoons of cream and beat again. Taste for seasoning. Roll into small balls about 1 inch in diameter and chill for about 1 hour.

When the balls are firm, roll them lightly in flour, then dip them in the whole eggs, first lightly beaten with the vegetable oil. Roll them in the bread crumbs and make sure the balls are well coated. Ideally, they should be chilled again but you can, if you wish, fry them immediately. Heat the fat to 375 degrees on the deep-fat thermometer. Fry the balls, a few at a time (too many in the frying basket at the same time would lower the temperature of the fat too much) until they are a golden brown. This should take no more than 2 or 3 minutes. Drain them on paper toweling and serve at once. If they must wait, they may be kept warm for 10 minutes or so in a 250-degree oven.

The lamb and leek balls make fine cocktail accompaniments speared on picks and dipped in a bowl of lemon sauce (p. 221).

Madras Lamb Curry

Serves 4

5 tablespoons butter, *2 for sautéing onions and garlic and 3 for frying lamb*
2 cups onions, *thinly sliced*
1 teaspoon garlic, *finely chopped*
2 cups cold roast leg of lamb, *cut into 1½- to 2-inch pieces, trimmed of all fat and gristle*
4 tablespoons lemon juice

1 teaspoon salt
3 tablespoons imported Madras curry powder ⎫
1 tablespoon flour ⎬ *combined*
1 tablespoon vegetable oil ⎭
1 cup stock: beef or chicken bouillon or a combination of both, fresh or canned

Preheat the oven to 325 degrees. Melt 2 tablespoons of the butter in a 2- or 3-quart heavy flameproof casserole that has a tight-fitting cover. Add the onions and garlic and fry them over moderate heat for about 10 minutes, stirring every now and then, until they are soft and lightly colored. Transfer them from the casserole to a small bowl.

Dip the pieces of meat in the lemon juice, sprinkle with a little salt, then roll the lamb pieces in the combined curry powder and flour, coating them heavily. Heat the remaining 3 tablespoons of butter and the tablespoon of vegetable oil in the casserole. When the foam subsides, fry the lamb over moderately high heat, a few pieces at a time, until each piece is a deep golden brown. Return the onions to the casserole, pour in the stock, and bring to a boil, stirring gently, to combine all the ingredients. Then cover the casserole tightly, and bake it in the center of the oven for about an hour.

Note: This extraordinarily simple and fine curry may be served with any of the condiments listed for turkey curry (p. 148). But most attractive and suitable, perhaps, would be to accompany it with a bowl of plain boiled rice, a cucumber-yoghurt sauce (p. 223), and a bowl of chutney.

Lahmajoon

Small Armenian Lamb Pies

Serves 4–6 PASTRY	2 cups flour
	1 package granulated yeast
	½ cup lukewarm water
	¼ cup vegetable shortening, *melted and cooled to lukewarm*

½ teaspoon salt

½ teaspoon sugar

1 tablespoon butter, *softened, for buttering baking sheet*

FILLING

1 cup firmly packed cold roast leg of lamb, *ground*

¼ cup onions, *finely chopped*

1 teaspoon garlic, *finely chopped*

3 tablespoons green pepper, *finely chopped*

2 tablespoons parsley, *finely chopped*

1 tablespoon fresh mint, *finely chopped;* or 1 teaspoon dried mint, *crumbled*

4 teaspoons tomato paste

¾ cup fresh tomatoes, *peeled, seeded, and finely chopped,* or ¾ of an 8-ounce can of tomatoes, *thoroughly drained and finely chopped*

½ teaspoon dried red pepper flakes or ¼ teaspoon Tabasco

¾ teaspoon salt

To make the pastry, dump the flour (which need not be sifted) into a large mixing bowl. Dissolve the yeast in the lukewarm water and stir in the melted, cooled shortening, salt, and sugar. Combine little by little with the flour, and knead the resultant dough for about 10 or 15 minutes, until it is smooth, shiny, and elastic. Form the dough into a ball and cut a 1-inch-deep cross into the top. Set it into the bowl, sprinkle with a teaspoon or so of flour, and cover the bowl with a damp dish towel. Let the dough rise in a warm place (80 to 90 degrees, to be exact) for about 2 hours, or until the dough doubles in bulk. Punch it down and let it rest for another 10 minutes, then roll the dough out, about ¼ inch thick, on a floured board. Cut it into rounds with a 2½-inch cooky cutter if you plan to use the pies as cocktail accompaniments or into larger rounds of up to 5 inches in diameter for more substantial fare. In any event, place the rounds on a buttered baking sheet and prepare the filling.

For the filling, mix the ground lamb, chopped onions, garlic, green pepper, parsley, and mint, the tomato paste and tomatoes, and the seasoning with a large spoon until they are thoroughly combined. Cover each round of pastry with approximately a ½-inch layer of filling and bake in a preheated 425-degree oven for about 20 minutes, or until the *lahmajoons* are crisp and brown. Slide them under a hot broiler for a few seconds, if you like, just before serving.

Gratin of Lamb Orloff

Serves 4–6   The recipe for this dish is exactly the same as the one for *gratin* of veal Orloff on page 65. Substitute 6 to 8 slices of lamb for the veal.

Lamb, Eggplant, and Almonds in the Persian Style

Serves 4–6

1 eggplant weighing about 1¾ pounds, or 2 eggplants weighing an equivalent amount
Salt
½ cup olive oil plus 2 tablespoons
2 medium onions, *thinly sliced* (*about 2 cups loosely packed*)
½ cup flour
6 tablespoons almonds, *blanched and slivered*

½ cup long-grain rice, *not* the converted type
1 cup (firmly packed) roast leg of lamb (preferably rare), *ground*
1 teaspoon garlic, *finely chopped*
Freshly ground black pepper
¼ teaspoon thyme
¼ teaspoon allspice
¾ cup chicken or beef stock, fresh or canned

SAUCE

1 cup yoghurt
½ cup cucumber, *peeled, seeded, and coarsely chopped*
1 tablespoon fresh dill, *finely chopped,* or 1 teaspoon dried dillweed

Salt
⅛ teaspoon cayenne

Cut the unpeeled eggplant into ½-inch slices, sprinkle the slices on both sides with about 1 tablespoon of salt in all, and lay them side by side on a large flat platter. Place a platter or plate on top of the slices and let them stand for about 1 hour, to drain.

Heat 2 tablespoons of the olive oil in a large heavy frying pan and, over moderate heat, fry the onions for about 8 minutes, turning them with a spoon until they are soft and slightly brown. With a slotted spoon transfer them to a small bowl. Pat the eggplant slices dry with paper toweling and dip them lightly in flour, shaking to remove any excess flour. Starting with 3 tablespoons of olive oil, heated almost to smoking in the frying pan, sauté the eggplant slices, a few at a time, until they are quite brown on both sides, but barely cooked through. Replenish the oil in the pan whenever necessary (see note, p. 46). As the eggplant slices are done, place them side by side on a large platter, and when finished, in the same pan lightly brown the slivered almonds over moderate heat. Remove the nuts with a slotted spoon to a small dish. Parboil the rice by dropping it into 2 cups of boiling salted water and boiling it briskly for 8 minutes. Drain at once, run cold water through it to stop its cooking, then put the rice aside. In a small mixing bowl combine the ground lamb with the chopped garlic, ½ teaspoon of salt, a few grindings of black pepper, the thyme, and the allspice, and mix thoroughly together.

Choose a 1-quart mold with straight sides (preferably a charlotte mold) in which to assemble and cook all the ingredients. Brush the pan with olive oil, then divide the eggplant into 3 parts and the meat, onions, and almonds in half. Arrange them in the pan in the following fashion: a layer of eggplant on the bottom, followed by half the meat, onions, and almonds; then another layer of eggplant, followed by the remaining meat, onions, and almonds. Finish with the remaining eggplant. Spread the parboiled rice evenly over the top of the eggplant, patting it down with a spatula so that the grains adhere to each other and cover the eggplant completely.

Preheat the oven to 350 degrees and in a small saucepan bring the ¾ cup of stock to a boil. Pour it into the mold without disturbing the rice, cover tightly with a sheet of aluminum foil, and set the mold in a small roasting pan. Pour enough boiling water into the pan to come halfway up the sides of the mold. Bake undisturbed for about 1 hour. If the rice isn't quite done at that time, cook for a few minutes longer. It is desirable to let the eggplant and lamb rest out of the oven for 5 minutes or so before unmolding it.

Meanwhile, make the sauce by combining the cup of yoghurt with the ½ cup of peeled, seeded, and coarsely chopped cucumber, the dill, salt, and cayenne.

To unmold the eggplant, first run a sharp thin knife around the inside of the mold. Place a warm platter over the top of the mold and, grasping mold and platter firmly together, turn them over. Before serving, remove any liquid which collects around the eggplant. This dish may be served either hot or cold; the sauce, in any event, is always served chilled.

Lamb alla Cacciatora in the Northern Italian Style

Serves 4–6

6 tablespoons olive oil, *4 for sautéing lamb and 2 for sautéing onions and garlic*

2 cups roast leg of lamb, *cut into 1- or 1½-inch cubes*

½ teaspoon salt

Freshly ground black pepper

1 teaspoon dried rosemary, *crumbled*

1 tablespoon flour

½ cup onions, *finely chopped*

1 teaspoon garlic, *finely chopped*

2 tablespoons red wine vinegar

¾–1 cup beef stock, fresh or canned, or, if pos sible, all or part unthickened gravy from the roast leg of lamb

2 anchovy fillets, *drained, washed, dried, and finely chopped*

1 tablespoon parsley, *finely chopped*

Preheat the oven to 475 degrees. Heat 4 tablespoons of the oil in a large heavy frying pan, add the pieces of lamb, and quickly sauté them over high heat until they are lightly browned and glistening with the olive oil. Transfer to a heavy 2-quart casserole, add the salt, a few grindings of black pepper, the rosemary, and 1 level tablespoon of flour. With a large spoon, mix together thoroughly until no trace of the flour remains. Cook the lamb, uncovered, in the center of the oven, turning the meat from time to time to prevent it from burning and to brown the flour evenly.

Meanwhile heat the remaining 2 tablespoons of olive oil in the frying pan, add the onions and garlic and sauté, stirring almost constantly, until they are soft and lightly colored. Pour in the vinegar, turn the heat up high, and boil the liquid away almost completely. Add ¾ cup of the stock and bring it to the simmering point.

Remove the casserole from the oven and turn the heat down to 325 degrees. Stir the simmering stock and onions into the lamb, cover the casserole tightly, and return it to the oven. Cook for about 40 minutes, checking every 15 minutes or so to make sure the sauce isn't thickening too much. If it does (it should be the consistency of a medium cream sauce), thin it with a few tablespoons of stock.

Ten minutes or so before the lamb is done, remove 4 tablespoons of sauce from the casserole and combine it with the chopped anchovies in a small bowl, beating them together until the anchovies almost completely dissolve. Stir the mixture into the casserole and simmer 10 minutes longer. Serve the lamb directly from the casserole or arranged on a hot platter, garnished, in either case, with the chopped parsley. Buttered white or green noodles or, in fact, any buttered *pasta* would be a suitable accompaniment.

Veal

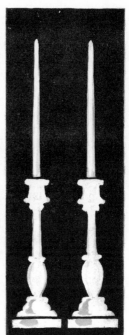

Veal

Veal Because the demand for veal in America is relatively limited, it is difficult to find the young milk-fed variety, which is grayish-pink, satiny, and finely grained. But it is worth searching for; veal at its best has a delicacy few other meats can approach.

Of course, much depends on how it is cooked. Since even the best veal has little interior fat—or what in beef is called marbling—it is at its least successful when simply roasted. Moreover, veal is always served well done. The only sensible way to cook it, therefore—as French and Italian cooks know so well— is to braise it. Then the meat is constantly enveloped in the aromatic steam produced by the stock, wine, and vegetables surrounding it, and the veal emerges, finally, tender, moist, and succulent, and with a natural sauce all its own.

Again, like all braised meats, braised veal can be reheated successfully. And when one improvises, using it in various hot dishes, or cold in *vitello tonnato*, for example, or in a salad, it maintains its original flavor remarkably well.

▶ ◀

A Classic Braised Veal in a Casserole

5-pound roast of veal, boned and tied: *neck, rump, shoulder, or loin*
3 tablespoons butter

2 medium onions, *thinly sliced*
2 medium carrots, *thinly sliced*
3 stalks celery, *thinly sliced*

3 tablespoons vegetable oil
Salt
Freshly ground black pepper
A bouquet consisting of 4 sprigs parsley and 1

bay leaf, *tied together with string*
½ teaspoon thyme
½ cup chicken stock, fresh or canned, *heated*
(optional)

Whatever the cut of veal, have it wrapped in a thin covering of fat and securely tied at 1-inch intervals so that it will keep its shape while braising.

Preheat the oven to 325 degrees. Choose a heavy, flameproof casserole equipped with a tightly fitting cover and just large enough to hold the veal comfortably. Melt 3 tablespoons of butter in the casserole, and when the foam subsides, add the sliced onions, carrots, and celery. Cook over low heat for 10 or 15 minutes until the vegetables are tender and lightly colored. Meanwhile, in a large heavy frying pan, heat 2 tablespoons of vegetable oil until it literally begins to smoke. Add the veal and brown it thoroughly on all sides. Transfer it then to the top of the vegetables in the casserole, sprinkle generously with salt and freshly ground black pepper, and toss in the bouquet. Cover the casserole tightly, heat it to the sizzling point on top of the stove, and place it in the lower third of the preheated oven. Depending on the diameter of the veal roast rather than its weight, it will take anywhere from 1½ to 2 hours to become tender. Baste after 30 minutes with its own juices and continue to baste thereafter every 15 minutes. (If, for some reason, the casserole is dry, add the ½ cup of heated stock.) The veal is done when its juices run yellow rather than pink after it is pierced with the point of a small sharp knife.

After cutting away the strings, carve the roast into thin even slices. Serve as a sauce the braising liquid, first strained, then degreased and boiled down in the uncovered casserole, until it reaches the intensity of flavor you desire.

▶ For this classic braised veal, cajole your butcher into giving you a solid piece of boned veal rather than one he has rolled. Attractive and neat as the rolled piece of veal may look, it will inevitably shred into strips when you carve it. The neck of veal is an unfamiliar cut to many cooks; should your butcher have some on hand it is well worth trying. Properly boned and tied, it makes a most attractive—and comparatively inexpensive—narrow cylinder of solid veal. Although it is streaked with bits of cartilage here and there, its flavor is good and it is easy to carve. The loin of veal, boned (the rack, that is), is of course the choicest cut, but is almost prohibitively expensive. Whatever the cut of veal you use, however—if it is meat of good quality—it will cook through in the braising time suggested in the recipe.

odds
and
ENds

A Classic Braised Veal in a Casserole 61

▶ Another and unusual way to serve the *vitello tonnato* improvisation on page 67 is to cut the cold veal into small cubes instead of slices, and then marinate them in the tunafish sauce. Before presenting them as hors d'oeuvres, roll the cubes in minced parsley and chives and spear each one with a toothpick.

▶ If it is the warm weather season, you might want to plan the *blanquette de veau* improvisation, chilled (the sauce will usually jell), sprinkled with the chopped dill, and accompanied by slices of lemon and a cold rice salad.

▶ There are many variations possible in the veal and herring salad improvisation on page 69. Although cold veal is used in Denmark to make this salad, Swedish cooks use any meat they may happen to have on hand—tongue is an especial favorite. And Scandinavian cooks in general will make a "fine" herring and meat salad by chopping all the ingredients together until they are soft but not mushy in texture. The salad can then be spread on bread as a base for the celebrated Danish open-faced sandwiches, or served in small lettuce cups, sprinkled with finely chopped hard-cooked eggs.

iMPROViSATiONS

Fricadelles of Veal with Caper Sauce

Makes about 30 one-inch fricadelles

6 tablespoons butter, *2 for sautéing onions, 2 softened for the meat mixture, and 2 for sautéing the fricadelles*

⅔ cup onions, *finely chopped*

1 teaspoon garlic, *finely chopped*

3 medium baked potatoes (about 1 cup of pulp, firmly packed) or 1 cup cold mashed potatoes

2 cups cold braised veal, *ground or finely chopped, free of all fat and gristle*

4 flat anchovy fillets, *washed, dried, and finely chopped (about 3 teaspoons)*

1 teaspoon lemon juice

2 tablespoons parsley, *finely chopped*

1 egg, *lightly beaten*

2 tablespoons heavy cream

Freshly ground black pepper

Salt

3 tablespoons vegetable oil

½ cup flour

CAPER SAUCE	2 tablespoons flour	¼ teaspoon lemon juice
	1 cup chicken stock, fresh or canned, or **all or part of the veal braising liquid, if available**	1 tablespoon parsley, *finely chopped*
	1 egg (yolk only)	Salt
	½ cup heavy cream	⅛ teaspoon cayenne
	2 tablespoons capers, *drained, washed, dried, and coarsely chopped*	

Melt 2 tablespoons of the butter in a small frying pan, add the chopped onions and garlic, and slowly sauté them for about 18 minutes; they should become soft but not brown. Transfer them, to a large mixing bowl. Add the freshly baked potato pulp (leftover mashed potatoes will do, but they will be nowhere nearly as good), the chopped or ground veal, the anchovies, lemon juice, and parsley. Beat vigorously with a large wooden spoon or in an electric mixer equipped with a pastry arm. When the mixture is quite smooth, beat in the egg and 2 tablespoons of cream. Season highly with freshly ground black pepper and more discreetly with salt, remembering that the anchovies are quite salty. Beat in, finally, 2 tablespoons of softened butter. Form the meat into small balls about 1 inch in diameter and place them in one layer on a platter or cooky sheet. Cover with waxed paper and chill for at least 1 hour.

When you are ready to cook the fricadelles, slowly heat 3 tablespoons of vegetable oil and 1 tablespoon of butter in a heavy 10-inch frying pan. Meanwhile sift ½ cup flour onto a double sheet of waxed paper and gently roll the fricadelles in the flour until they are thoroughly coated. When the fat in the pan is almost smoking (and not before), add 8 or 10 meatballs and shake the pan back and forth so that the fricadelles roll around in the pan almost constantly; this will help them keep their shape and brown evenly. Cook them as quickly as you can—at most for 3 or 4 minutes—and remove them with a slotted spoon to a heated platter or baking dish. Proceed similarly with the remaining fricadelles, adding a little more oil and butter to the pan if necessary.

When all the fricadelles are cooked, quickly make the sauce: pour off all but 2 or 3 tablespoons of fat from the pan and stir in, off the heat, 2 level tablespoons of flour. Mix thoroughly. Now, over this *roux* pour the cup of stock (or combined braising liquid and stock, hot or cold). Return the pan to the heat and with a whisk beat the sauce until it begins to thicken. When it reaches the boiling point and becomes quite smooth, turn down the heat and simmer slowly for 1 or 2 minutes. Meanwhile combine the egg yolk with the ½ cup of heavy cream, and then stir into it 3 tablespoons of the hot sauce before mixing the cream and egg with the sauce in the pan; add slowly, stirring constantly. When it comes to the boil, remove it from the heat at once. Add the capers, lemon juice, chopped parsley, salt, and cayenne. Taste for seasoning, pour the sauce over the fricadelles, and serve.

A Blanquette de Veau

Serves 4–6

3 tablespoons butter, *1 for cooking the onions and 2 for the roux*

2 cups chicken stock, fresh or canned (**use as part of this any remaining braising liquid from the original braised veal**), *½ cup for cooking the onions and 1½ cups for the sauce*

12 small white onions, *about 1 inch in diameter, peeled and left whole*

1 teaspoon lemon juice, *½ for cooking the mushrooms and ½ for the sauce*

½ pound mushrooms, *whole if small, quartered or sliced if large*

3 tablespoons flour

2 eggs (yolks only)

½ cup heavy cream

Salt

⅛ teaspoon cayenne

2 cups cold braised veal, *trimmed of all fat and gristle and cut into 1½-inch chunks*

2 tablespoons parsley, *finely chopped*

Plain boiled rice

In an enamel or stainless-steel saucepan that can be covered tightly, heat 2 tablespoons of the butter with the ½ cup of chicken stock. Season with a little salt and add the onions. Bring to a boil, cover the pan, and turn down the heat. Simmer the onions for about 30 minutes, turning them occasionally with a spoon so that they will be constantly moistened. Add a little extra stock if the original amount should cook away. The onions should be tender after the half hour of cooking. Remove them with a slotted spoon to a small bowl. Stir ½ teaspoon of the lemon juice into stock remaining in the pan, bring it to a boil and add the mushrooms. Cook them over high heat for about 5 minutes, stirring almost constantly. Remove them from the pan with a slotted spoon and put them in the same bowl with the onions.

Use the remaining liquid in the saucepan as part of the 1½ cups of stock to make the *velouté* sauce. In a separate enamel or stainless-steel saucepan, melt the remaining 2 tablespoons of butter and stir into it, off the heat, 3 tablespoons of flour. Add 1½ cups of stock, hot or cold, and with a whisk stir it briskly with the butter-and-flour *roux*. Bring the sauce to a boil over high heat, stirring almost constantly. When it thickens, turn the heat down and simmer the sauce undisturbed for about 5 minutes. Meanwhile, mix together, only just enough to combine them, the 2 egg yolks and the ½ cup of cream. Mix into it a few tablespoons of the hot *velouté* sauce, then reverse the process and pour the egg mixture into the pan of sauce. Stirring briskly, bring the sauce almost to a boil and season with the remaining ½ teaspoon of lemon juice, salt, and cayenne.* Add the cold cubed veal, the cooked white onions and mushrooms, but don't include any of the liquid which may have collected in the bowl. Cook gently until the vegetables and meat are heated through, sprinkle with the chopped parsley and serve with plain boiled rice.

* *Note:* The *blanquette* can easily be turned into a *blanquette de veau à l'indienne* by stirring into the *roux* of the *velouté* sauce 1 tablespoon or more of good curry powder and letting it cook with the flour and butter for a minute or so before adding the stock and completing the sauce.

Gratin of Veal Orloff

Serves 4–6	**6–8 thin (¼- to ½-inch) slices cold braised veal,** *well trimmed and all the same size, if possible*

SOUBISE SAUCE		
	2 tablespoons butter	Salt
	2 cups onions, *coarsely chopped*	⅛ teaspoon cayenne
	3 tablespoons raw rice (not converted type)	⅛ teaspoon lemon juice
	⅓ cup chicken stock, fresh or canned	2–6 tablespoons heavy cream
	1 egg (yolk only)	

MORNAY SAUCE		
	3 tablespoons butter	¼–½ cup heavy cream
	4 tablespoons flour	¼ cup imported Swiss cheese, *grated*
	1½ cups chicken stock, fresh or canned; use **part veal braising liquid if available**	Salt
		White pepper

½ cup bread crumbs
1 tablespoon butter, *softened and cut into small pieces*

Preheat the oven to 325 degrees. Prepare the *soubise* sauce by melting 2 tablespoons of butter in a small enamel casserole equipped with a tightly fitting cover. Add the chopped onions and, stirring continuously, cook them for a few minutes until they wilt slightly; don't let them brown. Mix in the rice and chicken.stock and bring to a boil. Cover the casserole tightly and slide it into the middle of the preheated oven and let it cook undisturbed for about 40 minutes. By then all the stock should be absorbed and the rice and onions tender. If they aren't, cook them a while longer. Force the rice and onion mixture through a food mill, or lacking that, run it through a fine sieve with the back of a large spoon. Beat in the egg yolk, salt, cayenne, and lemon juice. The purée will be very thick. Thin it with enough heavy cream so that the resulting *soubise* sauce just about holds its shape in the spoon. Then put it aside.

To prepare the *mornay* sauce, melt the 3 tablespoons of butter in a small enamel or stainless-steel saucepan and stir in, off the heat, the 4 level tablespoons of flour. Add to this *roux*, all at once, 1½ cups of stock, hot or cold, and beat it together with a wire whisk. Still beating, bring it to a boil over moderate heat, and when it begins to thicken turn the heat down to barely simmering and, stirring with a spoon, let the sauce cook slowly for a few minutes to rid it of any floury taste. Stir in ¼ cup of heavy cream and if the sauce seems too thick (it should flow fairly easily off the spoon), add as much of the remaining cream as necessary. Season with salt and white pepper to taste and add the grated cheese. If the sauce must stand for any length of time before being used, transfer it to a mixing bowl and cover it tightly with plastic wrap.

Choose a shallow oven-proof baking dish in which to assemble, cook, and finally serve the *gratin*. Spread a thin layer of the *mornay* sauce on the bottom of the dish. Cover the veal pieces one at a time with a fairly thick layer of the *soubise* sauce and lay them down the center of the dish, one slightly overlapping the other. When they are assembled, spread the remaining *soubise* on top and around the sides of the loaf, covering as much of the exposed meat as possible. Over this pour, spoonful by spoonful, the *mornay* sauce, masking the *soubise* sauce almost completely. Sprinkle the veal with the ½ cup of bread crumbs and dot it lightly all over with little bits of butter. The dish now can either be covered with plastic wrap and refrigerated until you are ready to cook it or cooked at once.

Preheat the oven to 375 degrees. Cook the *gratin* of veal in the center of the oven for about 15 or 20 minutes, or until the sauce begins to bubble. Slide it, then, under a hot broiler for a few seconds to brown its surface and serve at once.

Veal Paprikash

Serves 4

The recipe for this dish is exactly the same as the one for turkey paprikash on page 145. Substitute 2 cups of cold braised veal for the cooked turkey. And the veal may be cut into larger pieces than the turkey if you prefer.

Vitello Tonnato

Serves 4

6–8 slices of cold braised veal, *about ¼ inch thick and trimmed of all fat and gristle*

SAUCE

½ cup olive oil

3½-ounce can tunafish (canned in olive oil, if possible)

3 flat anchovies, *cut up*

1 egg (yolk only)

1 tablespoon lemon juice

⅛ teaspoon cayenne

3 tablespoons heavy cream

3 tablespoons veal braising liquid or chicken stock, fresh or canned

1½ tablespoons capers, *drained, washed, and dried*

GARNISH

1 tablespoon parsley, *finely chopped*

3–4 green onions (scallions), *cut into small rounds*

4 tomatoes, *sliced or quartered*

2 eggs, *hard-cooked and quartered or sliced*

Black olives, preferably the Italian type

1 lemon, *quartered or sliced*

In the container of an electric blender,° combine the olive oil, tunafish, anchovies, egg yolk, lemon juice, and cayenne. Blend only long enough to turn this into a thick, smooth purée, then scrape it into a small mixing bowl. Stir in the heavy cream and the braising liquid or chicken stock. If the sauce is still too thick, thin it with a little more cream or stock. It should have the consistency of a medium cream sauce. Add the capers and taste the sauce for seasoning. It may possibly need a little salt and more lemon juice.

Spread a thin layer of the tunafish sauce on the bottom of a glass or porcelain platter or baking dish. Lay the cold veal on it and mask with the remaining sauce. Cover the dish tightly with plastic wrap and refrigerate overnight, or a day longer, if possible.

To serve, arrange the slices of veal, slightly overlapping, down the center of an attractive serving platter, and cover them with the sauce. Sprinkle the meat with the combined chopped parsley and green onion rounds and surround it with the tomatoes, hard-cooked eggs, olives, and lemon.

* *Note:* To make the tunafish sauce by hand, mash the tunafish and anchovies to a paste with a fork. With the back of a large spoon rub it through a fine sieve set in a mixing bowl. Stir in the egg yolk, lemon juice, and cayenne, and then, with a whisk, beat in the olive oil 1 tablespoon at a time. Add as much of the cream and braising liquid or chicken stock as is necessary to thin the sauce to the consistency of a medium cream sauce. Stir in the capers and continue with the recipe as described above.

A Glazed Veal Loaf in the French Style

Serves 4

½ cup freshly made mayonnaise or a very good commercial brand

2 teaspoons shallots or scallions, *finely chopped*

2 tablespoons watercress, *finely chopped*

2 tablespoons parsley, *finely chopped*

1 tablespoon dried tarragon or 1 tablespoon fresh, *finely chopped*

1 tablespoon capers, *washed, dried, and finely chopped*

1 tablespoon sour pickle, *finely chopped*

3 anchovy fillets, *drained, washed, dried, and finely chopped*

4 tablespoons unsalted butter

Salt

⅛ teaspoon cayenne

Lemon juice

8–10 even slices cold braised veal, *cut about ¼ inch thick*

ACCOMPANI-MENTS

French potato salad (p. 112)

Tomatoes, *sliced*

Black olives

Lemon quarters

Ideally, your mayonnaise should be freshly made but a good unsweetened commercial brand will do if it must. In a small mixing bowl combine the mayonnaise with the shallots or scallions, watercress, parsley, and tarragon. Squeeze the chopped capers and chopped pickle in the corner of a towel to rid them of their extra moisture and then add them to the mayonnaise also. Stir in the chopped anchovies.

Cream the 4 tablespoons of butter by beating with a wooden spoon in a bowl until it is smooth and creamy. Beat it into the mayonnaise a teaspoon at a time, and add the salt, cayenne and lemon juice. Taste for seasoning. If the mayonnaise has become too soft at this point to hold its shape in a spoon, refrigerate it for 15 minutes or so to firm it slightly.

Trim the slices of veal so that they form symmetrical rectangular or square shapes. Spread each slice with the chilled mayonnaise, reconstructing the original shape as you proceed. When all the slices have been covered, frost the loaf almost as you would a cake. Smooth all of its sides with a spatula and chill until firm. Serve with French potato salad, sliced tomatoes, black olives, and lemon quarters.

Veal and Herring Salad in the Scandinavian Style with Pink Sour Cream Sauce

Serves 4–6

½–⅔ cup of ½-inch pieces of herring: *salt herring (soaked overnight in cold water), canned Matjes herring from Sweden, bottled Bismarck herring, bottled Danish herring in wine sauce, or pickled herring in sour cream*

2 cups cold veal, *cut into ½-inch cubes and trimmed of all fat and gristle*

2 cups cold boiled potatoes, *diced (½-inch cubes)*

1 cup fresh or canned cooked beets, *well drained,*

patted dry on paper toweling, and diced (¼-inch cubes)

½ cup apple, *peeled, cored, and coarsely diced*

⅓ cup onions, *finely chopped*

3 tablespoons dill pickle, *finely chopped*

2 tablespoons white wine vinegar

4 tablespoons fresh dill, *finely chopped*

Salt

Freshly ground black pepper

DRESSING

3 eggs, *hard-cooked and chilled*

1 tablespoon prepared mustard

2 tablespoons white wine vinegar

4 tablespoons vegetable oil

2–4 tablespoons heavy cream

SAUCE

½ pint sour cream

3 tablespoons beet juice from canned beets

½ teaspoon lemon juice

Whatever herring you use, place it in a sieve and wash it well under cold running water. Drain and dry it thoroughly with paper toweling. In a large mixing bowl combine the cut-up herring with the veal, potatoes, beets, apples, onions, and dill pickle, and with a large spoon toss all the ingredients together gently but thoroughly. Add the 2 tablespoons of vinegar and 3 tablespoons of the dill and toss again. Although most herrings are fairly salty, the salad will probably need extra salt. Add it to taste, and a few grindings of black pepper.

To make the dressing, remove the yolks from the hard-cooked eggs and with the back of a spoon rub them through a fine sieve into a small mixing bowl. (Chop the whites finely for later use.) Stir in the mustard and mash the yolks to a paste, then with a small whisk beat in the 2 tablespoons of vinegar and 4 tablespoons of oil, 1 tablespoon at a time. Beat in the heavy cream, using as much of it as you need to make the dressing fluid enough to run thickly off the spoon. Pour it over the salad and mix together lightly; take care not to mash any of the ingredients during the process. Taste again for seasoning, then refrigerate it for at least 3 hours before serving. The salad may be presented simply arranged on a platter or in a glass serving bowl with the garnish described below.

If you want to mold it, firmly pack the salad into any undecorated lightly oiled mold, soufflé dish, pan, or bowl. Cover it with plastic wrap and chill for at least 3 hours. To unmold, place a chilled serving platter upside down over the salad, then grasp the mold and platter together firmly and quickly invert them. Still holding them together, rap the platter gently on the table; the salad will slide out easily.

In whatever form you serve it, sprinkle the salad with the reserved chopped egg whites and dust it with the remaining tablespoon of chopped dill. A wreath of crisp watercress arranged around the salad not only makes an attractive garnish but is a fine accompaniment as well. Make the sauce by stirring the beet juice into the sour cream a tablespoon at a time, then season it with the lemon juice. Transfer it to a sauceboat and pass it separately with the salad.

Veal, Anchovy, and Watercress Salad

Serves 4–6

1½–2 cups cold braised veal, *cut into small batons or sticks about 2 inches long and ½ inch wide*

½ teaspoon salt

Few gratings of freshly ground black pepper

½ teaspoon powdered or Dijon mustard

2 tablespoons white wine vinegar

½ cup olive oil

1 tablespoon shallots or scallions, *finely chopped*
½ teaspoon garlic, *finely chopped*
2 tablespoons parsley, *finely chopped*
2-ounce can of rolled anchovies with capers, *drained*

2 hard-cooked eggs (yolks only), *rubbed through a sieve*
A bunch of crisp watercress, *chilled*

Naturally, the batons of veal needn't be precisely 2 inches long, but they should all be somewhat the same size, if possible. Make the vinaigrette sauce in a small bowl by dissolving the salt, black pepper, and mustard in 2 tablespoons of white wine vinegar. Slowly beat in the olive oil, then add the shallots or scallions and garlic. With a spoon toss the veal batons in the dressing making sure the meat is thoroughly coated. Marinate at room temperature for at least 1 hour or longer, stirring now and then so that the veal is continually moistened.

Compose the salad a few minutes before serving it. Arrange the marinated veal in the center of a chilled glass or crystal salad bowl and dot it with the drained rolled anchovies. Sprinkle the top with the chopped parsley and dust it lightly with the sieved egg yolks. Surround with a thick wreath of chilled watercress and serve.

PORK

Pork

More pork is consumed in the United States than any other meat except beef, but for some singular reason it is never considered impressive enough to serve on really important occasions. Other cuisines have no such inhibitions. The Chinese, Poles, and French, among others, have devised innumerable recipes for its use and serve them with style. And interestingly enough, many of the dishes require that the pork be previously cooked. These adventurous cooks are also aware of how attractive a dish of thinly sliced pork, served at room temperature, can be, accompanied, say, by chilled fresh melon as is suggested in one of the improvisations.

Because it is relatively free of fat and bone, a roast half of fresh ham is presented here as the basic recipe from which all the other pork recipes derive. Of course, a roast loin of pork or fresh picnic shoulder could be roasted instead or, if you prefer, braised, as in the recipe for braised veal on page 60, a method, preferred by many because it gives the pork a more pliable, less springy texture. But however you cook it, and whatever the cut, *all* pork responds remarkably well to being recooked. The only danger to avoid is overcooking, which does not so much toughen it, as would be the case with roast beef, for example, but is likely to cause it to shred or disintegrate—hardly a fitting end for so noble a meat.

▶ ◀

A Classic Roast Fresh Ham or Pork Shoulder

Half a fresh ham, butt or shank end, about 6 pounds
2 teaspoons whole black peppercorns, *coarsely crushed*

2 teaspoons salt
2 bay leaves, *coarsely crumbled*
1 teaspoon dry leaf thyme
2 medium onions, *sliced*

2 medium carrots, *sliced*

1½ cups chicken stock, fresh or canned, or ¾ cup each of canned bouillon and canned chicken

stock, *combined*

Lemon juice (optional)

Preheat the oven to 450 degrees. Score the ham by cutting through the rind and fat right down to the flesh with a long sharp knife. Make the cuts parallel to each other, 2 inches apart, first lengthwise then crosswise.

Mix the peppercorns (crushed coarsely either in a mortar or wrapped in a towel and bruised with a rolling pin), salt, bay leaves, and thyme in a small bowl. Press this mixture into the scored fat of the ham, insert a meat thermometer, if you have one, into the fleshiest part of the meat, then place the ham on a rack set in a roasting pan just about large enough to hold it.

Roast the ham undisturbed at 450 degrees in the center of the oven, then turn the heat down to 350 degrees. Scatter the sliced onions and carrots on the bottom of the pan. Basting is unnecessary. The ham should be fully done, with a crisp, crackly surface, at the end of about 4 hours, or when the thermometer reads 185 degrees. Let the ham rest for about 10 minutes outside the oven before carving and serving it.

Meanwhile, add 1½ cups of stock to the drippings and fat in the roasting pan, scraping up all the brown sediment on the bottom and sides of the pan. Bring the stock to a boil on top of the stove, and cook it briskly, uncovered, until it has reduced to about half its original volume. Strain it then through a sieve set over a saucepan, pressing down hard on the vegetables before throwing them away. Let the fat rise to the surface of the sauce and skim it carefully. Season the sauce lightly with salt and pepper and perhaps a drop or two of lemon juice; reheat and serve it in a sauceboat with the sliced ham.

► In place of the honeydew melon served with the cold ham on page 81, you might, for variety, use other fresh fruit, notably, fresh figs, fresh pineapple, or ripe, peeled sliced pears, or avocados sprinkled with lemon juice to prevent their darkening.

► The Chinese use not only cold shredded pork for their fried rice but often any other cooked cold meat, poultry, or seafood they may happen to have on hand. Any of the meats, fowl, and shellfish described in the classics in this book can therefore be substituted for the pork suggested in the fried rice and pork improvisation on page 78.

► And even small amounts of chopped peanuts, walnuts, or almonds may be added with discretion to the finished fried rice dish.

odds
and
ENds

▶ Should you on occasion have a cup or so of cold cooked pork left over for which you have no particular use, substitute it for the shredded raw pork in the egg roll improvisation on page 185. In that event, sauté the cooked pork for only ½ minute or so to heat it through instead of cooking it as the recipe calls for.

iMPROViSATiONS

Bigos

Polish Hunter's Stew

Serves 6–8

2 pounds sauerkraut, fresh if possible, otherwise canned or in plastic bags

3 tablespoons butter

1 cup onions, *finely chopped*

1 teaspoon garlic, *finely chopped*

6 medium mushrooms, *coarsely chopped*

1 medium tart apple, *peeled, cored, and coarsely chopped*

2 cups fresh cabbage, *finely shredded*

½ cup dry white wine

2–2½ cups chicken stock, fresh or canned (**include, if possible, in this amount as much pork braising liquid as you have**)

1 tablespoon tomato paste

8 dried prunes

A bouquet consisting of 6 parsley sprigs, celery tops with leaves, and 1 bay leaf, *tied together with string*

Salt

Freshly ground black pepper

1 pound Polish sausage (*Kielbasa*), *cut into 2-inch chunks*

1½ **cups roast fresh ham or pork,**° *cut into ½-inch cubes*

2 tablespoons fresh dill, *finely chopped*

Preheat the oven to 325 degrees. Drain the sauerkraut, wash it well under cold running water, then soak in cold water for 10 to 20 minutes depending upon its acidity. Squeeze it dry by the handfuls and put it aside. Ideally, sauerkraut, whatever the dish, should taste only mildly acidulated before being cooked.

Melt the 3 tablespoons of butter in a 4-quart casserole that has a heavy, tightly fitting cover, and cook the chopped onions, garlic, mushrooms, and apples for about 10 or 15 minutes. Stir them frequently and don't allow them to brown. Add the sauerkraut, first gently pulled apart with your fingers, the shredded fresh cabbage, white wine, 2 cups of stock, the tomato paste, prunes, and the bouquet. Mix together gently and bring the liquid to a boil over high heat. Add salt and freshly ground pepper to taste, cover the casserole tightly, and place it in the center of the preheated oven. Let it cook undisturbed for about 1 hour. If the cabbage seems dry at this point, add the other ½ cup of heated stock. In any case, cook it for ½ hour longer, then bury in the cabbage the cut-up Polish sausage and the pieces of ham. Cook from 40 minutes to 1 hour longer and before serving taste for seasoning. In Poland where the making and serving of *bigos* is as much a ritual as is the serving of *choucroute* in France, Polish cooks insist that *bigos* should be served only after it has been reheated and cooled once or twice a day for three days. Be that as it may, *bigos* is every bit as good eaten the moment it is done. Before serving, sprinkle the *bigos* with the finely chopped dill.

* *Note: Bigos* can be made, as it frequently is in Poland, with pot roast as well as with pork. And often the two meats are combined with fine effect.

Sweet and Pungent Pork in the Chinese Style

Serves 4	2 tablespoons soy sauce	
	2 cups cooked cold pork, *cut into ¾-inch cubes and trimmed of all fat*	
SAUCE*	½ cup red wine vinegar	2 medium carrots, *cut into 1 by ½ inch strips*
	4 tablespoons brown sugar	2 teaspoons cornstarch
	1 cup chicken stock or ¾ cup stock and ¼ cup cold water	1 tablespoon soy sauce
	2 medium green peppers, *seeded and cut into 1-inch squares*	
BATTER	¼ cup flour	1 egg
	¼ cup cornstarch	Vegetable oil or shortening for deep-frying
	4 tablespoons cold chicken stock or cold water	

Mix together in a small bowl the cubed pork and 2 tablespoons of soy sauce. Marinate for 1 hour or so, turning the pork in the sauce every now and then. Meanwhile make the sauce. Combine in a small saucepan the vinegar, brown sugar, and ¾ cup of the stock. Bring this to a boil and continue to boil vigorously until the liquid is reduced to about half its original volume. Add the green-pepper squares and carrot strips and cook them for about 5 or 6 minutes over fairly moderate heat—they should be tender but still slightly crisp. Mix to a paste the 2 teaspoons of cornstarch and a ¼ cup of stock or cold water, then stir it in the hot sauce, and cook for 1 or 2 minutes until it thickens and becomes translucent. Season with the tablespoon of soy sauce (more if you prefer) and put sauce aside.

Just before serving, prepare the batter by combining in a small mixing bowl the flour, 4 tablespoons of cold water or stock, and the egg, beating with a spoon until it is smooth. Add to the batter the pork and its marinating liquid. Stir the mixture gently and thoroughly so that each piece of pork is completely coated. Lift the pork cubes out of the batter with a slotted spoon and fry them in a basket, a few pieces at a time, in deep fat heated to 375 degrees.

Serve the lightly browned, crisp pork in a deep serving dish with the hot sweet and pungent sauce poured over and around it.

Note: Although many Chinese cooks frown upon it, you may, if you like, add a cup of well-drained canned pineapple chunks to the sauce for this sweet and pungent pork.

Fried Rice and Pork in the Chinese Style

Serves 4–6

⅓–½ cup vegetable oil

4 cups boiled rice, *chilled* (about 1⅓ cups raw rice)

2 **cups cold cooked pork,** *coarsely shredded*

2 tablespoons soy sauce

Salt

Freshly ground black pepper

3 eggs, *lightly beaten*

¼ cup scallions, *cut into ½-inch pieces and slivered lengthwise*

In a 10-inch frying pan, heat ⅓ cup of vegetable oil until it smokes. Add the rice and, with a large wooden spoon, stir it over moderate heat until the grains are thoroughly coated with oil and begin to color lightly. Add the remaining oil if the rice seems dry. This should take no more than 7 or 8 minutes. Mix in the shredded pork and cook 3 or 4 minutes or until it is heated through. Stir in the soy sauce and season with salt and pepper to taste.

Beat the eggs just long enough to combine them, then pour them over the hot rice and pork mixture. If the pan is a heavy one, it will retain enough heat from the first frying to cook the eggs through as you continually stir them with the rice. Naturally, if the pan has cooled, cook the mixture over fairly high heat. In any event the finished dish should not be too dry. Just before serving, sprinkle the fried rice with the slivered scallions.

Cassoulet with Pork

Serves 4–6   The recipe for this dish is exactly the same as the one for *cassoulet* with lamb on page 46. Substitute 2 cups of pork for the lamb, or use a combination of cooked pork and cooked lamb, if you have both on hand.

Pork with Water Chestnuts and Shredded Cabbage in the Chinese Style

Serves 4–6   The recipe for this dish is exactly the same as the one for beef with water chestnuts on page 24. Substitute 2 cups of cold cooked pork for the roast beef.

Galantine of Pork

Serves 6

2 cups thoroughly degreased chicken stock, fresh or canned
1 cup dry white wine
1 medium onion, *thinly sliced*
1 medium carrot, *thinly sliced*
1 leek (white part only), *thinly sliced*
A bouquet consisting of 4 sprigs parsley, 2 celery tops, and 1 small bay leaf, *tied together with string*
1 medium tomato, *coarsely chopped*
2-inch strip of lemon peel

10 black peppercorns
1 envelope unflavored gelatin
¼ cup cold stock or white wine or water
2 eggs (whites only)
2 cups roast fresh ham or pork, *free of all fat and gristle and coarsely chopped*
½ cup parsley, *finely chopped*
1 teaspoon garlic, *very finely chopped*
Salt
Freshly ground black pepper
Lemon slices (optional)

In a deep 2- or 3-quart saucepan, bring to a boil the chicken stock and white wine, the sliced onion, carrot, leek, the bouquet, chopped tomato, lemon peel, and whole peppercorns. Then half cover the pot and simmer at the lowest possible heat for about 40 minutes. Strain through a fine sieve, pressing down hard on the vegetables with the back of a spoon to extract every last drop of their moisture before throwing them away.

Measure the stock before returning it to the pan. There should be about 2 cupfuls. If less, add more stock; if more, boil down rapidly to the required amount. Soften the envelope of gelatin in ¼ cup of cold stock, wine, or water for about 3 minutes. With a rubber spatula scrape it into the hot stock and stir until it is thoroughly dissolved.

To clarify the aspic, beat the 2 egg whites to a froth and just before they stiffen stir them into the stock. Stirring constantly with a wire whisk, bring this mixture to a boil. When it begins to rise in the pot and threatens to boil over, turn off the heat at once, whisk once or twice more, and let the froth subside for at least 5 minutes. Meanwhile place a fine-meshed sieve over a small but deep bowl—deep enough so that the bottom of the sieve will not touch the surface of the aspic after it has drained through. Line the sieve with a kitchen towel moistened with cold water and wrung dry. Pour the entire contents of the waiting pan into it and let it drip through undisturbed. Taste for salt, then cool the aspic in or out of the refrigerator but don't let it set.*

In a large mixing bowl combine the chopped pork, parsley, garlic, and salt and freshly ground black pepper to taste. Mix them together gently but thoroughly and pack the mixture not too firmly into a quart-sized mold or loaf pan. Slowly pour over it the cooled but still liquid aspic and shake the pan gently to distribute the aspic throughout. Pour in just enough of the aspic so that it covers the meat and save the rest, if any, to be chilled, chopped, and used for a garnish. Refrigerate the *galantine* and chill for at least 3 or 4 hours, or until firm.

Unmold by running a sharp knife around the circumference of the mold, next dipping the bottom of the mold briefly in hot water. Place a chilled platter on top of the mold, then, holding the platter and mold tightly together, quickly turn them over. Rap sharply on the table to loosen the *galantine* and carefully lift off the mold. Serve with slices of lemon, if you wish.

* *Note:* Or make the aspic in a more professional way by cooling it over ice rather than in the refrigerator. Place the bowl of aspic in a larger bowl of crushed ice (or cubes in a few inches of water) and stir the aspic with a large metal spoon until it thickens to a syrup heavy enough to run sluggishly off the spoon. At this point combine it quickly with the cold ham and other ingredients. Should the aspic become too firm while you are stirring it (and this applies to the refrigerator method as well), simply warm it briefly until it returns to a liquid state and chill it once again to the point of setting, as the process is technically called.

Cold Roast Fresh Ham with Honeydew Melon

Serves 4

4–8 slices cold roast fresh ham or pork, *sliced about ⅛ inch thick*

8 slices of chilled ripe honeydew melon, *sliced about ½ inch thick and their rinds removed*

12 black olives, Mediterranean style, if possible

Lemon or lime quarters

Salt

Freshly ground black pepper

Trim the slices of fresh ham or pork of all their fat and arrange them overlapping down the center of a narrow chilled platter, intersecting each piece with a slice of chilled melon. If possible, the pork should be served at room temperature. Arrange the olives and lemon or lime quarters around the outside of the platter. The pork should be sprinkled lightly with salt and the melon with freshly ground black pepper.

Cold Pork and Fennel (or Celery) Salad

Serves 4–6

1½–2 cups cooked pork, *free of all fat and gristle, cut into julienne strips 1½ by ½ inches*

2 cups fennel or celery, *cut into julienne strips the same size as the pork*

2 cups Boston lettuce, *washed, dried, and shredded*

DRESSING

4 hard-cooked eggs (yolks only)

2 teaspoons Dijon mustard

½ cup olive oil

1 tablespoon white wine vinegar

¼ teaspoon lemon juice

1 scant teaspoon salt

¼ teaspoon cayenne

1–2 tablespoons heavy cream

The fennel or celery must be as crisp as possible and the julienned pork at room temperature for this salad to be at its best. Slice the stalks of fennel or celery into julienne strips about 1½ inches long and ½ inch wide and soak them in ice water for at least 1 hour. Meanwhile make the dressing by mashing the egg yolks and mustard together into as smooth a paste as possible, then beat in the olive oil about ½ teaspoon at a time. The mixture should be quite thick when you have used all the oil. Thin it by stirring in the vinegar and lemon juice. Season with the salt and cayenne, and beat in 1 tablespoonful of the heavy cream. If the sauce seems too thick, add as much of the remaining cream as you need to give it the consistency you desire. Taste again for seasoning.

Assemble the salad in a chilled glass or crystal bowl. First add the washed, dried, and chilled shredded lettuce and scatter the pork over it. Dry the fennel or celery pieces thoroughly with paper toweling and spread them carelessly over the top. Just before serving pour on the dressing and mix the salad at the table. Serve on chilled plates.

Notes

Cured Meats

CURED MEATS

In the past, the smoking and corning of beef were primarily preservative devices; it was only in time that the characteristic flavors they produced began to be prized for their own sake and cooking with these assertively flavored meats required other approaches than those used for fresh meat.

Smoking meat produces a markedly different flavor than corning or salting it. Thus smoked ham and smoked tongue can be used interchangeably in the following recipes while corned beef cannot. All three meats, however, despite the differences between them, reheat perfectly in their original form. Moreover, they lose none of their identity and little of their texture when they are recooked more elaborately.

► ◄

A Classic Braised Smoked Ham in the French Style

Half a smoked ham, butt or shank end, about
   6 pounds
3 tablespoons butter
½ cup onions, *thinly sliced*
½ cup carrots, *thinly sliced*
¼ cup celery, *coarsely chopped*
2 medium-sized leeks (white part only), *thinly sliced*

1 cup dry white wine
6–8 cups beef stock, fresh or canned, or canned beef bouillon and canned chicken stock, *mixed half and half*
A bouquet consisting of 6 sprigs parsley and 1 large bay leaf, *tied together with string*
Arrowroot (optional)

With a sharp knife remove the rind and all but a ¼-inch layer of fat from the ham. Score the ham by cutting through the fat right down to the flesh. Make the cuts parallel two inches apart, first lengthwise, then crosswise. Preheat the oven to 350 degrees. In a heavy casserole with a tightly fitting cover melt the 3 tablespoons of butter. When the foam subsides, add the sliced onions, carrots, celery, and leeks and cook them over moderate heat for about 10 minutes, stirring frequently with a wooden spoon. When the vegetables have colored lightly, place the ham on them, fat side up, and pour around it the cup of wine and 6 cups of the stock. The liquid should come a third the way up the sides of the ham; if it doesn't, add more stock. Add the bouquet and bring the stock to a boil on the top of the stove. Then cover the casserole tightly and place it in the middle of the oven, where it should cook slowly for about 1 hour, or until the ham can be easily pierced with a fork. For the best results, it is wise to baste the ham every 15 minutes or so. Keep an eye on the heat; the stock should only barely simmer. If it seems to be cooking more rapidly, turn the oven down to 325 degrees.

Serve the ham cut into ¼-inch slices. A simple sauce to accompany it can be made easily by straining the braising liquid and skimming it of its surface fat. Thicken the sauce, if you like, by bringing it to a boil with a little arrowroot first dissolved in cold water; the usual proportion is 1 tablespoon of arrowroot dissolved in 2 tablespoons of cold water for every 2 cups of braising liquid.

▶ Buy the best-quality precooked, mildly smoked ham you can find. Because most of the cheaper varieties are chemically cured and synthetically smoked, they should be avoided; they tend to be pulpy, oversalted, and oversmoked. Make certain to read the label on any ham you buy. Most commercial hams sold today are fully cooked but on occasion you may come across an uncooked cured ham. It is best to cook this type with a meat thermometer inserted in the thickest area; when it reads 165 degrees, the ham is done. A 6-pound uncooked half ham will take approximately twice as long to braise as a precooked ham of the same size.

odds and ENds

▶ Canned hams may be braised in the same fashion as the classic braised smoked ham in the French style described above. Care must be taken, however, since some inferior varieties of canned hams tend to be overcooked to begin with, not to overcook them further when braising them. Watch during the braising process for any signs of shredding, at which point remove the ham from the oven at once.

▶ So-called aged country hams, the aristocrat of all American smoked hams, are best cooked according to the labels attached to them. They are usually not successful braised, but country hams, however they are cooked, may be used effectively in any of the following ham improvisations.

▶ One of the many advantages of braising ham and tongue instead of cooking them in other ways is that you will have a sauce at hand automatically for the improvisations which follow. Although the ham and tongue improvisations can be made without them, the braising sauces do give these dishes a special flavor difficult to achieve with stock alone.

▶ A spectacular garnish for the ham *mousse* on page 96 (and for that matter, any of the smoked meat *mousses* in this section) is an imported Italian delicacy called *mostarda di frutta*. It is a condiment of preserved fruits—pears, cherries, apricots, plums, figs, watermelon, and pumpkin—in a piquant mustard sauce and is usually available in fine specialty food stores. The mustard-flavored fruits are not only dramatic and colorful to look at but are a fine foil for the flavor of the smoked meat.

iMPROVISATIONS

Garbanzo Soup with Ham and Broad Beans

Serves 4–6

3 tablespoons butter
½ cup onions, *finely chopped*
½ cup carrots, *finely chopped*
¼ cup celery, *finely chopped*
6 cups stock consisting of **1 cup ham braising liquid, if available,** plus canned or fresh chicken stock, or all chicken stock
Ham bone (optional)
A bouquet consisting of 6 sprigs parsley and 1 small bay leaf, *tied together with string*
1 pound 4 ounce can garbanzos (chick-peas),

drained of all their liquid and washed in cold water
1–1½ cups cooked ham, *cut into small cubes*
1 package frozen broad beans or string beans, *defrosted*
2 medium boiling potatoes, *peeled and cut into 1-inch cubes*
Salt
Freshly ground black pepper
1 tablespoon parsley, *finely chopped*

Over moderate heat melt the 3 tablespoons of butter in a heavy 3- or 4-quart soup pot. When the foam subsides, add the chopped onions, carrots, and celery and cook, stirring almost constantly, until the vegetables are wilted but not brown. Pour in the stock, add the optional ham bone and the bouquet, and bring to a boil. Then lower the heat and, with the pot half covered, simmer slowly for about ½ hour. Add the chick-peas, the ham, the broad beans (or string beans), and the cubed potatoes and continue to simmer until the potatoes are tender. Remove the ham bone. Season the soup with salt and freshly ground pepper to taste, and serve sprinkled with chopped parsley in large, deep soup plates.

Alsatian Choucroute Garnie

Serves 6–8

2 pounds sauerkraut, fresh if possible, otherwise canned or in plastic bags

3 tablespoons lard or goose fat, if possible

1¼ cups onions, *finely chopped*

½ cup carrots, *finely chopped*

½ teaspoon garlic, *finely chopped*

1 small tart apple, *peeled, cored, and coarsely chopped*

¼ cup gin

1 cup dry white wine

1½–2 cups chicken or beef stock, fresh or canned

¾-pound piece of salt pork, lean and mildly cured

A bouquet consisting of 4 sprigs parsley, 2 celery tops with leaves, and 1 small bay leaf, *tied together with string*

Salt

Freshly ground black pepper

4–8 slices braised smoked ham, *cut about ¼ inch thick*

Boiled potatoes

Preheat the oven to 325 degrees. Drain the sauerkraut,* wash it well under cold running water, then soak in cold water for 10 to 20 minutes, depending upon its acidity. Squeeze it dry by the handful and put it aside. It should be only mildly acidulated before being cooked.

Melt the lard or goose fat in a 4- or 6-quart casserole with a heavy, tightly fitting cover, and over moderate heat cook the chopped onions, carrots, and garlic for about 10 minutes, stirring occasionally. When the vegetables are soft but not brown, add the chopped apple and cook for a few minutes longer. Spread the matted kraut apart gently with your fingers and stir it into the vegetable mixture. Add the gin.** Cover the pot and cook the kraut gently for about 15 minutes, stirring it now and then. Pour in the cup of wine and 1½ cups of the stock, and over high heat bring it to a boil. Push the salt pork and bouquet beneath the kraut, add salt and a few grindings of pepper, and cover the pot. Braise in the middle of the preheated oven for 3 or 4 hours. After about 2 hours, if the *choucroute* seems dry, add another ½ cup of stock (which has first been heated), though it is unlikely that this will be needed.

A half hour or so before serving add the sliced ham to the casserole.***

To serve, mound the *choucroute* in the center of a large serving platter, arrange the ham slices over it, and surround with plain boiled potatoes. Pass it with a variety of mustards and pickles. Cold beer is really the perfect drink for the dish.

* *Note:* The sauerkraut should be fresh if possible, and the most likely place to find this would be in a German or Middle European grocery or delicatessen. The canned variety, of course, will do if it must; so will sauerkraut in bags. But, whatever the kraut, be certain to follow the directions in the recipe for washing and soaking and drying it if you don't want the *choucroute garnie* literally overpowered (as it so often is) by the brine in the kraut.

** *Note:* Ten or 15 juniper berries may be substituted for the gin, if you like. Wrap them in a small square of cheesecloth for easier removal when the *choucroute* is done.

*** *Note:* For a more elaborate *choucroute,* add to the ham a cooked Polish sausage (*kielbasa*), knockwurst, or any other sausage you prefer.

Jambon à la Crème

Serves 4–6

¼ cup shallots or scallions, *finely chopped*

⅓ cup white wine vinegar

2 teaspoons fresh tarragon, *finely chopped,* or 1 teaspoon dried tarragon

½ bay leaf

4 whole black peppercorns

2 sprigs parsley

½ cup chicken stock, fresh or canned, or, if available, **½ cup braising liquid from ham,** or a combination of both

2 eggs (yolks only)

½ cup heavy cream

Salt

⅛ teaspoon white pepper

1 tablespoon fresh tarragon or parsley, *finely chopped*

3 tablespoons butter

1 tablespoon vegetable oil

6–8 slices braised cooked ham, *cut about ¼ inch thick*

Combine in a small enamel or stainless-steel saucepan the shallots or scallions, wine vinegar, fresh or dried tarragon, bay leaf, peppercorns, and parsley. Bring to a boil, then simmer, uncovered, until the liquid has boiled down to about a tablespoonful. Strain into a small bowl, pressing down on the shallots or scallions and herbs before throwing them away.

In the same saucepan (washed, of course) heat the ½ cup of chicken stock. Meanwhile, beat the 2 egg yolks lightly and mix with the heavy cream. Now, spoonful by spoonful, add the hot stock to the cream mixture (not the other way around), then return it to the pan. Next add the tablespoon of reduced vinegar.

Stirring constantly, cook the sauce over moderate heat until it slowly begins to thicken. Raise the pan from the heat occasionally so that the sauce doesn't get too hot; if it boils, it will curdle. When it has thickened enough to coat the back of a spoon very heavily, it is done. Remove from the heat, taste for salt, add the white pepper, and mix in the chopped tarragon or parsley. If it is not to be served at once, keep it warm in the top of a double boiler set over tepid water. Stir it every now and then.

A little before serving, in a heavy frying pan set over moderate heat, heat the ham slices in a mixture of 3 tablespoons of butter and 1 tablespoon of oil. Don't let them brown. This dish can be presented quite simply, by serving the ham and the sauce separately; or more elaborately, by arranging the ham slices on a bed of chopped spinach masking them with the sauce.

Jambalaya

Serves 6

3 tablespoons bacon fat or 1 tablespoon butter and 2 tablespoons vegetable oil
¾ cup onions, *finely chopped*
2 medium-sized green peppers, *seeded and cut into 1½-inch strips*
1 cup raw rice
1 teaspoon garlic, *finely chopped*
1 pound 3 ounce can solid-pack tomatoes, *thoroughly drained and coarsely chopped*
½ teaspoon leaf thyme

1½ teaspoons chili powder
1 teaspoon salt
Freshly ground black pepper
1½–2 cups chicken stock, fresh or canned
¼ teaspoon powdered saffron
6 small pork sausages, *fully cooked and drained*
2 cups cooked ham, *cut into small cubes*
6–12 fresh oysters (optional) °
2 tablespoons parsley, *finely chopped*

In a 6- to 8-cup heavy casserole heat either the bacon fat or the butter-oil mixture and cook the finely chopped onions for about 10 minutes, until they are transparent but not brown. Add the green pepper strips and when they have wilted a bit but are still crisp stir in the cup of rice.

Stirring almost constantly, cook for a few minutes, until the grains of rice become slightly opaque, at which point add the garlic, the drained and chopped tomatoes, the thyme, chili powder, salt, and black pepper. Pour over this 1½ cups of hot chicken stock, sprinkle in the saffron and, mixing it all together with a large spoon, bring it slowly to a boil. Submerge the cooked sausages and chunks of ham in the casserole, cover it tightly, and transfer it to the lower third of a preheated 350-degree oven. Cook undisturbed for about 20 minutes. By then the rice should have absorbed most of the stock and become quite tender. Taste a few grains; if they seem too firm to the bite, cover the casserole and let it cook for a few minutes longer, adding a few more tablespoons of hot stock if the rice seems dry.

Ten minutes before serving, add the optional oysters, gently pushing them beneath the rice. Sprinkle the parsley on top and serve the jambalaya directly from the casserole.

* *Note:* Although the oysters in this jambalaya are indicated as being optional, they do lend an element of gastronomic surprise to the dish. It is decidedly worth including them.

Pipérade Basquaise

Serves 4

4 tablespoons olive oil or 4 tablespoons rendered fresh pork fat or duck or goose fat

½ cup onions or scallions, *finely chopped*

½ teaspoon garlic, *finely chopped*

2 small peppers (preferably 1 green and 1 red, or 2 green), *seeded and cut into strips 1½ inches long by ½ inch wide (about ¾ cup)*

1 pound fresh ripe tomatoes, *peeled, seeded, and coarsely chopped (about 1½ cups)*

1 teaspoon dried basil or 1 tablespoon fresh basil, *finely chopped*

½ teaspoon dried pepper flakes or ⅛ teaspoon Tabasco

1 tablespoon olive oil

1 tablespoon butter

1 **cup cooked ham,** *cut into julienne strips 1 inch long by ½ inch wide*

5 eggs

½ teaspoon salt

Freshly ground black pepper

1 tablespoon parsley, *finely chopped*, and/or 1 tablespoon fresh chives, *chopped*

Prepare the *pipérade* by first heating the 4 tablespoons of fat of your choice in a heavy 8-inch frying pan or, better still, in a small oval copper or enamel pan that you can bring to the table. Add the chopped onions and garlic and cook them for about 5 minutes over moderate heat, stirring them frequently until they are soft but not brown. Stir in the pepper strips, turning them in the fat now and then, letting them cook for about 10 minutes, at which point they should be tender but still crisp. Drain the chopped tomatoes thoroughly and add them to the pan, sprinkling in at the same time the dried or fresh basil and the pepper flakes or Tabasco. Raise the heat and cook the tomatoes briskly for a few minutes and stir constantly with a wooden spoon until all their moisture has evaporated. Be careful that the *pipérade* doesn't burn. Put it aside until you are ready to reheat and serve it.

At that point, combine 1 tablespoon each of olive oil and butter in an 8-inch heavy frying pan, and over moderate heat cook the julienned ham for a few minutes until the strips are thoroughly heated through. Remove them at once with a slotted spoon and spread them out on paper toweling to drain.

Meanwhile let the fat in the frying pan cool to lukewarm before pouring into it the eggs, lightly beaten with salt and pepper. Over low heat stir the eggs with a rubber spatula until they begin to form soft, creamy curds. Remove them from the heat when they are not quite set and gently spread them over the reheated *pipérade*. Let some of the colorful vegetables show through. Lightly scatter the ham over the top, sprinkle with the chopped parsley and/or chopped chives, and serve at once.

Gratin of Ham Orloff

Serves 4–6   The recipe for this dish is exactly the same as the one for *gratin* of veal Orloff on page 65, except for the optional addition of 2 teaspoons of Dijon mustard to the *soubise* sauce stirred into it after it is puréed. Substitute 6 to 8 slices of ham for the veal.

Croque Monsieur

Makes 8 small sandwiches

16 slices good white bread
1 cup imported Swiss cheese, *grated*
5–7 tablespoons heavy cream, *2–4 for the filling and 3 for the egg batter*
Salt

White pepper
8 **thin slices cooked ham,** *trimmed to about the same size as the bread*
3 eggs
4–6 tablespoons of clarified butter*

In a small bowl mash the grated Swiss cheese with 2 tablespoons of the cream, adding up to 2 more tablespoons of cream, if necessary, to make a thick, smooth paste. Season highly with salt and cayenne. With a small spatula spread the cheese evenly on all 16 slices of bread, leaving about ⅛ inch of rim exposed. Now cover 8 of the pieces of bread with slices of ham, and top each with the remaining cheese-spread bread. Press each sandwich together firmly and with a sharp knife trim off the crusts.

Beat together, just long enough to combine them, the 3 eggs and 3 tablespoons of the cream. Season with salt and a little white pepper. Dip each sandwich into the egg mixture and let soak for a few seconds before frying over moderate heat in the hot clarified butter, which has been poured into a large heavy frying pan. Turn the sandwiches only once and fry them slowly enough to ensure the cheese's melting before they are served.

* *Note:* To clarify butter, cut it first into pieces. In a small saucepan set over fairly low heat, melt the butter but don't let it brown. Remove the pan from the heat and skim all the foam from the top. Tilting the pan away from you, ladle off as much of the clear butter as you can and put it into a small bowl, taking care to avoid the milky solids that have settled at the bottom of the pan.

Jambon Persillé

Serves 6

3 cups thoroughly degreased chicken stock, fresh or canned, **and include, if you can, anywhere from 1 tablespoon to 1 cup of liquid remaining from braised ham**
1 cup dry white wine
1 small onion, *diced*
1 teaspoon dried tarragon or 1 tablespoon fresh tarragon, *finely chopped*
10 whole black peppercorns
A bouquet consisting of 4 sprigs parsley, 2 celery tops with leaves, and 1 small bay leaf, *tied together with string*
3 **cups cooked ham,** *cut into approximately 2-inch chunks*
1 envelope unflavored gelatin
¼ cup cold stock or water
2 eggs (whites only)
2 teaspoons tarragon white wine vinegar
Salt
6 tablespoons parsley, *finely chopped*

Combine the stock and wine in an enamel or stainless-steel saucepan. Add the diced onion, tarragon, peppercorns (tied in a cheesecloth bag, if you wish), the bouquet, and the ham. Bring to a boil, then lower the heat and simmer as slowly as possible, with the pan half covered, until the ham is quite soft but not falling apart. This may take from 15 to 30 minutes, depending upon how well cooked the ham was to begin with. Remove the ham with a slotted spoon and put it into a 1-quart glass or crystal bowl attractive enough to bring to the table and serve from. Press and mash the ham lightly with the back of a large spoon or fork and set it aside to cool.

Strain the cooking liquid through a fine sieve into a 2- or 3-quart deep saucepan, pressing down on the bouquet and vegetables with the back of a spoon before throwing them away. Bring the liquid to a boil and cook rapidly, uncovered, until it has reduced or cooked down to 2½ cups. (If you miscalculate and have less, add enough chicken stock to make up the difference.) Add the gelatin to ¼ cup of cold stock or water and let it soften for 5 minutes. Add it to the reduced stock and stir until it dissolves.

To clarify the aspic, beat the egg whites to a lightly thickened froth with a rotary beater and, just before it stiffens, stir into it the hot stock. Stirring constantly with a wire whisk, bring the mixture to a boil. Continue to cook and stir until the liquid begins to rise in the pot and threatens to overflow. At this point, turn off the heat immediately, whisk once or twice, and allow the froth to subside. Let it rest undisturbed for about 5 minutes.

Meanwhile, over a small but deep bowl, place a fine-meshed sieve lined with a kitchen towel that has first been moistened with cold water and wrung out. Pour the hot aspic into it. Don't move or jostle this mixture until the clear aspic has drained through completely. Add the 2 teaspoons of vinegar and taste for salt. Let cool to room temperature.

When the aspic is cool but not set, pour 1 cup of it over the ham in the serving bowl. Shake the bowl gently so that the aspic seeps through the ham gently. Chill thoroughly. Chill the remaining aspic in the refrigerator (or stirred over ice) until it becomes syrupy but not set. (If it sets, heat it again, returning it to its liquid state, then recool it.) Stir the chopped parsley into this aspic and pour it over the ham. Refrigerate until set.

Note: Apart from the hams, the only significant difference between the traditional *jambon persillé* as made in Burgundy and this improvised version is the powdered gelatin. In the French recipe the gelatin is produced naturally by cooking veal bones and other gelatin-forming ingredients with the stock before clarifying it.

Ham Mousse

Serves 6

¼ cup dry white wine or cold chicken stock
1 envelope unflavored gelatin (1 tablespoon)
1 cup chicken stock, fresh or canned
2 cups ground cooked ham, *firmly packed*
2 tablespoons Madeira
1 teaspoon tomato paste

⅛ teaspoon cayenne
Salt
½ cup heavy cream
½ cup cooked tongue, *cut into ¼-inch dice* (optional)
1 egg (white only)

Soften gelatin in ¼ cup of white wine or cold stock. Meanwhile bring the cup of chicken stock to a boil in a small saucepan. Stir in the gelatin and continue to stir it until it is thoroughly dissolved. Pour the stock into the jar of an electric blender,* add the ground ham, and purée at high speed until smooth. Scrape into a small mixing bowl and mix in the Madeira and tomato paste. Season with the cayenne and salt to taste, remembering that food which is to be chilled should be more highly seasoned than hot food.

Beat the cream in a chilled bowl until it is not quite stiff but firm enough to cling to the beater when it is lifted out of the bowl. Put it aside for a few minutes while you stir the bowl of puréed ham over ice until it begins to thicken and cling to the spoon. Stir in the optional diced tongue and carefully but quickly fold in the whipped cream. In a small bowl beat the egg white stiffly and fold it into the *mousse* also, making sure no streaks of white show when you have finished.

Pour the *mousse* into 1-quart mold—preferably a charlotte mold—or dish which has been lightly spread with vegetable oil. Chill for at least 2 hours, or until firm. Unmold by running a knife around the inside of the mold, then dipping the bottom into hot water for a second or two. Turn onto a chilled plate and serve at once, or refrigerate again.

* *Note:* To make the *mousse* by hand, rub the ground ham through a fine sieve with the back of a large spoon, then add the gelatin-stock mixture and beat together until smooth. Mix in the Madeira, tomato paste, cayenne, and salt and continue the recipe as described above.

A Classic Braised Smoked Beef Tongue with Madeira-Mustard Sauce

4–5 pound smoked beef tongue

4 tablespoons butter, *2 for sautéing and 2 for the sauce*

2 tablespoons vegetable oil

2 medium onions, *thinly sliced*

3 carrots, *thinly sliced*

2 stalks celery, *cut into 1-inch chunks*

3 cloves garlic, *peeled*

½ teaspoon thyme

A bouquet consisting of 4 sprigs parsley and 1 bay leaf, *tied together with string*

3-inch strip of lemon peel

2 cups beef stock, fresh or canned

1 cup Madeira

2 tablespoons flour

1 teaspoon Dijon mustard

2 tablespoons heavy cream

¼ teaspoon lemon juice

Salt

Most smoked tongues today do not require soaking before being cooked, but it might be well to ask your butcher about the specific one to buy. But whether you soak it or not, before braising the tongue it is necessary to parboil it. Place the tongue in a large kettle of cold water, bring it to a boil, then, on the lowest possible heat, simmer it, half covered, for about 1 hour. Make sure the tongue is completely immersed in the water during all this period. Remove the tongue and, without letting it cool, peel it. You should have little difficulty removing the skin with a small sharp knife if you do the operation while the tongue is still quite hot. If it is too hot to handle, use a kitchen towel to protect your hands.

For the braising, choose a casserole that is just about large enough to hold the tongue comfortably and has a tightly fitting cover. Preheat the oven to 325 degrees. Heat 2 tablespoons of the butter and the oil in the casserole and, over moderate heat, cook the onions, carrots, and celery in the fat for about 10 minutes until they are soft and lightly colored. Place the peeled tongue on top of them, add the garlic, thyme, bouquet, and lemon rind, and pour in the stock and the Madeira. The liquid should cover about a third of the tongue; if it doesn't, add a little more stock or water. Bring the casserole to a boil on top of the stove, then loosely drape over the tongue a sheet of aluminum foil and cover the casserole tightly. Braise the tongue in the center of the oven for about 2 hours. Basting is not necessary, but the tongue should be turned over in the liquid after the first hour of cooking. Replace the foil and the cover and cook the tongue until it can be easily pierced with a fork.

To make the Madeira-mustard sauce, strain the braising liquid through a fine sieve into a small bowl, pressing down hard on the vegetables before throwing them away. Melt the remaining 2 tablespoons of butter in a small saucepan and, off the heat, stir in the 2 tablespoons of flour. Mix to a smooth paste and pour over it, all at once, 1½ cups of the tongue braising liquid, skimmed of all its fat. (Save any remaining stock for later use.) Stir briefly with a whisk, then bring to a boil over moderate heat, stirring constantly until the sauce is fairly thick and smooth. Add the mustard, cream, and lemon juice, and a little salt if you think it needs it. Heat again without boiling and pass the sauce separately in a sauceboat.

► If you plan to make any of the tongue improvisations requiring the tongue braising liquid, it might be well, in the classic braised tongue recipe, to make less of the Madeira-mustard sauce than is suggested. In this way you will have more of the unthickened braising sauce on hand for later use.

► In Italy, *spaghetti alla carbonara* is always made with unsmoked bacon, or what the Italians call *pancetta*—never with tongue. But the braised smoked tongue (and ham as well) suggested for the *spaghetti alla carbonara* improvisation works surprisingly well, and the addition of heavy cream to the eggs, although it is scarcely traditional, prevents the *pasta* from becoming too dry as it often does.

IMPROVISATIONS

Spaghetti alla Carbonara

Serves 4–6

1 pound spaghetti
6 quarts water
Salt, 2 *tablespoons for the pasta-boiling water and some for seasoning spaghetti*

4 tablespoons butter, *softened*
4 strips lean bacon, *cut crosswise into ½-inch strips*

1–1½ **cups braised tongue,** *cut into julienne*
strips about ¼ inch wide and 1 inch long
1 teaspoon Italian red pepper flakes (optional)
or freshly ground black pepper

2 whole eggs plus 2 yolks
⅔ cup heavy cream
1 cup Parmesan cheese, *freshly grated*

Drop a pound of unbroken spaghetti into a large pot containing 6 quarts of rapidly boiling salted water. Stir the spaghetti from time to time with a large fork and let it cook as rapidly as possible, uncovered, anywhere from 10 to 14 minutes, depending upon how firm you prefer your *pasta.* Meanwhile prepare the other ingredients; having them within easy reach and all ready will determine the success or failure of this extraordinary *pasta* dish.

Cream 4 tablespoons of softened butter by beating, mashing, and stirring it in a mixing bowl with a wooden spoon until it is smooth, creamy, and light in color. Set it aside.

In an 8- or 10-inch frying pan, cook the bacon strips until they are almost but not quite done. Add the julienned tongue and, stirring constantly over fairly high heat, cook the meats together for 2 or 3 minutes until the bacon is crisp and the tongue is lightly colored. Stir in the optional pepper flakes or a few grindings of black pepper. Remove the pan from the heat.

Now beat the eggs and egg yolks together only long enough to combine them, stir in the heavy cream, and add ½ cup of the grated Parmesan cheese.

When the spaghetti is done, drain it at once in a large colander, lifting the strands with a fork to make certain they are free of all their cooking water. Have ready a 2- or 3-quart flame-proof bowl or casserole (which you have heated in a slow oven, or rinsed with boiling water, then dried). Drop the drained spaghetti into it and quickly stir in the creamed butter, lifting the strands over each other with two forks until they are well coated. Reheat the tongue and bacon pieces until they sizzle, then pour the entire contents of the pan over the buttered spaghetti. Mix together, then pour over it all the egg-cream mixture. Wielding your two forks quickly and vigorously, combine all the ingredients until they are thoroughly amalgamated. Theoretically, the heat of the bowl, spaghetti, tongue, and bacon should cook the eggs upon contact. To make certain of this, however, it might be well to place the casserole over low heat as you mix in the eggs and cream. But however you handle this somewhat tricky operation, make sure that you taste the spaghetti for salt before you serve it. There is nothing more disappointing to the palate than undersalted *pasta.* Serve the spaghetti without delay (it should not wait a moment after it is done) and pass the remaining ½ cup of grated cheese.

Sliced Braised Tongue with Prune, Raisin, and Almond Sauce

Serves 4

¼ cup red wine vinegar
3 tablespoons sugar
1 cup braising liquid from the tongue or beef
  bouillon, fresh or canned
1 teaspoon arrowroot dissolved in 2 tablespoons
  Madeira or cold water
⅛ teaspoon ground cinnamon

⅛ teaspoon ground cloves
8 prunes, *pitted*
4 tablespoons raisins
2 tablespoons whole almonds, *blanched*
1 tablespoon orange rind, *shredded*
1 teaspoon lemon juice
8–12 slices braised tongue

Mix the wine vinegar and sugar together in a small enamel saucepan and slowly bring it to a boil. Let it boil rapidly without stirring for about 5 minutes until it becomes a thick, heavy syrup and begins to caramelize. The caramel should be a dark mahogany brown when you remove it from the heat. Pour into it at once the cup of braising liquid or bouillon. Upon contact with the liquid the caramel will immediately harden. Bring the stock to a boil and stir with a spoon to dissolve it completely. Stir in the arrowroot-Madeira (or -water) mixture and cook it over moderate heat until the sauce thickens and becomes clear. Add the spices, the prunes, raisins, almonds, orange rind, and lemon juice and simmer over the lowest possible heat for about 5 minutes.

Reheat the sliced tongue in its own braising liquid or in a little beef or chicken stock, drain, and arrange the slices overlapping slightly down the center of a small heated platter. Pour the fruit sauce over the tongue and serve at once.

Tongue-Filled Spinach Roulade with Mustard Hollandaise

Serves 8
ROULADE

8 tablespoons butter, *2 softened for buttering
  pan and paper and 6 for sauce*
⅔ cup flour, *8 tablespoons for sauce plus some
  for flouring pan*
2 cups milk

4 whole eggs plus 1 additional white, *yolks and
  whites separated*
1 tablespoon butter
1 tablespoon vegetable oil } *combined*

2 packages frozen spinach, *thoroughly defrosted, squeezed dry by the handful, and finely chopped,* or 1 pound fresh spinach, *cooked, squeezed dry, and finely chopped*

1 tablespoon salt

½ teaspoon nutmeg, *freshly grated*

¼ cup dry white wine or cold chicken stock

2 tablespoons Madeira

FILLING

2 tablespoons butter

3 tablespoons flour

¾ **cup braising liquid from the tongue** or chicken stock, fresh or canned

1 egg (yolk only)
2 tablespoons heavy cream } *combined*

2 cups cooked tongue, *finely minced or coarsely ground*

1 tablespoon parsley or chives, *finely chopped*

Salt

Cayenne

MUSTARD HOLLANDAISE

¼ pound sweet butter, *softened and cut into small pieces*

3 large eggs (yolks only)

1 tablespoon lemon juice

½ teaspoon salt

¼ teaspoon cayenne

1 tablespoon salt butter, *cold*

1 tablespoon heavy cream, *cold*

2 teaspoons Dijon mustard

Brush 1 tablespoon of softened butter evenly over the bottom and sides of a 12 x 17 jelly-roll pan. Line the pan with a 22-inch strip of waxed paper and let the extra paper extend over the narrower ends of the pan. Brush another tablespoon of softened butter over the paper and make sure the surface is thoroughly covered. Toss a small handful of flour into the pan, then tip it from side to side so that the flour spreads evenly all over the surface of the paper. Turn the pan over and rap it smartly a few times to dislodge the excess flour. Preheat the oven to 325 degrees.

To prepare the sauce, melt 6 tablespoons of the butter in a heavy saucepan; off the heat, mix in 8 level tablespoons of flour. Stir until smooth. Pour in the 2 cups of milk. Beat vigorously with a whisk to partially dissolve the flour, then return the pan to the heat. Stirring constantly, bring the sauce to a boil. It will be very thick. Let it simmer for 1 or 2 minutes, remove the pan from the heat, and beat in, one by one, the 4 egg yolks.

In a small frying pan heat the oil-butter mixture and cook the chopped spinach, which you have squeezed as dry as possible, over fairly high heat until its moisture has completely evaporated and the spinach begins to stick lightly to the pan. With a rubber spatula scrape it at once into the sauce and mix it together vigorously. Season with salt and nutmeg. Beat the 5 egg whites (for the greatest volume, use balloon whisk in an unlined copper bowl) until they are stiff enough to cling to the beater solidly and their small peaks do not waver when the beater is lifted from the bowl. Mix 2 large tablespoons of it into the still-warm spinach sauce, then reverse the process and pour the sauce over the remaining egg whites in the bowl. With a rubber spatula fold them together gently but thoroughly. Although there should be no egg whites showing when you finish, be careful not to overfold them or the roulade will be heavy instead of light. Pour the mixture into the floured pan, spread it out evenly, and bake it in the center of the oven for 50 to 60 minutes. The roulade should be lightly browned on top when it is finished and a small knife plunged into its center should come out dry.

While the roulade is baking, or earlier, if you like, make the tongue filling. Melt in a small saucepan 2 tablespoons of butter; off the heat, stir in 3 level tablespoons of flour. With a whisk stir until smooth, then pour in, all at once, the ¾ cup of stock or braising liquid. Return the pan to the heat and, whisking constantly, bring the sauce to a boil. When it is smooth and thick, beat into the yolk-cream mixture. Heat again to boiling, and let it boil for 10 seconds then remove the pan from the heat. Add the tongue, mix in the chopped parsley or chives, and season to taste with salt and a few specks of cayenne.

When the roulade is done, turn it out on a triple thickness of waxed paper about 2 feet long. Remove the waxed-paper lining carefully, and spread the hot tongue filling over the roulade and roll it up like a jelly roll. Use the ends of the waxed paper as handles to help you cradle the roulade and lift it to the serving platter.* Let it remain on the waxed paper but cut away the exposed paper. Slice the roulade into 1- or 1½-inch slices and serve with the mustard hollandaise sauce.

To make the sauce, first melt the ¼ pound of sweet butter in a small saucepan without letting it brown. Keep it warm over the lowest possible heat. Meanwhile, in another saucepan, beat the 3 egg yolks with a whisk until they are thick, then beat in the lemon juice, salt, and cayenne. Add the tablespoon of cold butter, place the pan over moderate heat and, with a whisk, stir the yolks constantly until they begin to thicken and the butter is absorbed. Lift the pan off the heat every few seconds to cool it; if the eggs get too hot they will curdle. When the eggs have thickened enough to cling to the beater, remove the pan from the heat and quickly stir in the tablespoon of cold cream. Immediately begin beating in the hot melted butter from the first saucepan. Start adding it a few drops at a time and, as the sauce begins to thicken, pour the butter in a thin steady stream until you have used it all. Stir in the mustard, add the salt and cayenne, and serve in a warmed sauceboat.

* *Note:* The tongue-filled spinach roulade can be reheated without losing any of its quality. Instead of transferring the finished roulade to a serving platter, return it to the jelly-roll pan in which it was cooked. Cover the roulade securely with aluminum foil and refrigerate it or not as you will. A half hour or so before you plan to serve it, place the pan over a large skillet filled with simmering water. Let the water continue to simmer under the pan (replenishing it if it cooks away) until the roulade is thoroughly heated through. Remove the foil and transfer the roulade to a heated serving platter as described in the recipe text.

Jambalaya of Tongue

Serves 4   The recipe for this dish is exactly the same as the one for jambalaya with ham on page 91. Substitute 2 cups of cubed tongue for the ham, or use a combination of both should you have them on hand.

Choucroute Garnie with Tongue

Serves 4   The recipe for this dish is exactly the same as the one for Alsatian *choucroute garnie* on page 89. Substitute 4 to 8 slices of tongue for the ham, or use a combination of both should you have them on hand.

Scandinavian Herring and Tongue Salad

Serves 4–6   The recipe for this dish is exactly the same as the one for veal and herring salad in the Scandinavian style on page 69. Substitute 2 cups of cubed tongue for the veal.

Tongue Mousse with Mustard Mayonnaise

Serves 4–6

2 teaspoons vegetable oil
1 package unflavored gelatin
¼ cup cold water
¾ cup beef stock, fresh or canned
2 cups braised tongue (packed down), *finely chopped or ground*
3 tablespoons onions, *finely chopped*
3 tablespoons green pepper, *finely chopped*

3 tablespoons parsley, *finely chopped*
1 scant teaspoon salt
Freshly ground black pepper
1 teaspoon prepared mustard, preferably Dijon
1 teaspoon English dry mustard
2 tablespoons lemon juice
½ cup heavy cream, *chilled*

SAUCE

½ cup freshly made mayonnaise (p. 218) or a good, unsweetened commercial brand

4 tablespoons prepared mustard, preferably Dijon

GARNISHES
(OPTIONAL)

Hard-cooked eggs
Sliced tomatoes

Olives
Radishes

Oil a 1-quart ring mold or a loaf pan of an equivalent size by brushing it with 2 teaspoons of vegetable oil, then invert the pan onto a double thickness of paper toweling to drain.

Soften the powdered gelatin in the ¼ cup of cold water for 5 minutes. Meanwhile bring the ¾ cup of beef stock to a simmer in a small saucepan; stir in the softened gelatin. Simmer this quickly made aspic for a few minutes until the gelatin is completely dissolved, and then put it aside.

Combine in a large mixing bowl the tongue, onions, green pepper, parsley, salt, a few grindings of black pepper, the mustards, and the lemon juice. With a large spoon mix these ingredients together thoroughly. Beat the cream until it is not quite stiff but firm enough to cling lightly to the beater when it is lifted out of the bowl; refrigerate it covered with plastic wrap. Meanwhile set the pan of aspic into a bowl of ice to chill. Stir with a metal spoon until it begins to jell and threatens to solidify (if it takes you unawares and does set somewhat, don't worry). Stir the aspic into the tongue mixture quickly and if it has really jelled, mix vigorously to amalgamate it with the tongue. Gently fold in the whipped cream and keep folding until no streaks of cream remain. Pour this *mousse* into the oiled mold and refrigerate until it is firm at least 3 hours.

When you are ready to serve the *mousse*, run a sharp knife around the inside edge of the mold (if it is a ring mold, run the knife around the inside cone of the mold also), dip the bottom of the mold in hot water for a second or so, and wipe it dry with a towel. Place a chilled platter on top of it, grasp the platter and mold together and then invert them. Rap the plate smartly on the table to dislodge the *mousse*.

Surround the *mousse* with a garnish of your choice: sliced tomatoes, hard-cooked eggs, olives, radishes—almost anything you have on hand—and serve with a bowl of mustard mayonnaise, made by combining the ½ cup of mayonnaise with the prepared mustard.

Lingue Tonnato

Cold Tongue and Tunafish Sauce

Serves 4   The recipe for this dish is exactly the same as the one for *vitello tonnato* on page 67. Substitute 6 to 8 slices of tongue for the veal.

Tongue-Stuffed Eggs in the French Style

Serves 4–6

9 tablespoons butter, *1 for duxelles, 4 for cream sauce, 2 softened for blending egg mixture, and 2 softened for topping*

1½ tablespoons shallots or scallions, *finely chopped*

⅛ pound mushrooms, *finely chopped (½ cup)*

8 hard-cooked eggs, *chilled and cut lengthwise*

4 tablespoons flour

1 cup milk

1 cup heavy cream

½ cup braised tongue, *ground*

1 teaspoon Dijon mustard

Salt

White pepper

2 tablespoons chives or parsley, *finely chopped*

¼ cup imported Swiss cheese, *grated*

2 tablespoons bread crumbs

To prepare ½ cup of *duxelles*, melt 1 tablespoon of the butter in a small frying pan and add the chopped shallots or scallions. Sauté for about 1 minute without letting them color, then mix in the chopped mushrooms. Stirring every now and then, cook the mixture over low heat for about 10 minutes, or until the mushrooms are dry but not brown.

With a small knife cut the hard-cooked eggs in half lengthwise. Carefully remove the yolks and with the back of a spoon rub them through a fine sieve into a mixing bowl. Melt 4 tablespoons of the butter in a small saucepan. Off the heat, add 4 tablespoons of flour and stir until smooth. Pour over it, all at once, the cup of milk and ½ cup of the cream and mix with a whisk until the flour has partially dissolved. Return the pan to the heat, and whisking continually, bring the cream sauce to a boil. It will be very thick. Add 8 tablespoons of the hot sauce to the sieved egg yolks and put the remaining sauce aside. Also stir into the yolks the ground tongue, *duxelles,* mustard, salt to taste, a little white pepper, the chopped chives or parsley, and, finally, 2 tablespoons of softened butter. Beat with a large spoon until the mixture is smooth. If for some reason it seems too dry, beat in another tablespoon or so of the reserved cream sauce.

Using a small spoon, fill each egg white with the stuffing, mounding it into a dome from end to end at least ½ inch above its surface. Heat the remaining cream sauce slightly if it has become cold and thin it with the remaining ½ cup of cream. Stir in, off the heat, the ¼ cup of grated Swiss, add salt to taste, and spread 2 or 3 tablespoons of the sauce over the bottom of the baking dish, which should be just about large enough to hold the stuffed egg halves comfortably. Lay the eggs in this, side by side, and mask each one with the remaining sauce. Sprinkle with bread crumbs, dot with bits of softened butter, and put the dish aside, covered with plastic wrap, until you are ready to bake it.

Preheat the oven to 375 degrees. Bake the eggs, uncovered, in the center of the oven for about 20 minutes, or until the sauce begins to bubble. Slide the eggs under a hot broiler briefly to brown them just before serving.

Salad of Fresh Spinach, Orange, and Tongue

Serves 4–6

1 pound fresh young spinach, *washed and thoroughly dried, the leaves stripped from their stems*

2 navel oranges, *peeled, trimmed, and separated into sections*

1½–2 **cups cold braised tongue,** *cut into julienne strips ½ inch wide and 1½ inches long*

3 teaspoons onion, *grated*
1 teaspoon salt
¾ teaspoon freshly ground black pepper
1 tablespoon prepared mustard, preferably Dijon

2 tablespoons white wine vinegar
1 teaspoon lemon juice
⅔ cup olive oil or a mixture of olive and vegetable oils

To prepare the dressing, combine the grated onion, salt, pepper, mustard, vinegar, and lemon juice in a small mixing bowl. Mix into a smooth paste; with a wire whisk then beat in, little by little, the ⅔ cup of oil. Continue to beat until the dressing thickens.

In a chilled glass salad bowl arrange the spinach leaves, orange sections, and tongue. Pour the dressing over them and toss thoroughly. Unlike most green salads, this salad is somewhat improved if it is allowed to stand 10 minutes or so before being served on chilled plates.

► ◄

A Classic New England Corned Beef and Cabbage

6-pound corned beef, first cut of the brisket, if possible
2-pound firm green cabbage, *cored and quartered*

8–12 new potatoes, about 1½ inches in diameter
6 tablespoons butter, *melted*
2 tablespoons parsley or chives, *finely chopped,* or a combination of both

ADDITIONAL
VEGETABLES
(OPTIONAL)

Carrots
Parsnips
Turnips
Onions

Put the corned beef in a large heavy soup kettle and cover with cold water. Make sure the water rises to at least 2 inches above the surface of the meat. Bring it to the boiling point, then turn the heat down to its lowest point (a bubble or two should break on the water's surface every few seconds), half cover the pot, and simmer the meat at this rate anywhere from 4 to 6 hours, or until it can be easily pierced with a fork. Add more hot water to the pot from time to time, if necessary.

In parts of New England, the accompanying cabbage and potatoes (and other vegetables as well, such as carrots, parsnips, turnips, and onions) are added to the simmering beef 30 minutes or so before it is done. For a fresher, less briny flavor, many cooks prefer to cook the additional vegetables separately; also the cored and quartered cabbage, cooked for about 15 minutes in its own pot of boiling water; and the potatoes, peeled or not, boiled separately too.

But however you cook the vegetables, serve the dish as follows: slice the corned beef thinly and arrange the slices overlapping down the center of a large heated platter; surround the meat with the cooked vegetables, douse them with the melted butter, and sprinkle them with the herbs. Horseradish and a variety of mustards and pickles make excellent accompaniments, as do glasses of cold beer.

► Your butcher should be able to tell you whether the corned beef has been heavily corned (or salted, that is) or not. If it has been mildly cured, no soaking is necessary, but heavily cured beef should be soaked in cold water—and the water changed 3 or 4 times—anywhere from 4 to 6 hours.

► It is a waste of time and material to cook corned beef in anything but plain unseasoned boiling water. No matter how lightly corned the meat, the brine inevitably released in the water during the cooking process will cancel out the flavor of any vegetables, seasonings, or herbs you might be tempted to add and, consequently, have not the slightest effect upon the meat itself.

► For any of the corned beef improvisations that follow a can of corned beef of superior quality may, in a pinch, be used to round out an insufficient amount of corned beef remaining from the classic recipe. Unfortunately, even the best canned corned beef tends to be pulpy, so use it with discretion. Far better would be a few slices of the cooked corned beef which is sold in better delicatessens, although it is usually formidably expensive.

► If you have any leftover corned beef hash or red flannel hash from the improvisations on pages 111 and 110, respectively, use what you have as substitute fillings for any of the stuffed vegetable recipes on pages 198 through 214.

IMPROVISATIONS

Pâté of Corned Beef in Croustade

*Serves 6–8
as a cocktail
accompaniment*

¼ pound butter, *creamed*

2 cups cooked corned beef, *ground—twice, if
possible*

1 tablespoon onion, *grated*

3 tablespoons heavy cream

2 teaspoons prepared mustard

1 teaspoon English dry mustard

1 teaspoon lemon juice

2 tablespoons parsley, *finely chopped*

2 tablespoons chives, *finely chopped*

¼ teaspoon salt

¼ teaspoon freshly ground black pepper

2 teaspoons Worcestershire sauce

A fresh French or Italian bread, about 8½ inches
long and 3½ inches in diameter

Cream the butter in a mixing bowl by beating it with a large spoon for a few minutes until it is smooth and pale in color. Then, a few tablespoons at a time, beat in the corned beef and, one after the other, the onions, cream, mustards, lemon juice, parsley, chives, salt, pepper, and Worcestershire sauce. Your task will be greatly facilitated if you own an electric mixer with a pastry arm, but if you do not, continue to beat the *pâté* by hand until it is as smooth as you can possibly get it. Taste for seasoning, remembering that when the *pâté* is chilled, its flavor will be considerably muted.

Slice 2 inches or so off the ends of the bread. With your fingers and the aid of a long thin spoon, remove as much of the soft insides of the bread as possible without damaging or breaking through the crust. When the bread is a hollow tube, stand it on one end on a sheet of waxed paper and carefully fill it with the soft *pâté,* packing it down as you proceed. If there isn't enough *pâté* to fill the bread, simply cut off the hollow portion. Wrap the *croustade* in waxed paper and refrigerate for a few hours until the *pâté* is firm. Slice into ⅛- or ¼-inch rounds with a serrated knife and serve as a cocktail accompaniment. You may, if you like, briefly heat the bread in a hot oven, to crisp the crust, but do this with caution; if the *croustade* becomes too hot the *pâté* will soften too much to slice.

Note: All the *pâtés* in this book may be presented in this fashion.

Glazed Corned Beef with Orange-Horseradish Sauce

Serves 4–6

¾ cup light brown sugar
1½ cups orange juice
1 tablespoon lemon juice
2 teaspoons English dry mustard
1 teaspoon chili powder
⅛ teaspoon cayenne

1–2 teaspoons horseradish, *freshly grated or bottled*
A solid 2-inch piece of cooked corned beef weighing 2–3 pounds
12–16 whole cloves

Preheat the oven to 375 degrees. In a small saucepan combine the brown sugar, orange and lemon juices, mustard, and chili powder. Stirring almost constantly, bring the marinade to a boil, then let simmer for 5 minutes or so. Meanwhile insert the whole cloves on the fatty side of the beef (if there is enough fat, score it as if it were a ham), leaving an inch or so between them. Place the corned beef, fat side up, on a rack in a roasting pan just about large enough to hold it, pour over approximately half the simmering marinade, and slide the pan into the center of the oven. Remove the remaining marinade from the heat and put it aside; it will be the base for the sauce.

Roast the corned beef for about ½ hour, basting it with the marinade in the pan every 10 minutes or so. When the beef is brightly glazed, remove it to a heated platter and serve it in thin slices accompanied by the reheated reserved marinade to which you have added 1 (or 2, if you like its pungent flavor) teaspoons of freshly grated or commercial bottled horseradish. If the horseradish is bottled, first drain, then squeeze it dry in a towel.

Red Flannel Hash

Serves 4

¼ pound salt pork, *finely diced*
½ cup scallions or onions, *finely chopped*
¼ cup green pepper, *finely chopped*
2 cups cooked corned beef, *ground or finely chopped*

1½ cups freshly cooked or canned beets, *not too finely chopped*
4 tablespoons parsley, *finely chopped, 2 for seasoning hash and 2 for garnishing*

2 cups cooked baking potatoes, *freshly boiled,*   Salt
   cooled, and not too finely chopped   Freshly ground black pepper
6 tablespoons heavy cream

Render the diced pork by frying it in a 10-inch heavy frying pan over moderate heat. Stir almost constantly with a wooden spoon until the fat has dissolved, then remove the brown bits and put them aside. Pour half the fat into a dish and save it until later.

Heat the remaining fat in the frying pan and, over moderate heat, cook the scallions or onions and green pepper for about 5 minutes, or just long enough for them to soften without browning. Scrape them into a large mixing bowl. Add the corned beef, beets, the chopped parsley, and potatoes, and moisten them with the heavy cream. Season with salt to taste and a few gratings of black pepper and mix all the ingredients together gently but thoroughly. If you wish, add the brown pork bits you saved earlier.

Over moderate heat, warm the reserved pork fat in the same frying pan, then add the corned beef mixture. Pat it down gently with a spatula. Cook over moderate heat for about 40 minutes, shaking the pan every now and then to make sure the hash doesn't stick to the bottom. As the hash cooks, the pork fat will inevitably rise to the surface; tip the pan and skim it from the sides with a small spoon or bulb baster. During the last 10 minutes of cooking, to ensure that the hash will be free of most of its fat, lay a double thickness of paper toweling on top like a blotter, pressing it down gently into the pan. Repeat this blotting procedure as often as you think necessary.

When the hash is done, have ready a large circular heated platter. If you prefer to fold the hash over omelette fashion, under no circumstances attempt this maneuver unless you are certain the hash hasn't stuck to the bottom of the pan, which, more often than not, it tends to do. A far more reliable procedure is to place the platter on top of the frying pan and turn the hash out. If, by some chance, part of the crust sticks to the pan, remove it with a spatula and patch it into place. Sprinkle the top with the remaining 2 tablespoons of chopped parsley.

Corned Beef Hash

Serves 4   The recipe for this dish is exactly the same as the one for roast beef hash on page 21. Substitute 2 cups of cooked corned beef for the roast beef.

French Potato Salad with Julienned Corned Beef

Serves 4

4 cups firm potatoes, *sliced ¼ inch thick (about 6 medium potatoes)*

2 tablespoons beef or chicken stock, fresh or canned, *heated*

1½ teaspoons salt

½ teaspoon English dry mustard

½ teaspoon prepared mustard

Freshly ground black pepper

2 tablespoons white wine vinegar

1½ **cups cold cooked corned beef,** *cut into julienne strips 1½ inches by ½ inch*

5 tablespoons olive oil

2 tablespoons scallions, *finely chopped*

1 tablespoon parsley, *finely chopped*

Watercress sprays

Drop the potato slices into boiling salted water and cook them briskly until they are tender but not falling apart. Drain them, place them in a large frying pan, and shake gently over low heat to dry them. Put them in a large mixing bowl and, while they are still hot, pour over them 2 tablespoons of the hot stock. Stir gently until the stock is absorbed, then add, first mixed together in a small dish, the salt, mustards, a few gratings of black pepper, and the vinegar. Stir in the julienned corned beef, then the olive oil, 1 tablespoon at a time. Follow this with the scallions and parsley. To be at its best, the salad should not be refrigerated but served at room temperature surrounded with sprays of crisp watercress.

Corned Beef Mousse with Mustard Mayonnaise

Serves 4–6

The recipe for this dish is exactly the same as the one for the tongue *mousse* on page 104. Substitute 2 cups of chopped or ground corned beef for the tongue.

Salad of Fresh Spinach, Orange, and Corned Beef

Serves 4–6

The recipe for this dish is exactly the same as the one for the salad of fresh spinach, orange, and tongue on page 106. Substitute 1½ to 2 cups of cold cooked corned beef for the tongue.

Notes

Poultry

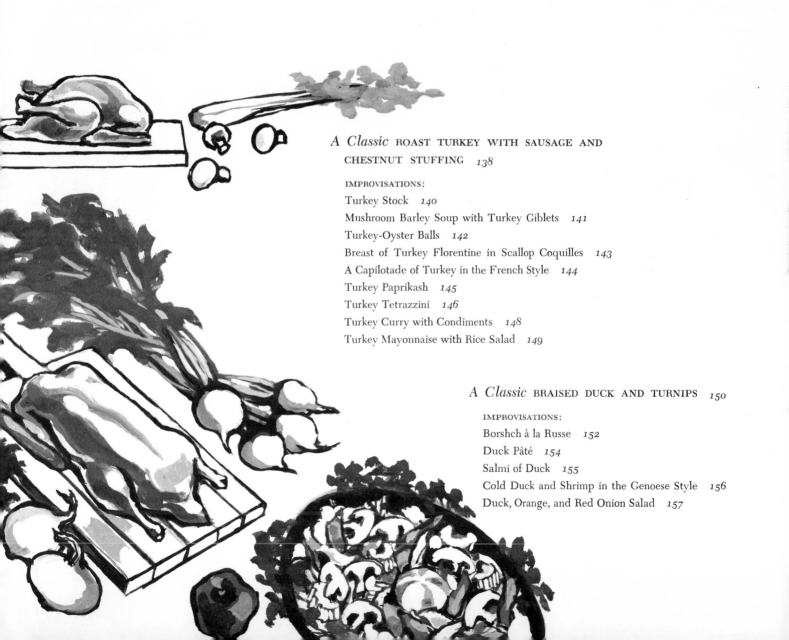

PoulTRY Because chickens, turkeys, and ducks are more easily overcooked than other

meats, reheating or recooking them presents something of a problem. How long and in what fashion the birds were originally cooked are of course important considerations, and the recipes that follow—some traditional and others improvisational—have often taken these factors fully into account.

Roast chicken or turkey can no more be reheated successfully in their original forms than can any other roasted meat, but, on the other hand, they are remarkably good simply served unadorned at room temperature. To recook them successfully, it is best to heat them gently in a sauce. Not only will the birds then be spared further cooking (which would surely make them tasteless) but the sauce will reintroduce, as it were, some of the moisture lost in the first roasting and cooling process. And even more importantly, the sauce, if it is a judiciously seasoned one, will thoroughly absorb and mask the characteristic aftertaste typical of most recooked roasted poultry.

Boiled chicken and braised duck are easier to reheat and recook. Moist and sauced to begin with, these fowl can stand more securely on their own; in fact, they need be only gently reheated in their original stock or sauce to make perfectly respectable dishes. More elaborate treatment, however, gives these cooked birds more interest, and many of the recipes suggested for them have their roots in some of the greatest dishes of the past.

If you are willing to settle for results somewhat short of perfection, cooked turkey may be substituted in those chicken dishes which require that the cooked meat either be ground or served with highly seasoned sauces. At best, turkey has considerably less flavor than chicken and its loss of character when recooked is particularly apparent in dishes in which a chicken flavor is expected to dominate.

The braised duck suffers from no such disadvantage. The only problem confronting the cook who wants to reuse it is that there is always so little left. But the flavor of a braised duck is so pervasive that used even in the smallest amounts, as in the *pâté* or orange and red-onion salad improvisations, it makes itself known as few other meats can. Even the merest scraps of cooked duck are worth hoarding for just such dishes.

With the enormous quantity of fresh chickens and turkeys of all ages and sizes always available, there seems little reason to use the frozen varieties. However, our Long Island ducks appear to emerge from the ordeal of freezing with their quality comparatively unimpaired. But still, the fresh birds are more desirable.

► ◄

A Classic Roast Chicken in the French Style

2 young chickens, about 3 pounds each
10 tablespoons butter, *4 softened for rubbing inside chickens and 6 melted for rubbing chickens all over and for basting*
1 teaspoon lemon juice
½ teaspoon salt
1 tablespoon parsley, *finely chopped*

Freshly ground black pepper
2 tablespoons vegetable oil
2 medium onions, *thickly sliced*
2 medium carrots, *cut into ½-inch chunks*
2 stalks celery, *cut into ½-inch chunks*
Salt
2 cups chicken stock, fresh or canned

Wash the chickens under cold running water and dry them quickly and thoroughly with paper toweling. Cream the 4 tablespoons of softened butter by beating it vigorously with a wooden spoon for a few minutes and then mix into it, little by little, the lemon juice. Stir in the salt and parsley and spread the seasoned butter, equally divided, inside the chickens. Meanwhile, truss the chickens with white kitchen cord and rub them all over with some of the melted butter, which you have mixed with the vegetable oil. Save the remainder for the basting.

Preheat the oven to 475 degrees and choose a shallow roasting pan just large enough to hold the 2 chickens comfortably. Place the birds on their sides on the rack and slide the pan into the center of the hot oven. Let them roast undisturbed for about 10 minutes, then with a kitchen towel turn them over onto their other side. With a pastry brush baste them with the butter-oil mixture and again let the chickens roast undisturbed for 10 minutes. Now turn the chickens on their backs, at the same time lowering the oven heat to 400 degrees. Baste the chickens thoroughly and salt them heavily. Scatter the onions, carrots, and celery in the bottom of the pan underneath the rack, and continue to roast the chickens 40 minutes or so longer. Baste every 10 minutes with the butter-oil mixture, and when that runs out use the juices in the bottom of the roasting pan. All in all, the chickens should be done after a total of about 1 hour 10 minutes. To test for doneness, lift one of the chickens with a wooden spoon inserted in the tail opening. If the juice which runs out is yellow, the chicken is done; if the juice is faintly pink, roast the chickens 5 or 10 minutes longer. When they are done, remove them to carving board and let them rest for about 8 minutes before carving and serving.

In the meanwhile, pour into the roasting pan the 2 cups of chicken stock. Bring it to a boil on the top of the stove and scrape into it all the brown sediment clinging to the bottom and sides of the pan and the vegetables. Cook briskly until the sauce reaches the intensity of flavor you desire. Then strain it through a sieve, pressing down on the vegetables with the back of a spoon before throwing them away. Skim the surface of most of its fat, season the sauce, and pass in a gravyboat with the chicken.

► A can or jar of cooked chicken of the highest quality can be used with discretion to amplify any chicken or turkey improvisation for which you don't have quite enough of your own cooked fowl. And similarly, a pair of blanched sweetbreads, should you have them on hand, can do wonders, cut up and added to any white-sauced improvisation for which you need extra cooked chicken.

► Bits of cold cooked chicken, turkey, or duck may be finely chopped, seasoned with salt, white pepper, and a little lemon juice and chopped tarragon. Moistened with mayonnaise, the spread may be used for small sandwiches, canapés, and the like.

IMPROVISATIONS

Chicken and Rice in the Style of the Basque Country

Serves 4–6

1 pound hot Italian sausages
1 cup chicken stock, fresh or canned
A strip of orange peel (removed with a rotary peeler), *1 inch wide by 3 inches long*
4 tablespoons olive oil
2 medium green peppers, *seeded and cut into julienne strips ½ inch by 1½ inches*
1 teaspoon garlic, *finely chopped*
1½ pounds firm ripe tomatoes, *peeled, seeded, and coarsely chopped*

Salt
Freshly ground black pepper
2 teaspoons imported Hungarian sweet paprika
1 teaspoon oregano
5 cups cooked rice (1⅔ cups raw rice), *cold*
1 teaspoon butter
4–6 substantial pieces of cold roast chicken: *wings, thighs, breast, etc.—substantial scraps will do if they must*
1 tablespoon parsley, *finely chopped*

Choose a heavy frying pan just about large enough to hold the sausages and cover them with the cup of chicken stock—or a little more, if necessary. Add the orange peel and bring the stock to a boil. Turn the heat down to moderate, let the sausages simmer for about 5 minutes, then prick them with the point of a knife in 2 or 3 places to allow the fat to escape. Pierce them again after 5 more minutes of cooking, then remove the sausages from the pan and let them drain and cool on paper toweling. Reserve the cooking stock but first skim it of all its fat.

Heat the 4 tablespoons of olive oil in a small heavy frying pan and cook the julienned green peppers over moderate heat for about 10 minutes, or until they are tender. Add the chopped garlic, cook for 1 or 2 minutes without browning, then add the thoroughly drained chopped tomatoes. Mix in the paprika and oregano, salt and freshly ground pepper to taste, and cook the vegetables quickly for about 5 minutes. Stir them almost constantly and take care not to burn them. When most of the liquid has cooked away, remove the pan from the heat.

Preheat the oven to 350 degrees. Arrange the cooked rice (first seasoned with salt) in a lightly buttered 3- or 4-quart casserole. Pour over it ½ cup of reserved chicken-sausage stock. Place the chicken pieces on top and spread the tomato-pepper sauce around and in between them. Slice the sausage into ½-inch pieces and arrange them around the edge of the casserole.

Bring the casserole to a boil on top of the stove, then transfer it to the center of the oven and let it bake for about 20 minues, or until the chicken is heated through. Sprinkle with the parsley and serve directly from the casserole.

A Paella Sevillana

Serves 4–6

4 small sausages: *chorizos, hot or sweet Italian sausages, or good fresh pork sausages*

3 tablespoons olive oil

2 tablespoons butter

¾ cup onions, *finely chopped*

1 teaspoon garlic, *finely chopped*

1 medium green pepper and 1 medium red pepper, *seeded and cut into julienne strips 2 by 2½ inches*

1 cup raw rice

¾ pound fresh ripe tomatoes, *peeled, seeded, and coarsely chopped,* or 1 cup canned tomatoes, *drained and coarsely chopped*

1–1½ cups chicken stock, fresh or canned, *heated*

¼ teaspoon powdered saffron

Salt

Freshly ground black pepper

2–2½ cups cold roast chicken, *cut into 2-inch chunks**

1 package frozen artichoke hearts, *defrosted*

8–12 large uncooked shrimp, *shelled and deveined*

1 dozen small cherrystone clams, *scrubbed,* or mussels, *scrubbed and bearded*

1 tablespoon parsley, *finely chopped*

Pimiento strips (optional)

In a shallow frying pan cover the sausages with cold water and bring the water to a rapid boil. Briskly cook the sausages, uncovered, piercing them with the point of a knife occasionally to allow their fat to escape. When the water has completely cooked away, turn the heat down to moderate and slowly brown the sausages in the fat which will have settled to the bottom of the pan. Remove them and drain on paper toweling. Cut the sausages into 2-inch lengths and reserve.

Preheat the oven to 350 degrees. Heat the oil and butter in a heavy 3-quart casserole or a *paellera* and slowly cook the chopped onion and garlic for about 3 or 4 minutes. Add the green and red pepper strips and cook for about 15 minutes longer. Into this stir the cup of unwashed raw rice and cook it slowly with the vegetables in the fat, stirring constantly until most of the grains turn slightly opaque or white. Be careful not to let them burn. Stir in the chopped tomatoes and 1 cup of the hot chicken stock, in which you have first dissolved the saffron. Season highly with salt and pepper. Bring the casserole to a boil on top of the stove, then transfer it to the center of the hot oven, where it should cook for about 15 minutes, or until the rice is almost but not quite done. Remove the casserole from the oven, and if the mixture seems dry at this point moisten it with the remaining ½ cup of stock heated to boiling. Bury beneath the surface of the rice the chicken, artichoke hearts, shrimp, and clams or mussels. Cover the casserole tightly, return to the oven, and let it cook until the bivalves open. During that time the chicken will have heated through, and the shrimp and artichokes should be thoroughly cooked. Serve either directly from the casserole or arrange the *paella* on a large platter. However you serve it, sprinkle the top with finely chopped parsley.

* *Note:* This *paella* Sevillana may be amplified with other previously cooked foods you may have on hand: cubes of ham, small pieces of lobster or pork, peas, or mushrooms. And for a decorative effect, you can garnish the *paella* platter with strips of pimiento.

Chicken Cocktail Croquettes with Lemon Dill Sauce

Serves 6–8

2 tablespoons butter	⅛ teaspoon cayenne
3 tablespoons flour	1–2 teaspoons lemon juice
¾ cup chicken stock, fresh or canned	1½ cups (packed down) cold roast chicken, *finely chopped*
1 egg (yolk only)	
2 tablespoons heavy cream	1 tablespoon parsley, *finely chopped*
¾ teaspoon salt	

DUXELLES
(¼ CUP)

1 tablespoon butter	⅛ pound mushrooms, *finely chopped* (½ cup)
1½ tablespoons shallots or scallions, *finely chopped*	2 tablespoons Madeira

COATING

½ cup flour	½ cup bread crumbs ⎫ combined
2 eggs, *lightly beaten with 1½ tablespoons vegetable oil*	½ cup almonds, *ground* ⎭
	Deep fat for frying

LEMON DILL
SAUCE

3 eggs (yolks only)	1 cup chicken stock, fresh or canned
1 tablespoon arrowroot	1 tablespoon lemon juice
1 teaspoon salt	2 tablespoons fresh dill, *chopped*
⅛ teaspoon cayenne	

Melt 2 tablespoons of butter in a small saucepan. Then, off the heat, mix in 3 tablespoons of flour. Pour over, all at once, ¾ cup of stock and stir with a whisk until the flour dissolves. Return the pan to the heat and, stirring constantly, bring the sauce to a boil. It will be very thick. Simmer for 1 or 2 minutes to remove any floury taste. Meanwhile combine the egg yolk with 2 tablespoons of cream, then add to it a few tablespoons to the hot sauce. Pour the egg mixture into the sauce and, continually stirring, bring it to a boil again. Let it boil for 10 seconds, then turn off the heat and season with the salt, cayenne, and 1 teaspoon of the lemon juice.

To prepare the *duxelles,* melt 1 tablespoon of butter in a small frying pan and add the chopped shallots or scallions. Sauté over moderate heat for about 1 minute without letting them color, then mix in the chopped mushrooms. Stirring every now and then, cook the mixture over low heat for about 10 minutes, or until the mushrooms are dry but not brown. Pour in the Madeira, raise the heat and, stirring constantly, cook the wine away entirely.

In a mixing bowl combine the sauce with the chopped chicken, *duxelles,* and chopped parsley. Taste for seasoning; it will most likely need more salt and possibly a little more lemon juice. Spread this mixture ½ inch thick on a small platter, cover tightly with plastic wrap, and chill in the refrigerator for at least 2 hours, or even as long as overnight.

When ready to use, form the now-firm chicken mixture into the balls about 1 inch in diameter. Roll them lightly in flour, shaking off the excess, then dip in the eggs, which have been lightly beaten with the oil. Coat thoroughly with the bread-crumb–almond mixture and chill again.

Fry the balls a few at a time in deep fat heated to 375 degrees. They should take no longer than 1 or 2 minutes to turn a delicate golden brown. Drain on paper toweling. If they must wait, keep them warm in a 250-degree oven.

The lemon sauce can be made at any time and reheated. In the top of a double boiler, combine the egg yolks, arrowroot, salt, and cayenne. Beat together with a whisk, then add the stock. Cook this directly over the heat, stirring almost constantly until it begins to thicken. Don't let it actually boil or it may curdle. When the sauce is thick enough to cling to the spoon, stir in the lemon juice and chopped dill. Taste for seasoning. Keep the sauce warm (in a small chafing dish) and use it as a dipping sauce for the croquettes, which should be pierced with ornamental toothpicks or tiny forks.

Chicken Cocktail Fritters

Serves 6–8 This recipe calls for exactly the same ingredients and amounts as does the chicken cocktail croquette recipe on page 121, except that the following fritter batter should be substituted for the coating suggested for the croquettes.

FRITTER BATTER	1 cup flour, *sifted before measuring*	3 tablespoons vegetable oil
	¾ cup warm water	1 egg (white only)
	½ teaspoon salt	Deep fat for frying

Prepare the batter about 2 hours before you plan to use it. In a small mixing bowl combine the water, salt, and oil and add the flour (sifted before measuring), stirring it in little by little and continuing to stir it only until a fairly smooth paste is formed. Overbeating develops the gluten in the flour and produces a rubbery batter. Let the paste rest for a couple of hours.

In the meanwhile, prepare the chicken balls exactly as described in the chicken croquette recipe, chilling them as suggested but omitting the coating procedure. In its place, just before frying, roll the balls lightly in flour.

A few minutes before cooking, beat the egg white stiff and carefully fold it into the waiting flour mixture. Heat the fat to 375 degrees on the deep-fat thermometer. Dip the chicken balls into the batter and drop them, 3 or 4 at a time, into the hot fat. They will puff up. Turn them in the fat with a slotted spoon until they are brown all over, then drain on paper toweling. They may be kept warm in a 250-degree oven for 15 minutes or so if they must wait. They are at their best and crispest, however, if served the moment they are done.

Gratin of Roast Chicken in the Style of the Savoie

Serves 4	4 tablespoons butter, *3 for the roux and 1 softened for topping*	⅛ teaspoon cayenne
	4 tablespoons flour	1 teaspoon Dijon mustard
	1 cup chicken stock, fresh or canned	3 tablespoons Swiss cheese, *grated*
	¼ cup dry white wine	¼ cup bread crumbs
	½–¾ cup heavy cream	**4–6 substantial pieces of cold roast chicken:**
	1 teaspoon fresh tarragon or ½ teaspoon dried	*thighs, breasts, wings, legs—large scraps will*
	Salt	*do if they must*

Melt 3 tablespoons of the butter in a small enamel or stainless-steel saucepan and when it is completely melted but not brown mix in, off the heat, the 4 level tablespoons of flour. Stir this *roux* until it is smooth, then pour in the chicken stock and wine. Beat together with a wire whisk until the *roux* has somewhat dissolved, return the pan to the heat, and cook, stirring constantly with the whisk, until the sauce thickens. Turn the heat down and let the sauce simmer as slowly as possible for about 5 minutes, stirring with a spoon every now and then. The sauce should be quite thick. Thin it with ½ cup of the heavy cream, and if it still seems too thick add the remaining cream, 1 tablespoon at a time, until the sauce runs sluggishly off the spoon when it is lifted from the pan. Add the tarragon, salt, cayenne, mustard, and Swiss cheese and stir until well combined with the sauce. Simmer a moment or two to dissolve the cheese, and taste again for salt. The sauce should be well seasoned, not bland.

Choose a shallow baking dish that is just large enough to hold the chicken in one layer and attractive enough to serve from at the table. Spread a thin layer of the sauce on the bottom of the pan and arrange the chicken pieces skin side up. Sprinkle each piece very lightly with salt, then with a large spoon coat the pieces thoroughly one by one with the remaining sauce. Sprinkle the bread crumbs over the top and dot with the tablespoon of softened butter, cut into small bits. If you don't intend to bake the chicken at once, cover the dish tightly with plastic wrap and refrigerate.

When you are ready to cook the chicken, preheat the oven to 375 degrees. Place the baking dish in the center of the oven and leave it there for about 20 minutes, or until the sauce begins to bubble and the chicken is heated through. Slide it under the broiler to brown the surface lightly, then serve at once.

Pollo Tonnato with Rice Salad

Serves 4–6

TUNA
MAYONNAISE

1 whole egg plus 1 yolk
½ teaspoon salt
⅛ teaspoon cayenne
1 cup olive oil or ½ cup each olive oil and vegetable oil

2 flat anchovy fillets, *washed, dried, and coarsely chopped*
3½-ounce can tunafish—imported and packed in olive oil, if possible
1 tablespoon lemon juice

2 cups cold roast chicken, *skin, fat, and gristle removed, cut into ¾-inch dice*

RICE SALAD	1 cup raw rice (*see text of recipe if you wish to substitute cooked rice*)	2 tablespoons coarsely chopped pimiento (canned or bottled), *thoroughly drained and patted dry with paper toweling*
	2 cups chicken stock, fresh or canned	¾ cup tiny cooked peas (canned or frozen), *cold*
	1½ teaspoons salt	1 teaspoon lemon juice
	3 tablespoons white wine vinegar	1 teaspoon lemon peel, *finely chopped*
	Freshly ground black pepper	
	4 tablespoons olive oil	

GARNISH (OPTIONAL)	Parsley sprigs or watercress	Black olives (Mediterranean varieties)
	Tomatoes, *peeled and sliced*	Lemons, *sliced or quartered*
	Artichoke hearts, *marinated*	

This tuna mayonnaise is most easily made in the blender.° At high speed, blend the whole egg and the additional yolk, ½ teaspoon salt, and the cayenne for about 35 seconds. Turn down the speed to moderate, then slowly, and in the thinnest of streams, start pouring the oil into the center of the whirling eggs. When half the oil has been absorbed, the mayonnaise will begin to thicken. When the remaining oil has been dribbled in, the mayonnaise will have achieved the proper, thick consistency. Turn off the blender. Mash the drained tunafish and anchovies in a small bowl, then add to the mayonnaise. Turn the blender to high speed and blend the mixture for 5—but at the most 10—seconds, or just long enough to combine the fish and mayonnaise into a smooth, thick mass. Stir in the lemon juice. The mayonnaise should fall lazily off a lifted spoon; if it is too thick, thin it with a little more lemon juice, or, if you wish, a few teaspoons of chicken stock or heavy cream. Scrape the mayonnaise into a small bowl. If it must wait for any length of time, cover tightly with plastic wrap to prevent its surface from darkening. Two hours—or even longer—before serving, combine the chicken with the mayonnaise, making sure each piece is thoroughly coated. Cover tightly.

For the rice salad, it is preferable to use freshly cooked rather than previously cooked rice, but should you have 3 cupfuls of leftover cooked rice, steam it in a colander over hot water for a few minutes before making the salad with it. To prepare freshly cooked rice for this dish, bring the 2 cups of chicken stock to a boil in a small saucepan, then pour in the unwashed rice. Add ½ teaspoon of salt, cover the pan tightly, and lower the heat to the barest simmer. In about 15 minutes all the stock will have been absorbed by the rice and the rice itself will be tender but still slightly firm, as it should be. Transfer the rice to a large mixing bowl and let it cool to lukewarm. Then stir in—with a fork, never with a spoon, which would mash it—the wine vinegar, 1 teaspoon of salt, and a little pepper. When the vinegar has been thoroughly absorbed, add the oil, 1 tablespoon at a time, then gently mix in the chopped pimiento, peas, and lemon juice. Taste for seasoning, remembering that because the salad will be served cold—or better still, at room temperature—it must be more highly seasoned than if served warm.

The *pollo tonnato* may be served in a number of ways. The simplest, of course, is to mound the mayonnaise-coated chicken in the center of a serving platter, surround it with either sprigs of parsley or watercress, and pass the rice separately. Or, more elaborately, the rice may be packed into a 1-quart oiled ring mold, chilled for an hour or so, then unmolded onto a circular platter. The center of the ring can then be filled with the *pollo tonnato* and sprinkled with a little chopped parsley. For a more elaborate presentation, the rice can be surrounded with overlapping slices of peeled tomatoes, marinated artichoke hearts, black olives (the imported Mediterranean varieties), and small slices or quarters of lemon, or for that matter, anything else that suits your fancy. No matter how you serve the *pollo tonnato*, hot garlic bread and a bottle of chilled Soave would be fine accompaniments.

* *Note:* To make the tuna mayonnaise by hand, mash the tunafish and anchovies to a paste with a fork. With the back of a large spoon rub it through a fine sieve set in a mixing bowl. Stir in 2 egg yolks (instead of the whole egg plus the additional yolk used for the blender version), the lemon juice, salt, and cayenne, and then, with a wire whisk, beat in the oil 1 tablespoon at a time. The mayonnaise should have the consistency of a medium cream sauce; if it is too thick, thin it with a little more lemon juice, or, if you wish, with a few teaspoons of chicken stock or heavy cream. Then continue the recipe as described above.

Chicken, Raw Mushroom, and Rice Salad in the Italian Style

Serves 4–6

¼ pound fresh white mushrooms, *thinly sliced*
Juice of 3 lemons, *strained* (*4 tablespoons*)
½ teaspoon dried oregano, *crumbled*

½ teaspoon garlic, *finely chopped*
3 tablespoons olive oil
Freshly ground black pepper

⅔ cup raw rice (*see text of recipe if you wish to substitute cooked rice*)

1⅓ cups chicken stock, fresh or canned

1¼ teaspoons salt

½ cup fennel or celery, *cut into julienne strips 1 inch by ½ inch*

1½–2 cups cold roast chicken, *all fat and gristle* removed and cut into julienne strips 1 inch by ½ inch or into ¾-inch chunks

2 tablespoons parsley, *finely chopped*

Tomatoes, *peeled and sliced*

Black olives

Watercress

If the mushrooms are sandy, wipe them with a damp paper towel, but under no circumstances wash or peel them. Cut the stems off level with the cap (save them for another purpose) and slice the mushroom caps lengthwise as thinly as possible. Mix them with the lemon juice in an enamel or glass or stainless-steel mixing bowl. After the mushrooms appear to have absorbed the juice, add the crumbled oregano, garlic, olive oil, and a few grindings of black pepper. Marinate for at least 2 hours, stirring every now and then so that the mushrooms are well coated with the marinade.

For the rice salad, it is preferable to use freshly cooked rather than previously cooked rice, but should you have 2 cupfuls of leftover rice steam it for a few minutes in a colander placed over hot water before making the salad with it. To prepare freshly cooked rice, bring the 1⅓ cups of chicken stock to a boil and pour in the ⅔ cup of unwashed rice. Add ¼ teaspoon of the salt, cover the pan tightly, and lower the heat to barely simmering. In about 15 minutes all the stock will have been absorbed by the rice and the rice itself will be tender but still slightly firm. Transfer it to a large mixing bowl and let it cool to lukewarm. Then stir in—with a fork, never with a spoon, which would mash the rice—the mushrooms and all their marinade, the fennel or celery, 1 teaspoon salt, the chicken pieces, and 1 tablespoon of the parsley. Mix together gently but thoroughly and taste for seasoning. Ideally, the salad should rest outside the refrigerator for at least 1 hour before serving, but of course it can be served at once, if it must. Pile loosely in the center of a platter and surround with sliced peeled tomatoes, black olives, and watercress. Dust the top of the salad with remaining parsley.

A Classic Poule au Pot, Henry V

1 fowl, about 5–6 pounds
1 teaspoon salt
2 tablespoons butter
2 tablespoons vegetable oil } *combined*
2 medium onions, *halved*
2 medium carrots, *cut into 2-inch pieces*
3 stalks celery, *cut into 2-inch pieces*

A bouquet consisting of 6 sprigs parsley, 1 well-washed leek (white part only), split and with a bay leaf inserted inside, *tied together with string*
1 veal knuckle, *sawed into 2-inch pieces*
4–5 quarts water or equal amounts of water and canned chicken stock or all canned chicken stock

STUFFING

2 tablespoons butter
½ cup onions, *finely chopped*
¾ cup raw rice
1½ cups chicken stock, fresh or canned
½ pound well-seasoned fresh sausage meat
1–2 chicken livers

4 tablespoons parsley, *finely chopped*
½ teaspoon thyme
4–6 tablespoons heavy cream
Salt
Freshly ground black pepper

VEGETABLE
GARNITURE
(OPTIONAL)

The same vegetables as those listed for the *pot-au-feu* on page 5 and cooked in the same fashion

Quickly wash the fowl and its giblets under cold running water and dry thoroughly with paper toweling. Rub the cavity with a teaspoon of salt.

For the stuffing, melt 2 tablespoons of butter in a small casserole or saucepan and cook the onions for about 5 minutes, letting them color slightly. Stir in the rice and over moderate heat stir the grains until they become somewhat opaque and turn a milky white. Be careful not to let them burn. Pour in the hot stock and bring it to a boil. Turn the heat down to the barest simmer and cook with the pan tightly covered for about 12 or 13 minutes, or until the rice is almost but not quite done. It will finish cooking in the fowl. Drain it if any liquid remains, then transfer the rice to a large mixing bowl.

Fry the sausage meat (starting it in a cold pan) over moderate heat and break it up with a fork as it begins to render its fat. When the sausage is crumbled and lightly brown, strain it of all its fat, reserving 2 tablespoons. Add the sausage meat to the rice. Then heat the 2 tablespoons of pork fat to sizzling and in it quickly cook the chicken livers, turning them constantly until they are brown all over but still pink inside. Chop them finely and add to the rice and sausage mixture. Now add the chopped parsley, and thyme. Stir gently and thoroughly with a fork and moisten with heavy cream, using less than 6 tablespoons if you prefer a drier stuffing. Season well with salt and freshly ground pepper and let the mixture cool before stuffing the chicken with it.

Stuff the chicken without packing the stuffing in too tightly; the rice will expand somewhat as it cooks and it is wiser to understuff rather than overstuff the fowl. Sew up the openings and with strong cord truss the bird so that it will keep its shape as it cooks.

Heat the butter-oil mixture in a large heavy frying pan and quickly brown the fowl on all sides, turning it in the hot fat with two large spoons or a kitchen towel, to avoid puncturing the skin. When it is golden brown all over (this should take at least 15 minutes), place it in a large soup kettle or casserole. Surround it with the washed giblets, the cut-up vegetables, the veal knuckle, and the bouquet and pour in the liquid. The liquid should rise at least 2 inches above the fowl. Add more water or stock if it doesn't. Over high heat bring this to a boil and skim the surface of all scum as it rises to the top. After it reaches the full boil, turn the heat down, half cover the pot, and simmer the chicken for 2 to 3 hours, depending upon the tenderness of the bird. Be careful not to overcook it. A fairly reliable test for doneness is to remove the bird from the broth and pierce the thigh with the point of a knife. If the liquid which spurts out is light amber, the fowl is done; if it is lightly tinged with pink, cook it a while longer.

To serve, place the bird on a serving platter and let it rest for about 15 minutes before carving it. Meanwhile, if you like, serve the thoroughly degreased broth in bouillon cups with a little cooked vermicelli and/or a sprinkling of chopped parsley. When the chicken is carved, arrange the pieces attractively on a large heated platter and either mound the stuffing in the center of the dish or surround the chicken with it. In either case, moisten the whole with a little hot broth.

If you have decided to add the garniture of vegetables, follow the procedure for cooking and serving them as described in the *pot-au-feu* recipe on page 6.

▶ The lemon sauce on page 221 is a fine accompaniment for the *poule au pot*. Make it with the *poule au pot* stock.

▶ The remaining chicken broth from the *poule au pot* may be used as a base for any soup or sauce calling for a white stock. If you have no immediate use for the extra broth, it can be refrigerated, after being cooled, in a tightly covered jar or a bowl covered with plastic wrap. Every four days bring the stock to a boil, cool it, uncovered, then cover again and refrigerate as before. More easily, of course, you can freeze the stock and avoid the reboiling process.

▶ If you have any stuffing left from the *poule au pot*, shape it into small balls (bound with a little beaten egg if they don't hold together) and poach them in broth as a garnish for clear bouillon. Or dip the balls in egg, then crumbs, and deep-fry them like the chicken cocktail croquettes (p. 121) and serve them as hors d'oeuvres.

▶ Any remaining *blanquette* of chicken (p. 138) may be served chilled (the sauce will jell), sprinkled with a little chopped fresh tarragon or dill. For a fine warm-weather dish, accompany it with lemon quarters, a cold rice salad made with tiny peas, and hot French or Italian bread.

iMPROViSATiONS

Chicken Gumbo Soup

Serves 4

4 tablespoons butter
½ cup onions, *finely chopped*
¼ cup celery, *thinly sliced*
2 tablespoons green pepper, *finely chopped*
1 teaspoon garlic, *finely chopped*
1 package frozen okra, *defrosted and thinly sliced (2 cups)*
1 pound 3 ounce can solid-pack tomatoes, *drained and coarsely chopped*
4 cups chicken stock, fresh—**preferably using some of the *poule au pot* stock**—or canned

1 small bay leaf
1½–2 cups cold cooked chicken, *cut into ½-inch dice*
2 teaspoons *filé* powder
Salt
Freshly ground black pepper
A few drops Tabasco (optional)
1 tablespoon parsley, *finely chopped*
1 cup cooked rice, *hot*

Melt the butter over moderate heat in a 2- or 3-quart saucepan and sauté the onions, celery, pepper, and garlic for about 5 minutes, stirring constantly, so that the vegetables color just slightly. Add the sliced, defrosted okra and, still stirring, cook until the okra stops "roping" or, in other words, until the thin white threads the vegetable produces when heated more or less disappear. Now pour over the vegetables the chopped tomatoes and chicken stock and bring to a boil. Turn the heat down to barely simmering, add the bay leaf, and cook with the pan half covered for about ½ hour. At this point, stir in the chicken pieces and the *filé* powder. Heat briefly to warm the chicken through, but don't allow the soup to boil or the *filé* powder (powdered sassafras) will string unpleasantly and spoil the texture of the gumbo. Season with salt, pepper, and a few drops of Tabasco—if you like—and just before serving, sprinkle with the chopped parsley.

Traditionally, gumbos are served with a small mound of cooked rice in each soup plate over which the gumbo is ladled. It may, of course, also be served without the rice.

Gratin of Chicken Hash in Cream

Serves 4–6

2 cups cooked chicken, *minced*
1½ cups heavy cream, *½ cup for chicken and 1 cup for sauce*
3 tablespoons butter, *2 for the sauce and 1 softened for the topping, cut into bits*
3 tablespoons flour

½ teaspoon salt
⅛ teaspoon cayenne
1 egg (yolk only)
4 tablespoons Parmesan cheese, *grated*
2 tablespoons bread crumbs

Combine the minced chicken with ½ cup of the heavy cream and cook it in the upper part of a double boiler set over boiling water for about 15 minutes. Stir every now and then until the cream is completely absorbed. Transfer the chicken to a mixing bowl.

In a small saucepan melt 2 tablespoons of butter and add, off the heat, 3 level tablespoons of flour. Stir with a wooden spoon until the *roux* is smooth. Pour over, all at once, the remaining cup of heavy cream and stir with a wire whisk. Return the pan to the heat and, still stirring, bring the sauce almost to the boil. It should be quite thick. Simmer as slowly as possible for about 5 minutes to remove any residual floury taste, then beat in the egg yolk. Quickly bring the sauce to a boil and let it boil for about 10 seconds, stirring constantly. Stir in the salt and cayenne.

Thoroughly mix half the sauce into the minced chicken and taste for seasoning. It will undoubtedly need more salt. Butter an oval 3- or 4-cup baking dish and spread the hash in it as evenly as possible. Mix into the remaining sauce 2 tablespoons of the grated Parmesan cheese, add more salt—if you think it needs it—then, with a rubber spatula, spread it over the hash, masking it as completely as you can. Sprinkle the remaining cheese and bread crumbs on top and dot with the bits of softened butter.

If the dish must wait, it can be refrigerated—even for a day or so. When you are ready to cook it, preheat the oven to 375 degrees and bake for about 15 or 20 minutes, or until it begins to bubble slightly. Just before serving, slide it under the broiler to brown the top, then serve at once.

Chicken-Oyster Shortbread

Serves 4–6	1 cup yellow cornmeal	4 teaspoons baking powder
THE CORN	1 cup flour	1 egg, *lightly beaten*
BREAD	1 teaspoon sugar	4 tablespoons butter, *melted and cooled*
	¾ teaspoon salt	1 cup milk

THE CHICKEN	4 tablespoons butter	12 oysters, *shucked*
AND OYSTERS	5 tablespoons flour	1½ **cups chicken,** *free of all skin and gristle and*
	1¾ cups chicken stock, fresh or canned	*cut into ¾-inch chunks*
	½ cup heavy cream	1 tablespoon parsley, *finely chopped*
	½ teaspoon salt	2 tablespoons pimiento (canned or bottled),
	⅛ teaspoon cayenne	*coarsely diced*
	1 teaspoon lemon juice	

Preheat the oven to 425 degrees. To prepare the corn bread (which may be made hours ahead and reheated), sift into a mixing bowl the cornmeal, flour, sugar, salt, and baking powder. Beat the egg lightly, add the 4 tablespoons of melted butter, and stir in the cup of milk. Beat the dry and liquid ingredients together with a spoon, rotary or electric beater, but take care not to overbeat it. At most, the mixture should be beaten for about 1 minute. Pour the batter into a buttered 8-inch-square or 8 x 12-inch baking pan and bake in the center of the oven for 20 to 25 minutes, or until the bread comes slightly away from the edge of the pan and is lightly browned on top. Turn out on to a cake rack to allow air to circulate around the bread as it cools.

In a small enamel or stainless-steel saucepan, melt 4 tablespoons of butter without letting it brown. Off the heat, add 5 level tablespoons of flour and mix thoroughly. Pour over, all at once, the 1¾ cups of chicken stock and stir with a wire whisk until the *roux* is almost completely dissolved. Return the pan to the heat and, still stirring, bring the sauce almost to the boil. It will be quite thick. Simmer as slowly as possible for about 5 minutes to remove any residual floury taste, then stir in the ½ cup of heavy cream. Season with the salt, cayenne, and lemon juice, adding more of any of them if you think the sauce too bland.

Next poach the oysters. In a small pan bring the oyster liquid (add water, if necessary, to cover) to a boil. Immerse the oysters and simmer slowly for about 5 minutes until they become plump. Don't overcook. Drain the oysters carefully and add to the sauce. Stir in the chunks of chicken also. Taste for seasoning again and heat slowly, without letting the sauce boil. Set aside until ready to use.

A few minutes before serving, preheat the oven to 325 degrees. Cut the cornbread into approximately 4-inch squares, and carefully slice each square horizontally into halves. Heat the bread in the oven for 5 minutes, or only long enough to warm it through. Meanwhile reheat the chicken and oysters. Arrange the bottom halves of the cornbread on a heated platter, spoon the chicken mixture generously over each half, reserving a little of the sauce. Top each bottom cornbread square with its mate and dribble the reserved sauce over them. Sprinkle with the chopped parsley and diced pimiento and serve at once. Tiny peas or lima beans would be a fine vegetable accompaniment for this old American dish.

Gratin of Crêpes Stuffed with Chicken and Mushrooms

Serves 4–6

16–20
crêpes

CRÊPE BATTER			
	1 cup milk	½ teaspoon salt	
	¼ cup cold water	3 tablespoons butter, *melted and cooled*	
	1¼ cups flour	3 tablespoons butter, *melted* ⎱ *combined*	
	3 eggs	1 tablespoon vegetable oil ⎰	

SAUCE		
	4 tablespoons butter	1 cup heavy cream
	6 tablespoons flour	¾ teaspoon salt
	2 cups chicken stock, fresh or canned	⅛ teaspoon white pepper
	2 eggs (yolks only)	¾ teaspoon lemon juice

FILLING		
	4 tablespoons butter, *2 for the* duxelles *and 2 softened for topping, cut into bits*	1 tablespoon parsley, *finely chopped*
	3 tablespoon shallots or scallions, *finely chopped*	1 tablespoon fresh tarragon, *finely chopped,* or ½ teaspoon dried
	¼ pound mushrooms, *finely chopped (1 cup)*	4 tablespoons imported Swiss cheese or Parmesan, *grated,* or a combination of both
	4 tablespoons Madeira	
	2 cups cold cooked chicken, *cut into approximately ½-inch chunks*	

To make the *crêpe* batter in a blender, put the milk, water, flour, eggs, salt, and butter in the blender jar. Blend at high speed for a few seconds, then, with the machine off, scrape down the sides of the jar with a rubber scraper. Blend again, this time for about 40 seconds. Ideally, the batter should rest for about 2 hours before being used, but it can be used at once, if you wish, at a slight sacrifice of tenderness.

To make the batter by hand, combine the flour and eggs in a mixing bowl, then slowly mix in the milk and water and salt. Beat with a whisk or beater until the floury lumps disappear, strain it through a fine sieve, and stir in the melted butter.

Use a 6-inch frying pan in which to make the *crêpes*. Heat the pan until a drop of cold water flicked on its surface evaporates instantly. Using a pastry brush, grease the pan with the butter-oil mixture, then lift it over the bowl of batter. Ladle 2 tablespoons (more or less) into the pan and rotate the pan until the batter covers the entire surface. The pan should be hot enough so that the batter grips on contact. Immediately tilt the pan over the bowl and pour off the excess batter. You may have to lose a few *crêpes* until you perfect this technique, but the paper-thin *crêpes* you will finally make are worth it. Cook each *crêpe* over fairly high heat until a faint rim of brown shows around the edge. Turn the *crêpe* over and cook for a few seconds before sliding it onto a plate. Continue with the remaining batter in the same fashion; you should end up with at least 16 perfect *crêpes* and, after a little practice, with about 20. There is no need to trim them into perfect circles; since they are to be rolled, whatever imperfections they have will be masked.

To prepare the sauce, melt the 4 tablespoons of butter in a 2- or 3-quart saucepan, then, off the heat, stir in the flour. Add, all at once, the 2 cups of chicken stock and stir with a wire whisk until the *roux* is almost completely dissolved. Cook over moderate heat, stirring constantly, until the sauce is smooth and thick. Combine the 2 egg yolks with ½ cup of the cream and mix into it a few tablespoons of the simmering sauce. Then reverse the process and slowly pour the egg-cream mixture into the saucepan, continuing to stir. Bring the sauce to a boil and let it boil for about 10 seconds before removing it from the heat. Season with the salt, cayenne, and lemon juice.

To prepare ½ cup of *duxelles* for the filling, melt 2 tablespoons of butter in a small frying pan and add the chopped shallots or scallions. Sauté for about 1 minute without letting them color, then mix in the chopped mushrooms. Stirring every now and then, cook the mixture over low heat for about 10 minutes, or until the mushrooms are dry but not brown. Pour over the Madeira, raise the heat and, stirring constantly, cook the wine entirely away. Scrape the *duxelles* into a mixing bowl. Add the chicken pieces and the parsley, tarragon, and 1 cup of the reserved sauce. Mix thoroughly and taste for seasoning.

Spread a scant 2 tablespoons of the chicken mixture across the lower third of each *crêpe* and roll up without tucking in the ends. Lay them side by side, in a buttered baking dish just about large enough to hold them. Thin the remaining sauce with the remaining ½ cup of heavy cream and carefully mask each *crêpe* with it. Sprinkle the grated cheese over the top and dot with the bits of the softened butter.

When you are ready to serve the *crêpes* (carefully covered, they may be refrigerated for a day or two before baking if they are not for immediate use), preheat the oven to 375 degrees and bake the *crêpes* for about 20 minutes, or until the sauce begins to bubble. Before serving, slide the pan under the broiler briefly to brown the cheese.

Kurnik

A Russian Chicken Pie

Serves 6

PASTRY

¼ pound sweet butter, *chilled and cut into ½-inch pieces*

3 tablespoons lard or vegetable shortening, *chilled*

2 cups flour, *sifted*

1 egg (yolk only)

¼ cup ice water

½ teaspoon salt

¼ teaspoon sugar

FILLING

10 tablespoons butter, *6 for the sauce, 2 for the duxelles, and 2 softened for topping, cut into bits*

6 tablespoons flour

2 cups chicken stock, fresh or canned

¾ cup heavy cream, *½ cup for the sauce and ¼ cup for thinning*

1 teaspoon lemon juice

Salt

⅛ teaspoon cayenne

3 tablespoons shallots or scallions, *finely chopped*

¼ pound mushrooms, *finely chopped* (1 cup)

4 tablespoons Madeira

1½ cups cooked rice, *cold* (½ cup raw rice cooked)

4 eggs, *cooked and coarsely chopped*

Freshly ground black pepper

4 tablespoons fresh dill, *finely chopped*

2 cups (packed down) cold cooked chicken, *cut into 1-inch chunks*

⅓ cup Parmesan cheese, *grated*

To prepare the pastry, combine in a large mixing bowl the cut-up butter, lard or shortening, and flour. Quickly rub through the thumb and forefingers of both hands until the fat and flour are well mixed and most of the lumps have disappeared. Don't allow the mixture to become oily; small bits of unassimilated fat here and there won't affect the final result. Mix the egg yolk, water, salt, and sugar together and pour over the flour. Toss together until all the flour particles are moistened sufficiently to adhere to each other. Quickly and lightly press the dough together into a compact ball and dust it lightly with a small handful of flour. Wrap in waxed paper and chill for 2 hours or more.

If you own an electric mixer equipped with a pastry arm, the dough may be made in a matter of minutes in precisely the same fashion. Simply use the pastry arm to mix the fat and flour together and either mix the egg and water in with your hands or combine it with 3 or 4 beats of the mixer. Be careful not to overmix. Then chill.

Preheat the oven to 425 degrees and thoroughly butter a 9 x 1½-inch cake pan with a removable bottom. Quickly roll the dough into a circle about 12 inches in diameter and a little less than ¼ inch thin. Lift it with the rolling pin and carefully fit it into the buttered pan. With a pair of scissors trim the extra pastry within ½ inch of the top of the circle and fold this back on itself, pressing it gently against the side of the pan to form a ropelike rim all around the top of the pie. If you wish, mark this decoratively with the prongs of a fork pressed gently around its circumference. Chill the shell for at least 15 minutes before filling.

Meanwhile melt in a small saucepan 6 tablespoons of the butter. Off the heat mix into it 6 level tablespoons of flour and when the mixture is smooth pour in the 2 cups of stock. Stir with a whisk until the flour dissolves; return the pan to moderate heat and, stirring constantly, bring the sauce to a boil. It will be very thick. Simmer for 1 or 2 minutes, then add the ½ cup of the heavy cream, the lemon juice, salt, and cayenne. Set aside and cool, stirring the sauce every now and then to prevent a crust from forming on its surface.

To prepare the *duxelles,* melt 2 tablespoons of the butter in a small frying pan and add the chopped shallots or scallions. Sauté over moderate heat for about 1 minute without letting them color, then mix in the chopped mushrooms. Stirring every now and then, cook the mixture over low heat for about 10 minutes, or until the mushrooms are dry but not brown. Pour in the Madeira, raise the heat and, stirring constantly, cook the wine away entirely.

Construct the pie by first spreading the bottom of the shell with the cold rice. Scatter over it the chopped eggs and season them with salt, freshly ground pepper, and 2 tablespoons of the dill. Mix together the *duxelles* and chicken and arrange them evenly over the eggs, then cover completely with 1½ cups of the cooled sauce. Shake the pan gently so that some of the sauce will seep down through the chicken. Sprinkle the grated Parmesan over the top and dot here and there with small pieces of the softened butter.

Bake in the hot oven for 20 minutes, then turn down heat to 375 degrees and bake for about 30 minutes longer. When the pie is done, run a sharp knife around the inside rim of the pan, and set the pan on top of a tall coffee can or jar. Remove the rim by gently pulling it downwards, leaving the pie itself perched on the can or jar. If you think you can remove the pie from its base without breaking the crust, by all means do so; if not, transfer the pie, base and all, to a serving plate. Whichever method of serving you choose, sprinkle the pie with the remaining dill and serve accompanied by the remaining sauce, reheated and thinned with the remaining ¼ cup of heavy cream.

Note: Wedges of *kurnik,* or, for that matter, the whole pie, may be baked in advance and reheated quite successfully whenever you wish to serve it.

Blanquette of Chicken

Serves 4–6   The recipe for this dish is exactly the same as the one for the *blanquette de veau* on page 64. Substitute 2 cups of chicken for the veal.

▶ ◀

A Classic Roast Turkey with Sausage and Chestnut Stuffing

THE BIRD	
9-pound turkey	2 medium onions, *thinly sliced*
Salt	2 medium carrots, *thinly sliced*
Freshly ground black pepper	2 stalks celery, *cut into 3-inch pieces*
3 tablespoons butter, *softened*	2 cups chicken stock, fresh or canned
A thin slice of salt pork large enough to cover turkey breast	

THE STUFFING	
4 tablespoons butter, *2 for sautéing onions and 2 for sautéing livers*	3 tablespoons parsley, *finely chopped*
	1 tablespoon salt
¾ cup onions, *finely chopped*	½ teaspoon freshly ground black pepper
½ pound sausage meat	1 teaspoon lemon juice
The turkey liver and 2 chicken livers, *coarsely chopped*	20 fresh chestnuts, *peeled and cooked*, or canned whole chestnuts packed in water
2 cups dry white bread crumbs, *coarsely grated*	3–4 tablespoons heavy cream
½ teaspoon thyme	

The stuffing may be made any time beforehand, but make sure it has time to cool before you stuff the turkey with it. To prepare the stuffing, melt 2 tablespoons of the butter in a large heavy frying pan, add the chopped onions, and sauté them slowly until they are a light even brown, then stir in the sausage meat, breaking it up with a fork as it begins to cook. When the meat has lightly browned, transfer the entire contents of the pan into a small sieve set over a bowl. Allow the fat to drain through; meanwhile, in the same frying pan, melt the remaining 2 tablespoons of butter. Quickly brown the chopped turkey and chicken livers. While they are still slightly pink, scrape them with a rubber spatula into a large mixing bowl. Stir in the drained sausage mixture, the bread crumbs, thyme, parsley, salt, pepper, and lemon juice. Mix together gently.

If you plan to use fresh chestnuts, peel them. This is most easily done by first cutting a long gash in the flat underside of each chestnut; then bring them to a boil in cold water, boiling them for a couple of minutes. With a small sharp knife peel them while they are still hot. Cook the peeled chestnuts in simmering salted water or chicken stock to cover for about 30 minutes, or until they are tender but still slightly on the firm side. Drain. If you prefer to use canned chestnuts, make sure you buy the ones packed in water, not syrup. They need only be drained.

Purée 10 of the chestnuts in an electric blender or food mill and stir the purée into the stuffing; crumble the remaining chestnuts coarsely and add them also. Moisten the stuffing with the heavy cream, using more or less of it depending upon how moist you like your stuffing.

Salt and pepper the inside of the turkey before stuffing it, then fill the body cavity loosely. If you have enough stuffing left over, stuff the breast also. Sew all the openings and truss the turkey with heavy cord. Preheat the oven to 350 degrees.

Rub the turkey all over with the 3 tablespoons of softened butter, sprinkle with salt, and lay the slice of salt pork over the breast. Scatter the sliced onions, carrots, and celery on the bottom of a shallow roasting pan and set the turkey on a rack directly over the vegetables. Roast for 2 hours, basting every 20 minutes or so with the drippings in the pan. After the first hour, add a couple of tablespoons of water or stock to the pan *after* each basting of the turkey. At the end of 2 hours, test the turkey for doneness by inserting the point of a sharp knife in the thigh. If the juice which squirts out is yellow, the turkey is done; if the yellow is tinged with pink, cook it for a few minutes longer.

When the turkey is done, lift it onto a platter and cut away the trussing cords. Let it remain on the platter for at least 15 minutes before carving it. Meanwhile make a clear gravy by pouring the 2 cups of chicken stock into the roasting pan. Bring to a boil and scrape up all the brown particles adhering to the bottom of the pan. Continue to boil until the flavor of the gravy pleases you, then strain it into a small saucepan. Skim it carefully, heat again, and serve in a sauce boat.

▶ A 10- to 12-pound turkey may of course be used in place of the 9-pound bird suggested for the classic roast turkey. For the larger turkeys increase the amount of stuffing by a quarter or third of the original amount and roast the turkey 8 to 10 minutes longer per extra pound. Periodically test for doneness after the 2-hour roasting period by piercing the thigh of the bird as described on page 139. Do not, under any circumstances, rely on the curious concept that a turkey is considered done if its leg can be moved freely in its socket. If you roast your turkey to that state of pliability, you may be sure it will be woefully overdone.

▶ If you prefer to roast your turkey without stuffing it, plan on a somewhat shorter roasting time; unstuffed birds always take less time to cook than stuffed ones.

▶ The *gratin* of chicken hash in cream on page 131 can be made with almost as much success with roast turkey, if the turkey you use is breast meat.

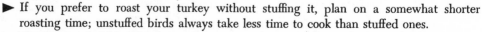

IMPROVISATIONS

Turkey Stock

Makes about
2 quarts

Carcass of roast turkey, skin, meat scraps, wing tips, and giblets

Any chicken giblets, backs, necks, etc. (optional)

2½ quarts cold water or all or part canned chicken stock

1 large onion, *quartered*

2 medium carrots, *scraped and cut into chunks*

2 stalks celery with their leaves, *cut up*

1 large leek (white part only), *well washed*

A bouquet consisting of 4 sprigs parsley and 1 small bay leaf, *tied together with string*

8 whole black peppercorns

1 medium tomato, *coarsely chopped*

½ teaspoon thyme

Salt

Break up the turkey carcass and place it in a 4- or 5-quart soup pot; toss in any bones, nondescript scraps of turkey meat you don't plan to use, the wing tips, and washed giblets and pour over this 2½ quarts of water and/or chicken stock. Add a little more stock or water if the turkey isn't quite covered. Bring to a boil, skim the scum which will soon rise to the surface, then add the onion, carrots, celery, leek, bouquet, peppercorns, chopped tomato, and thyme. Salt rather lightly and turn the heat down to barely simmering—the surface of the stock should scarcely move. Half cover the pot and simmer for a minimum of 2 hours, 3 if possible.

When the stock is finished, strain it through as fine a sieve as possible. Remove the giblets for later use, then press down on the vegetables with a large spoon before throwing them away.

If you plan to use the stock at once (served simply with cooked rice or *pasta* and sprinkled with chopped parsley), let it rest a few minutes and carefully skim off most but not all the fat. Otherwise, let the stock cool a bit, then refrigerate. The fat will rise to the surface and solidify after a few hours; it can be lifted off, then, quite easily.

This stock will keep, refrigerated, for 3 or 4 days, after which it can be brought to a boil, cooled, and refrigerated again for a similar period. To keep for longer periods, freeze it.

Note: Any turkey stock remaining can be used successfully wherever chicken stock is required in a recipe. Though the turkey itself may often lack flavor, its stock is quite intense.

Mushroom Barley Soup with Turkey Giblets

Serves 4–6

4 tablespoons butter, *2 for sautéing vegetables and 2 for roux*
⅓ cup onions, *finely chopped*
¼ cup carrots, *finely chopped*
¼ cup celery, *finely chopped*
2 quarts turkey stock (p. 140)
6–8 dried mushrooms, *coarsely chopped (about 2 tablespoons)*

½ cup pearl barley
2 tablespoons flour
The cooked turkey giblets, *roughly diced*
Salt
Freshly ground black pepper
2 tablespoons fresh dill or parsley, *finely chopped*

Melt 2 tablespoons of the butter in a 3- or 4-quart saucepan, and in it slowly cook the chopped onions, carrots, and celery until they color lightly. Add the 2 quarts of turkey stock, bring it slowly to a boil, then turn the heat down to simmering. Meanwhile pour ½ cup of the hot stock over the dried mushrooms and let them soak for about 10 minutes. Then drain, coarsely chop, and add the mushrooms with their liquid to the soup. Stir in the ½ cup of barley, half cover the pan, and simmer the soup slowly for about 1 hour.

Ten minutes or so before the soup is done, melt 2 tablespoons of butter in a small frying pan. When the foam subsides, stir in 2 level tablespoons of flour. Stirring with a wooden spoon almost constantly, cook over low heat until the flour turns a delicate golden brown. Watch carefully—

under no circumstance must this burn. With a rubber spatula scrape this brown *roux* into the simmering soup. Stir gently until it is thoroughly absorbed and the soup becomes opaque and somewhat thickened. Cook slowly for 15 or 20 minutes, skimming the soup of as much of its surface fat as you can. Now add the roughly chopped, cooked giblets (retrieved from the original turkey stock), season well with salt and freshly ground black pepper, and serve sprinkled with the chopped dill or parsley. Pumpernickel spread with sweet butter goes well with this.

Turkey-Oyster Balls

Makes 24 small balls

½ cup cold water
½ cup dry white wine
Salt
8 large fresh oysters, *shucked*
1 cup cooked turkey, *finely ground or chopped*
2 tablespoons butter
2 tablespoons shallots or scallions, *finely chopped*
4 eggs (yolks only), *2 for binding turkey mixture and 2 for coating*

1 teaspoon lemon juice
4 tablespoons heavy cream, *2 for turkey mixture and 2 for coating*
½ teaspoon Tabasco
1 tablespoon celery leaves, *finely chopped*
½ cup dry bread crumbs
½ cup almonds, *finely ground*
Vegetable oil or shortening for deep-frying

Combine in a small enamel saucepan the water and white wine and ¼ teaspoon of salt. Heat to the boiling point, then turn the heat down so that the liquid barely simmers. Add the oysters and poach them no more than 1 or 2 minutes; their edges will curl and they will shrink considerably. Remove them from the pan at once, cool, then chop them rather finely. Mix them in a small bowl with the ground turkey.

Melt the 2 tablespoons of butter in a small frying pan and in it slowly cook the chopped shallots or scallions until they are soft but not brown—a matter of 3 or 4 minutes. With a rubber scraper transfer them to the turkey-oyster mixture. Now thoroughly mix in 2 of the egg yolks, then the lemon juice, 2 tablespoons of the cream, ½ teaspoon of salt, the Tabasco, and the chopped celery leaves. The mixture should be quite smooth. Taste for seasoning; it may very well need more salt. Scoop up about a teaspoon at a time and roll into ¾-inch balls with the palms of your hands, moistening your hands with cold water whenever necessary. (For easier handling, if you have the time, chill the paste first before forming it into balls.) Chill the balls for at least ½ hour before you coat them. For the coating, mix the remaining 2 egg yolks with the remaining 2 table-spoons of cream in a small bowl. Combine the bread crumbs and ground almonds (both can be spun in the blender to pulverize them) and spread them on a plate or a sheet of waxed paper. Coat 1 ball at a time by first dipping it in the egg-cream mixture then rolling it in the bread-crumb–almond mixture. Lay the coated balls on a platter lined with waxed paper and chill once more.

To fry, heat enough vegetable oil or shortening in a frying kettle so that the balls can be immersed in it completely. For the best results use a deep-fat thermometer. When it reads 385 degrees, fry the balls—4 or 5 at a time—until they are a deep golden brown. This should take no more than 1 minute or so. Serve at once if possible, or keep the turkey-oyster balls warm in a 250-degree oven but not for too long or they will become soggy.

Breast of Turkey Florentine in Scallop Coquilles

Serves 4

6 tablespoons butter, *2 for sautéing spinach, 3 for sauce, and 1 softened for topping*
2 packages frozen chopped spinach or 1 pound fresh spinach, *cooked*
1 tablespoon Madeira
4 tablespoons flour
1½ **cups turkey stock** (p. 140) or canned chicken stock

⅓ cup heavy cream
⅛ teaspoon cayenne
Salt
2½ tablespoons Parmesan cheese, *freshly grated*
2½ tablespoons Swiss cheese, *freshly grated*
2 **cups cooked breast of turkey**, *cold, cut into 1½-inch dice*
4 teaspoons dry bread crumbs

For the best results, defrost the frozen spinach—if not completely, then at least to the point where it can easily be broken up with a fork. Melt 2 tablespoons of the butter in an enamel or stainless-steel saucepan and add the spinach. Cover the pan tightly and cook the spinach over moderate heat until all its frozen particles have thoroughly dissolved. Remove the cover, turn up the heat and, stirring almost constantly, boil away all the accumulated liquid. When the spinach is quite dry, press it in a sieve for good measure, to remove any extra moisture, then purée it through a food mill (*not* a blender) or, lacking that, force it through a coarse sieve with the back of a spoon. Stir in the Madeira and set it aside while you make a *velouté* sauce.

Melt 3 tablespoons of the butter in an enamel saucepan, then lift from the heat and stir in the 4 level tablespoons of flour. Mix this to a paste and add to it, all at once, the hot or cold turkey stock or canned chicken stock. Return the pan to the heat and, stirring constantly with a wire whisk, bring the sauce to a boil. Cook until it is thick and smooth. Simmer for 5 minutes or so to rid it of any raw flour taste and stir in the heavy cream. Add the cayenne and salt to taste. Mix 3 tablespoons of this sauce into the spinach purée, then transform the remaining sauce into a *mornay* sauce by stirring in 2 tablespoons each of the freshly grated Parmesan and Swiss cheeses. Cook for 1 minute or so to dissolve the cheese.

Prepare 4 scallop shells—the large ones—by buttering each one lightly. Divide the puréed spinach among them equally, leaving a ½-inch border exposed around each shell. Similarly, divide the diced turkey and arrange the pieces neatly on each spinach bed. Spoon the *mornay* sauce (if it seems too thick, thin it with a little more cream) over the turkey and spinach, masking them completely. Sprinkle each shell with a teaspoon of bread crumbs and then a sprinkling of the remaining Parmesan and Swiss cheeses. Dot lightly with the bits of softened butter.

The shells may be baked at once or covered tightly with plastic wrap and refrigerated all day or even overnight. Before serving, bake them for about 15 minutes in a preheated 375-degree oven until they begin to bubble (naturally, if you have just removed them from the refrigerator they will take a little longer), and then brown them briefly under a hot broiler.

Capilotade of Turkey in the French Style

Serves 4

½ cup onions, *finely chopped*

2 tablespoons shallots or scallions, *finely chopped*

½ teaspoon garlic, *finely chopped*

3 tablespoons butter, 2 *for sautéing onions, shallots or scallions, and garlic, and 1 softened for topping*

2 tablespoons white wine vinegar

1 medium tomato, *peeled, seeded, and finely chopped (about ½ cup)*

1 teaspoon tomato paste

¾ **cup turkey stock** (p. 140) or canned chicken stock

½ teaspoon sugar

1 small bay leaf

Salt

Freshly ground black pepper

2 tablespoons turkey gravy (optional)

1 tablespoon capers, *drained, washed, and dried*

4–8 pieces of roast turkey: a thigh, wing, thick slice of breast, etc.

½ cup dry bread crumbs

2 tablespoons parsley, *finely chopped*

Buttered peas

French or Italian bread, *hot*

In French country cooking, *capilotade* is the name of a dish in which fairly substantial joints or pieces of chicken are reheated in a piquant sauce. In this version, large pieces of roast turkey do quite as well, if not better, and benefit, moreover, from being gratinéed or browned in the oven before being served.

To make the sauce, lightly and slowly brown the finely chopped onions, shallots or scallions, and garlic in 2 tablespoons of the butter. Then pour the vinegar into the sauté pan, raise the heat and, stirring almost constantly, boil the vinegar completely away. Add the chopped tomatoes and tomato paste and stir in the stock. Bring this all to a boil and immediately reduce the heat to barely simmering. Add the sugar and bay leaf and season quite highly with salt and freshly ground pepper. Cook the sauce slowly, uncovered, for about 20 minutes; it should be quite thick when it is done. If it isn't, cook it a while longer. Stir in the turkey gravy—thickened or not—if you have it, and add the capers.

Although the turkey pieces may now be immersed in this sauce, heated through (without boiling), and served simply with a sprinkling of chopped parsley, the dish will have more character if it is treated in the following fashion. Preheat the broiler, then add the turkey to the simmering sauce and baste it for about 10 minutes to heat it through. Take care not to let the sauce boil or the turkey may toughen. Now transfer the hot turkey to a small shallow baking dish, spread the sauce over it, and sprinkle heavily with the bread crumbs. Dot with small pieces of softened butter and brown quickly under the broiler. Sprinkle with chopped parsley and serve with buttered peas, fried eggplant, perhaps, and hot French or Italian bread.

Turkey Paprikash

Serves 4

4 tablespoons butter
½ cup onions, *finely chopped*
1 medium green pepper, *cut into very thin slivers (about ¾ cup)*
1 tablespoon flour
1 tablespoon imported Hungarian paprika
1½ **cups turkey stock** (p. 140) or canned chicken stock
⅛ teaspoon sugar

Salt
1 egg (yolk only)
½ cup sour cream
¼ teaspoon lemon juice
2 **cups cooked turkey,** *cold, cut into 1½-inch dice*
2 tablespoons fresh dill or parsley, *finely chopped*
Cooked noodles with butter
Bread crumbs, *buttered*

Melt the butter in a small enamel frying plan, add the chopped onions, and cook over low heat for 8 to 10 minutes, stirring occasionally until they color lightly. Stir in the thinly slivered green pepper and cook 3 to 5 minutes longer; allow them to soften without browning.

Combine in a small bowl the flour and paprika, then, off the heat, mix this thoroughly into the sautéed onions and pepper. Now with a wire whisk beat in, little by little, the turkey or canned chicken stock, return the pan to the heat and, still beating, bring the sauce to a boil. It will get quite thick and smooth. Turn the heat down then to barely simmering, add the sugar and a little salt and let the sauce cook slowly for 10 minutes or so. At this point mix the egg yolk with the sour cream and stir it into the simmering sauce 1 tablespoon at a time. Under no circumstance let it come to a boil. When the sauce is quite hot, fold in the diced turkey, and season with the lemon juice and more salt if you think it needs it. Heat the turkey through without letting it actually cook, however, or it may become stringy or tough. And if it must wait for any length of time, keep it warm over hot water in the top of a double boiler.

Serve the paprikash sprinkled with the chopped fresh dill or parsley and accompany it with hot buttered noodles over which you have scattered crisp buttered bread crumbs.

Turkey Tetrazzini

Serves 4–6

½ pound *spaghettini* or *linguine*
10 tablespoons butter: *2 melted for the pasta, 3 for the mushrooms, 3 for the sauce, 1 softened for the topping, and 1 for buttering the casserole*
Salt
Freshly ground white pepper
½ pound mushrooms, *thinly sliced*
4 tablespoons flour
1½ cups turkey stock (p. 140) or fresh or canned chicken stock

1 egg (yolk only)
½ cup heavy cream
1 tablespoon Madeira
2½–3 cups cooked turkey, *cold, cut into 1-inch dice*
¼ cup Parmesan cheese, *freshly grated* ⎱
2 tablespoons dry bread crumbs ⎰ combined

Drop the unbroken strands of *spaghettini* or *linguine* into at least 4 quarts of briskly boiling salted water and cook the *pasta al dente*—as the Italians call it—or literally, until it is slightly resistant to the teeth. Ignore the directions on the backs of most *pasta* boxes; the timings are invariably too long. Eight or possibly 9 minutes of cooking is quite sufficient for *spaghettini,* and because it is flatter, 1 or 2 minutes less for *linguine.* When it is done drain the *pasta* in a colander, and after lifting the strands with two forks to rid them of any lurking water, transfer the *pasta* to a mixing bowl. Immediately stir into it the 2 tablespoons of melted butter and season highly with salt, and coarsely ground white pepper. Put the bowl aside while you prepare the other ingredients.

Melt 3 tablespoons of the butter in an enamel or stainless-steel frying pan. When the foam subsides, toss in the sliced mushrooms. Cook briefly over high heat—2 or 3 minutes perhaps—turning the mushrooms constantly with a wooden spoon until they have thoroughly absorbed the butter and have wilted without browning. Remove them at once to another small bowl. Now melt another 3 tablespoons of the butter in a saucepan and stir in, off the heat, the flour. Mix it to a paste and add, all at once, the turkey or chicken stock. Return the pan to the heat and, stirring almost constantly with a wire whisk, bring the sauce to a boil. Cook until it is smooth and thick, then turn the heat down to a simmer and cook the sauce slowly for about 5 minutes to rid it of any raw-flour taste. In a small bowl mix together the egg yolk and the cream. Stir in 2 tablespoons of the simmering sauce, then reverse the process and slowly pour the now-heated cream mixture into the pan of sauce, stirring all the while. Cook for a few seconds and remove from the heat. Season the sauce quite highly with salt and a little white pepper, add 1 tablespoon of Madeira, and fold in the sautéed mushrooms and diced turkey. You are now ready to assemble the casserole.

Choose a 1½-quart casserole attractive enough to bring to the table. Butter it well and put in half of the cooked *pasta.* Cover this with half of the turkey mixture, then spread over it the remaining *pasta.* Spoon the rest of the turkey, mushrooms, and sauce over the top, sprinkle it evenly with the combined cheese and bread crumbs, and dot all over with bits of softened butter. The casserole may now be cooked at once or refrigerated, tightly covered, all day or overnight.

Before serving, bake it in the center of a preheated 350-degree oven. The turkey *tetrazzini* should take about 40 or 50 minutes to cook through. Or more precisely, when the sauce bubbles and the top begins to brown, it is done. If necessary, slide it under the broiler briefly to brown it a little more.

Turkey Curry with Condiments

Serves 4–6

2 tablespoons butter
1 cup onions, *finely chopped*
½ cup celery, *finely chopped*
1 small tart apple, *peeled, cored, and finely chopped*
½ teaspoon garlic, *finely chopped*
2 tablespoons flour
3 tablespoons curry powder
1 teaspoon tomato paste

2 cups turkey stock (p. 140) or fresh or canned chicken stock
½ cup heavy cream
1 teaspoon lime juice
Salt
2–3 cups cold cooked turkey, *cut into 2-inch dice*
Boiled rice

CONDIMENTS

Currants or raisins, *soaked in cognac, sherry, port, or Madeira*
Coconut (fresh or canned), *shredded*
Scallions, *thinly sliced*
Bacon, *crisp and crumbled*
Chutney
Avocados, *sliced and sprinkled with lemon or lime juice*

Almonds, *toasted and slivered*
Hard-cooked eggs, *sieved*
Bombay duck, *heated and crumbled*
Pappadums, *deep-fried or pan-fried in butter*
Cucumber-yoghurt sauce (p. 223)

In a large enamel frying pan melt the butter. Stir in the chopped onions and celery and sauté slowly. When the vegetables are soft but not brown, mix in the chopped apple and garlic and continue to cook until the apple is soft enough to be mashed with the back of a spoon. Remove the pan from the heat.

In a small bowl combine the flour and the fresh curry powder. Add this to the mixture in the frying pan, stir in the tomato paste, and mash it into as smooth a paste as possible. Stirring constantly, cook over low heat for about 3 minutes. Now, little by little, pour in the 2 cups of turkey or chicken stock, beating slowly with a whisk; then add the cream. Over moderate heat bring the sauce to a boil, still stirring. When it is quite thick and smooth, lower the heat to barely simmering and cook for about 20 minutes with the pan partially covered. Then strain the sauce through a fine sieve into a small casserole, pressing down on the vegetables with the back of a large spoon to extract all their juices before throwing them away. Stir in the lime juice and salt to taste; if at this point the sauce seems too thick, thin it with a little more cream or stock. Now you need only heat the cooked turkey in this, but be careful that the sauce doesn't boil or the turkey may toughen or shred.

Serve with plain boiled rice and any or all of the following condiments: dried currants or raisins, soaked for a few hours in cognac, sherry, port, or Madeira; fresh or canned shredded coconut; thinly sliced scallions; crumbled, crisp bacon; chutney; sliced avocados sprinkled with lemon or lime juice; toasted slivered almonds; sieved hard-cooked eggs; Bombay duck (a dried, salted boned fish fillet from India), heated under the broiler or in the oven and then crumbled; pappadums (crisp, highly seasoned Indian wafers which are served in place of bread), deep-fried in oil or cooked in foaming butter. An unusual and cooling condiment might be added if you wish: the cucumber-yoghurt sauce on page 223.

Turkey Mayonnaise with Rice Salad

Serves 4

3 cups cooked rice (1 cup raw rice), *warm*
Salt
Freshly ground black pepper
¼ cup tarragon white wine vinegar
⅔ cup olive oil
¼ cup green pepper, *finely chopped*
3 tablespoons pimiento, *finely chopped*
½ cup mayonnaise, preferably freshly made (p. 218)

2 teaspoons prepared mustard, preferably Dijon type
2 **cups cooked turkey (preferably breast)**, *cold, cut into 1½-inch dice*
2 hard-cooked eggs, *chilled and thinly sliced*
1 tablespoon fresh chives or scallion tops, *finely chopped*
1 tablespoon parsley, *finely chopped*
French or Italian bread, *warm*

Cook 1 cup of rice, preferably the imported Italian short-grain rice or long-grained Carolina rice in at least 4 quarts of briskly boiling salted water. When the rice is thoroughly cooked but still slightly firm, drain it in a colander, then pour boiling water over to seperate the grains. Transfer the rice to a large bowl and let it cool a bit while you make the dressing. (If you use previously cooked leftover rice instead, steam it first in a colander set over boiling water.)

Mix 1 teaspoon of salt and ½ teaspoon of freshly ground pepper into the tarragon vinegar. With a wire whisk slowly beat in the olive oil. Pour the dressing over the still-warm rice and toss it thoroughly with two large forks. When it is well combined, add the chopped green pepper and pimiento. Toss again and taste for seasoning; it will probably need more salt and pepper. Remember that when the rice is cold the flavor of the seasoning will flatten out considerably, so don't be overly discreet.

In another mixing bowl combine the ½ cup of well-seasoned mayonnaise with 2 level teaspoons of mustard. Fold the cubed turkey into this and make sure each piece is well coated. Do not refrigerate, but let the turkey marinate at room temperature in the mayonnaise for about 1 hour.

When you are ready to assemble the salad, choose a 1½-quart glass or crystal salad bowl and chill it. Arrange the cold (not chilled) rice salad on the bottom of the bowl, spread the turkey mayonnaise over it and decorate the mayonnaise with overlapping slices of cold hard-cooked eggs. Sprinkle copiously with the chives or scallion tops and parsley and serve with warm French or Italian bread.

► ◄

A Classic Braised Duck and Turnips

DUCK STOCK
(OPTIONAL)

2 tablespoons butter
1 tablespoon vegetable oil
1 small onion, *sliced*
1 medium carrot, *sliced*

1 stalk celery
Necks, gizzards, hearts, and wing tips of the ducks, *washed and dried*
2 cups chicken stock, fresh or canned

---

2 ducks, about 5 pounds each
¼ pound rendered fresh pork fat or 4 tablespoons vegetable oil
4 tablespoons butter, *2 for browning onions and carrots and 2 for turnips*
2 medium onions, *thinly sliced, 1 for duck*
2 medium carrots, *thinly sliced*
Freshly ground black pepper
A bouquet consisting of 6 sprigs parsley, 2 celery

tops with leaves, and 1 large bay leaf, *tied together with string*
½ teaspoon leaf thyme, *crumbled*
3 pounds white turnips, *peeled and cut into even-sized quarters or olive shapes*
1½ cups brown duck stock (*see text of recipe*) or chicken stock, fresh or canned
½ teaspoon lemon juice
1 tablespoon parsley, *finely chopped*

To make a brown duck stock, melt 2 tablespoons of butter and 1 tablespoon of oil in a heavy 2- or 3-quart saucepan, then brown the small sliced onion, the sliced carrot, and the stalk of celery. Add the washed and dried necks, gizzards, hearts, and wing tips of the ducks and sauté until they are a deep golden brown. Pour in 2 cups or so of fresh or canned chicken stock, bring it to a boil, then lower the heat and simmer the stock, half covered, for 30 minutes to 1 hour.

Meanwhile wash the ducks quickly under cold running water, then dry thoroughly with paper toweling. Rub the inside of each duck with 1 teaspoon salt and truss the ducks securely with heavy white cord. Heat the rendered pork fat or vegetable oil in a large heavy frying pan; when it almost begins to smoke, add the ducks and regulate the heat so that they brown quickly and evenly without burning. This should take, all in all, about 15 to 20 minutes. Preheat the oven to 325 degrees.

Now heat 2 tablespoons of the butter in a casserole that is large enough to hold the two ducks comfortably and has a tightly fitting cover. When the foam subsides, slowly and lightly brown the sliced onions and carrots, stirring from time to time. Place the browned ducks on top of the vegetables, sprinkle them lightly with salt and pepper, and cover the casserole tightly. Place in the center of the preheated oven and cook without basting for about 1 hour.

During this time, in a large frying pan, quickly and lightly brown the cut-up turnips in 2 tablespoons of hot butter and put them aside until you are ready to use them.

When the ducks have cooked their allotted hour, remove them from the casserole and pour the vegetables and braising liquid into a fine sieve set over a mixing bowl, pressing down hard on the vegetables to extract their juices before throwing them away. Tip the bowl. With a large spoon skim off and discard all the surface fat. Return the remaining brown juices to the casserole and replace the ducks. Surround them with the turnips lightly sprinkled with salt. Pour over the turnips enough brown duck stock—first straining it and skimming off the fat—to cover them almost completely, and bring to a boil on top of the stove. Cover the casserole again and return it to the oven where it should cook slowly until the turnips are tender but not falling apart. This should take no longer than 15 or 20 minutes. By now the ducks should be thoroughly cooked and may be carved and served surrounded by the turnips, and accompanied by the braising liquid seasoned with lemon juice and some extra salt. However, if you like your ducks browner, and many people do, you may preheat the oven to 500–550 degrees and glaze the ducks set on a rack in a jelly-roll pan or baking pan. Ten minutes in the hot oven should give the ducks a deep, even brown; but be careful not to let them burn.

▶ Of all the birds sold frozen today, the Long Island duckling appears to survive the ordeal most successfully. Although the fresh birds are, of course, more desirable, frozen ducks retain their flavor and texture to a remarkable degree—that is, if they are defrosted properly. Let the duck thaw in the refrigerator, or at room temperature, if you like, which will take considerably less time. Never soak it in either cold or warm water to hasten the process. And most important of all, don't braise the duck until it is thoroughly defrosted.

▶ For variety, you might occasionally cook this classic braised duck with a garniture of olives instead of the suggested turnips. Be sure, however, to blanch the olives (the mild, ripe green California types are the best) in boiling water for a few minutes before adding them to the duck braising liquid. Use as many olives as you wish and cook them for about the same length of time you would the turnips.

▶ Although none of the improvisations calls for duck stock, it can be made precisely the same way as the turkey stock on page 140. Since duck stock tends to have a pronounced, almost gamy, flavor—not always to everyone's taste—it should be used with discretion whenever it is employed as a substitute for chicken or turkey stock.

▶ There is no reason why substantial pieces of cold (room temperature, really) roast turkey or chicken couldn't be substituted for the cold braised duck in the cold duck and shrimp in the Genoese style improvisation, although the combination might surprise a Genoan.

odds
and
ENds

IMPROVISATIONS

Borshch à la Russe

Serves 8

2 **braised duck carcasses,** *broken up, picked clean of all meat shreds*

1½ pounds shin of beef

2 pounds beef marrow bones, *sawed into 2-inch pieces*

A veal bone, *sawed into 2-inch lengths* (optional)

2 medium onions, *quartered*

3 medium carrots, *cut into chunks*

2 leeks (white part only)

3 quarts stock: half canned beef bouillon and half canned chicken stock or all fresh chicken or beef stock

A bouquet consisting of 6 sprigs parsley, 3 celery tops with leaves, and 1 large bay leaf, *tied together with string*

5 cups cooked beets, fresh or canned, *julienned*

5 cups red cabbage (white will do, if it must), *shredded*

1 pound fresh tomatoes, *peeled, seeded, and coarsely chopped* (about 1½ cups), or ¾ of a 1 pound 3 ounce can solid-pack tomatoes, *drained*

Salt

Freshly ground black pepper

2 tablespoons butter

2 tablespoons flour

1 medium raw beet, *grated into 3 tablespoons cold water*

¼ cup fresh dill, *chopped*

½ cup or more of cold braised duck, *cut into julienne strips*

½ pint sour cream

In a large 6-quart casserole or soup kettle combine the duck carcasses, shin of beef, beef marrow bones and optional veal bone, onions, carrots, and leeks. Add the stock and over high heat bring to a boil. Skim thoroughly as the surface scum begins to form, and when the stock is comparatively clear, turn down the heat to barely simmering, add the bouquet, and cook the soup, half covered, for 1½ to 2 hours, skimming every now and then. When it is done, strain it through a large sieve, pressing down on the vegetables and the duck carcasses with the back of a large spoon to extract all their moisture before throwing them away. Save the boiled beef for any of the *pot-au-feu* improvisations or for some other purpose.

Return the soup to the washed pot, add the julienned beets, shredded cabbage, chopped tomatoes, and salt and pepper to taste. Bring to a boil, then simmer as slowly as possible for about 1 hour. At this point, thicken the *borshch* by melting 2 tablespoons of butter in a small frying pan and stirring into it 2 tablespoons of flour. Cook this *roux* slowly over the lowest possible heat, stirring constantly, until the flour browns lightly. Scrape it into the soup and stir it until it dissolves. Simmer for at least 15 minutes. However, if you plan to serve the *borshch* cold, do not use the *roux* to thicken it.

Ten minutes before serving, stir the strained beet juice into the *borshch*, squeezing the grated pulp to rid it of its moisture before throwing it away. Taste the *borshch* again for seasoning, add the chopped dill, and pour into a heated soup tureen. Add a few pieces of cold julienned duck to each serving and top with about 1 tablespoon of sour cream.

To serve the *borshch* cold, strain it, chill it, and serve in chilled plates or cups with a sprinkling of dill and a spoonful of sour cream.

Duck Pâté

Serves 4–6

8 tablespoons butter, *2 for sautéing livers and 6 for the pâté*

2 duck livers or 4 chicken livers, *washed and dried*

¼ cup cognac or Calvados or Applejack

1–1½ cups cooked duck, *ground or finely chopped, trimmed of all skin, fat, and gristle*

3–6 tablespoons heavy cream

Salt

⅛ teaspoon cayenne

¼ teaspoon lemon juice

1–2 tablespoons black truffles (optional), *coarsely chopped*

In a small heavy frying pan melt 2 tablespoons of the butter over fairly high heat. When the foam subsides, add the washed and dried duck or chicken livers and cook them briskly, turning them with a spoon for 2 to 4 minutes. When the livers are quite brown on the outside but still pink within, remove the pan from the heat and flame them with the cognac or apple brandy. The safest way to do this is simply to heat the brandy to lukewarm in a small saucepan and set it alight with a kitchen match. Pour it into the frying pan, a little at a time, shaking the pan continuously, until the flame dies out. Scrape the livers and every bit of the liquid and brown sediment in the frying pan into the jar of an electric blender. Add the ground duck and 3 tablespoons of the cream. Blend at high speed until the duck and livers are reduced to a smooth purée. If at any point the blender clogs, add more cream. Remove the purée from the jar and rub it through a fine sieve to eliminate any bit of stray bone or gristle which may have escaped you earlier.

Now cream the remaining 6 tablespoons of butter by beating it in a bowl or in an electric mixer until it is smooth and light yellow in color. Beat into it, a little at a time, the duck purée, and continue to beat until the paste is as smooth and creamy as you can get it. Season well with salt to taste and the cayenne, and stir in the lemon juice. Fold in the chopped truffles (if you have them) and pack the *pâté* into small crocks from which it may be served.* Chill for at least 6 hours or overnight. Crusty French bread goes well with this, or, if you prefer, warm triangles of toast.

* *Note:* To prevent the surface of the *pâté* from turning an unpleasant brown after it is exposed to air, sprinkle the top with chopped parsley before you serve it, or seal it with a thin layer of warm clarified butter (p. 44) which, when it chills, will form a solid shield over the top.

Salmi of Duck

Serves 4

3 tablespoons butter

4 tablespoons onion, *finely chopped*

1 small leek (white part only), *finely chopped*

1 small carrot, *finely chopped*

2 stalks celery, *finely chopped*

2½ tablespoons flour

1 teaspoon tomato paste

2 cups stock: **duck braising liquid** plus chicken stock, fresh or canned, or 1 cup each of canned bouillon and canned chicken stock

¼ cup Madeira

½ teaspoon thyme

A bouquet consisting of 4 sprigs parsley and 1 small bay leaf, *tied together with string*

Duck carcass, *broken up,* **and/or gizzard, wing tips, etc.**

¼ teaspoon lemon juice

Slices of cold braised duck, or the legs, thighs, etc.

In a 2- or 3-quart heavy saucepan melt the butter. When the foam subsides, add the chopped onions, leek, carrot, and celery. Stirring occasionally, sauté over moderate heat for about 10 minutes, until the vegetables are soft but not brown, then remove the pan from the heat and stir in the flour. Mix it to a paste with a wooden spoon and return the pan to the heat. Stirring continuously, cook this flour-and-butter *roux* until the flour colors lightly and gives off a faint nut-like odor. Make certain it does not burn. Stir into it, then, the tomato paste and add, all at once, the 2 cups of stock, hot or cold. Mix with a whisk until the *roux* and liquid are somewhat amalgamated, then cook over high heat, still stirring, until the stock comes to a boil and thickens slightly. Add the Madeira, the thyme, the bouquet, and the broken-up duck carcass (and/or other duck leftovers). Reduce the heat and, with the pot half covered, simmer the sauce as slowly as possible for at least 1 hour, preferably 2. With a large spoon skim the sauce of its surface fat and scum every 15 minutes or so. When the sauce is done, it should have a fine rich flavor and be lightly thickened. Strain it through a fine sieve, pressing down hard on the vegetables and duck bones to rid them of all their moisture before throwing them away. If, at this point, the sauce lacks character or is too thin, bring it to a boil and cook rapidly, uncovered, until it reaches the desired degree of thickness and intensity of flavor. Taste for seasoning and add the lemon juice.

If your cooked duck pieces are substantial ones, wrap them in foil and heat them in a preheated 350-degree oven until warmed through. Coat with the sauce and serve. If, however, you intend to serve the duck sliced, immerse the slices in the hot sauce and simmer—do not boil—them long enough to thoroughly heat them through.

Cold Duck and Shrimp in the Genoese Style

Serves 4
SAUCE

3 hard-cooked eggs (yolks only)
1 egg (yolk only)
1 teaspoon mustard, preferably Dijon
½–¾ cup olive oil
2–3 teaspoons white wine vinegar
1 tablespoon duck braising liquid, if possible, heated to boiling, or 1 tablespoon chicken stock or water, *also boiling*
4–6 substantial pieces braised duck, trimmed *of all fat, warmed to room temperature*
8–12 cooked, shrimp, *cold*

8–12 black olives, Mediterranean if possible
Lemon quarters
2 teaspoons capers, *washed, dried, and finely chopped*
1 tablespoon sour pickle, *finely chopped*
3 small anchovy fillets, *washed, dried, and finely chopped*
1 tablespoon parsley, *finely chopped*
1 tablespoon shallots or green scallions, *finely chopped*

Make the sauce by mashing the 3 hard-cooked egg yolks, the raw yolk, and mustard in a medium-sized mixing bowl, until it is smooth and thoroughly free of lumps. With a small wire whisk beat in—½ teaspoonful at a time—the olive oil. After you have incorporated ¼ cup of the oil, increase the amount you add to 1 teaspoonful at a time, until ½ cup of the oil has been used. If the mayonnaise—for that is what it really is—seems unmanageably thick, beat in as much of the remaining ¼ cup of oil as needed. Still beating, add 2 teaspoons of the vinegar, and finally the boiling stock or water.

Squeeze the chopped capers and pickles in a towel to rid them of their extra moisture and stir them into the mayonnaise along with the chopped anchovies, parsley, and shallots or scallions. Taste for seasoning. The sauce may possibly need some more vinegar to attain its characteristic bite, but add it with discretion.

At its best, the duck should be served at room temperature and the shrimp chilled. Arrange them attractively on a large platter, intersecting them with the olives and lemon quarters. Pass the sauce separately in a sauceboat.

Duck, Orange, and Red Onion Salad

Serves 6
VINAIGRETTE
DRESSING

2 tablespoons white wine vinegar
½ teaspoon salt
Freshly ground black pepper

6 tablespoons olive oil
¼ teaspoon lemon juice

---

1 pound chicory or escarole leaves, *washed and thoroughly dried*
4 small or 2 large navel oranges, *peeled down to the flesh and either sliced or sectioned*
1 large red onion, *peeled, thinly sliced, and separated into rings*

1½ **cups braised duck,** *chilled and cut into thin slivers*
2 tablespoons parsley, *finely chopped*

Make the vinaigrette dressing in a small bowl, first combining the vinegar with the salt and a few gratings of freshly ground pepper, then beating in the olive oil, 1 tablespoon at a time. Add the lemon juce and taste the dressing for seasoning.

Place the chicory or escarole leaves in the bottom of a chilled glass or crystal salad bowl and arrange the sliced or sectioned oranges on top. Spread the red onion rings on this as symmetrically as you like and scatter the slivered duck on top. Sprinkle lightly with the chopped parsley and just before serving add the dressing. With two large spoons mix it together gently but thoroughly at the table, then serve on chilled salad plates.

Fish and Shellfish

Fish and Shellfish

We cook meat primarily to break down its tissues and thus tenderize it, but we cook fish for other reasons. Almost always tender and pliable to begin with, fish is fried, broiled, poached, or baked either to change its texture or to intensify its flavor. Because most fish responds instantaneously to heat, cooking it properly—that is, not overcooking it—demands unwavering attention on the part of the cook. And recooking the fish demands even greater care.

Of the multitude of fish available to us, our soles and salmon are surely the most popular. Each type has a distinct personality of its own: the soles, in their many varieties, delicate and fragile; and salmon, dense and sturdy. These characteristics have played a large part in determining the type of recipes suggested in this section. Of course, many lesser-known fish have similar characteristics and there is no reason why any delicate white-fleshed fish could not be used in place of the sole and a heavier-fleshed fish substituted for the salmon. However, seasonings should be amplified for the blander specimens or muted for the more assertive ones.

Shellfish, and particularly lobsters, while they may appear to share many of the characteristics of ordinary fish, are really on a culinary plane of their own. For one thing, their price alone makes us approach them with trepidation. But, consolingly, lobsters are easy to cook, especially if you boil them precisely as described in the classic boiled lobster recipe. For many lobster fanciers, this method is the best. If you prefer more elaborate lobster cookery, there is opportunity enough in the recipes that follow to cut as many international capers as you might wish. Cooked shrimp may be used in place of the lobster in many of the lobster improvisations and the more appropriate ones are listed at the end of this section.

Classic Poached Fillets of Sole

COURT-
BOUILLON

½ cup dry white wine
1 cup water
1 teaspoon lemon juice
1 small onion, *thinly sliced*
1 small carrot, *thinly sliced*
A bouquet consisting of 4 sprigs parsley, 1 small bay leaf, 2 celery tops with leaves, *tied together with string*

¼ teaspoon thyme
8 black peppercorns
½ teaspoon salt

3½ pounds filleted fish: either lemon sole, gray sole, or flounder, *all skin and small bones removed*

Salt
2 tablespoons butter, 1 *for buttering dish and 1 for dotting fish*

Combine in a small saucepan the wine, water, lemon juice, vegetables, bouquet, thyme, peppercorns, and salt for the *court-bouillon*. Bring it to a boil, then turn down the heat to barely simmering and cook for about 20 minutes with the pan half covered. Then strain it and let it cool.

Meanwhile preheat the oven to 350 degrees. Wash the fillets quickly in cold water and dry them on paper toweling. For easier handling and serving, cut the fillets into 2- or 3-inch pieces before cooking them, and sprinkle them lightly with salt. Butter the bottom of a shallow glass or enamel baking dish just about large enough to hold the fish in one layer. Lay the fish pieces side by side, folding them in half lengthwise if they are very thin. Pour enough *court-bouillon* over the fillets to come halfway up the sides of the fish. If you don't have enough *court-bouillon*, add a little cold water. Dot each piece of fish with a little butter and heat the baking dish on top of the stove until the liquid begins to simmer. Then loosely cover the dish with a large piece of waxed paper—somewhat larger than the dish itself—and place it in the center of the hot oven.

The fish should be done in about 10 minutes—in 12, if the pieces are particularly thick. In any event, the fish should be opaque, and firm to the touch. Remove the pieces from the pan with a slotted spatula and arrange them, overlapping, down the center of a large heated platter. Serve with the lemon sauce on page 221, using the strained *court-bouillon*, if you like, in place of the chicken stock. (Be sure to save whatever *court-bouillon* may be left; it will keep several days.) Or serve the fish with the hollandaise sauce on page 220, or simply with melted butter seasoned with a little lemon juice and a little finely chopped parsley, chives, or dill.

► Although this classic poached sole calls for American sole, almost any other firm-fleshed, closely grained fish, properly filleted, may be used instead. The choices among them are almost limitless: bluefish, fluke, flounder, halibut, whiting, dab, freshwater trout, red snapper, small mackerel, lake perch, pike, and scrod.

► Frozen filleted fish does well enough in the classic poached sole recipe and the improvisations based upon it, but it does seem a pity to use frozen fish when there is so much fine fresh fish almost always available. Be sure that any frozen fish you buy has not been defrosted and then refrozen. Certain indications that it has (and this unscrupulous, dangerous practice is more prevalent than one might think) are a layer of solid ice in the package, a perceptible darkening of the fillet's color, and pulpy, soft flesh which tends to disintegrate after the fish has been defrosted. And, needless to say, be wary of any particularly unpleasant fishy odor.

► Should you, by some mischance, overcook your sole in this classic poached sole, it might be consoling to know that although the fish may flake badly when hot, it will become quite firm when cool. The same applies to the simmered salmon on page 170. The overcooked fish will scarcely have the flavor of fish properly cooked, but it can still be used with effect in most of the improvisations, particularly the cold ones.

**odds
and
ENds**

IMPROVISATIONS

Chaussons of Sole with Lemon Sauce

Serves 4–6

PASTRY

¼ pound sweet butter, *chilled and cut into ¼-inch pieces*

3 tablespoons lard or vegetable shortening, *chilled*

2 cups flour, *sifted*

½ teaspoon salt

⅓ cup ice water

4 tablespoons butter, *2 for the duxelles, 1 for the filling sauce, and 1 softened for buttering the cooky sheet*

3 tablespoons shallots or scallions, *finely chopped*

¼ pound mushrooms, *finely chopped (1 cup)*

3 tablespoons Madeira

1 tablespoon flour

½ cup plus 2 tablespoons heavy cream, *the ½ cup for the filling and the 2 tablespoons for the egg wash*

½ teaspoon salt

⅛ teaspoon cayenne

2 teaspoons parsley, *finely chopped*

1 tablespoon chives, *finely cut*

½ teaspoon lemon juice

1½ cups poached sole, *flaked*

1 egg (yolk only)

Lemon sauce (p. 221)

In a large mixing bowl combine the cut-up butter, lard or shortening, flour, and salt. Quickly rub through the thumb and forefingers of both hands until the fat and flour are well mixed and most of the lumps have disappeared. Don't allow the mixture to become too oily, but small bits of un-assimilated fat here and there won't affect the final result. Pour the ice water over the flour all at once. Toss together with both hands until all the flour particles are moistened sufficiently to adhere to each other. Quickly and lightly press the dough together into a compact ball and dust it lightly with a small handful of flour. Wrap in waxed paper and chill for 2 hours or longer.

To prepare the *duxelles,* melt 2 tablespoons of the butter in a small frying pan and add the chopped shallots or scallions. Sauté over moderate heat for about 1 minute without letting them color, then mix in the chopped mushrooms. Stirring every now and then, cook the mixture over low heat for about 10 minutes, or until the mushrooms are dry but not brown. Pour in the Madeira, raise the heat and, stirring constantly, cook the wine away entirely. Remove the pan from the heat and scrape the *duxelles* into a small bowl.

Over moderate heat, melt 1 tablespoon of the remaining butter into the frying pan in which the *duxelles* were prepared. Add the *duxelles,* warm through for a moment or two, and stir in the level tablespoon of flour. Pour in ½ cup of the cream, mix together thoroughly, cook until the flour is absorbed and the sauce thickens, then scrape the mixture into a small bowl. Add the salt, cayenne, parsley, chives, and lemon juice. Carefully fold in the flaked poached sole and be careful not to mash the fish during the process. Taste for seasoning and cool thoroughly before using.

Preheat the oven to 425 degrees and butter a heavy cooky sheet. Remove the dough from the refrigerator at least 15 minutes before you intend to use it. When it is pliable enough to handle, divide it roughly into 2 parts and, on a floured surface, roll out each part into a large circle about ⅛ inch thick. With the lightly floured rim of a 10-inch flan ring or cake pan, cut the circles into two 10-inch rounds.* If, during this process, the pastry has softened too much to handle easily, transfer the circles to a cooky sheet and chill them for a few minutes in the refrigerator before proceeding.

Place the fish mixture, divided in half, on the lower third portion of each pastry circle, leaving about 1 inch of clear pastry at the bottom end. Brush this end with a little cold water. With the help of a small metal spatula lift the top two thirds of clear pastry up and over the fish mixture and press the edges into the moistened area, thus sealing it. Reinforce this sealed edge further by folding it back on itself (about ¼ inch) and pressing the tines of a fork along the entire length of this strip. (*Chausson* means "purse" in French, which is what your finished *chaussons* should resemble.)

With a large spatula gently turn the *chaussons* over onto the buttered cooky sheet and brush them lightly with the egg yolk, which you have mixed with the remaining 2 tablespoons of cream. Cut a ½-inch slit in the center of each *chausson* and bake them for 10 minutes in the center of the preheated oven. Turn the oven temperature down to 350 degrees and continue to bake for another 20 or 30 minutes, or until the *chaussons* are brown all over and the pastry is thoroughly cooked.

Serve, either cut in half or in thick slices. Pass a bowl of lemon sauce (p. 221) preferably made with the *court-bouillon* (if you have any) in which the sole was originally cooked. If not, thoroughly degreased chicken stock will do quite as well.

* *Note:* These 10-inch *chaussons* can be transformed easily into small turnovers by cutting the circles of dough into 3- or 4-inch rounds or triangles. Follow the *chausson* recipe precisely, using less of the fish filling, of course, for each turnover and baking them for a short period. They make perfect hors d'oeuvres and can be baked ahead of time and reheated in a moderate oven when you are ready to serve them. And literally any cooked filling devised for the improvisations in this book may be used in place of the sole filling.

Fish Pudding in the Norwegian Style

Serves 4–6

5 tablespoons butter, *1 softened for buttering the mold and 4 for the sauce*

2 tablespoons fine dry bread crumbs

3 slices good white bread (crusts removed and discarded), *crumbled (about ¾ cup)*

⅓ cup heavy cream

3 tablespoons shallots or scallions, *finely chopped*

5–6 anchovy fillets, *drained, washed, dried, and finely chopped (about 1 tablespoon)*

2 cups poached sole, *cold, finely flaked*

2 tablespoons fresh dill, *finely cut*

1 teaspoon lemon juice

½ teaspoon salt

⅛ teaspoon cayenne

3 eggs (yolks and whites separated)

Choose a 4-cup soufflé dish, ring, or charlotte mold in which to bake the pudding. Thoroughly butter the inside of the mold and toss in the bread crumbs. Tip the mold from side to side so that the crumbs spread evenly all over the buttered surface, then turn the mold over and rap it gently to dislodge the extra crumbs. Preheat the oven to 325 degrees.

Soak the crumbled bread in the heavy cream for about 5 minutes. Meanwhile melt the remaining 4 tablespoons of butter in a small frying pan and, over moderate heat, sauté the shallots or scallions for 2 or 3 minutes without letting them brown. Add the chopped anchovies and cook 1 or 2 minutes longer, stirring constantly, until they have almost completely dissolved. In a large mixing bowl combine the soaked bread, the entire contents of the frying pan, the flaked fish, dill, lemon juice, salt, and cayenne, and with a large spoon (or the pastry arm of an electric mixer, if you have one) beat for at least 5 minutes, or until the mixture is perfectly smooth. Still beating, add the egg yolks one at a time, then taste for seasoning. Beat the egg whites (at room temperature and preferably with a large balloon whisk in an unlined copper bowl) until they are stiff enough to cling to the beater solidly without their small peaks wavering when the beater is lifted from the bowl. With a rubber spatula vigorously mix a heaping tablespoon of the whites into the fish mixture, then, gently but thoroughly, fold in the rest. Pour into the prepared mold, smooth the surface of the mixture, and cover tightly with aluminum foil.

Bake in the lower third of the oven for 1 to 1¼ hours in a pan of hot water, which should come halfway up the sides of the mold. When the top of the pudding is firm to the touch, it is done.

Let it stand outside the oven for about 5 minutes before unmolding it. To unmold the pudding easily, first run a sharp thin knife around the circumference of the mold. Then place a warm platter over the top of the mold and, grasping mold and platter firmly together, turn them over. Remove any liquid that collects around the pudding. Serve with a separate bowl of hollandaise sauce (p. 220) into which you may stir 1 teaspoon or so of finely chopped dill, if you wish.

Individual Soufflés of Sole and Cheese in Coquilles

Serves 4

4 tablespoons butter, *3 for the sauce base and 1 softened for buttering the shells*

3 tablespoons flour

¾ cup plus 2 tablespoons milk

3 whole eggs plus 2 additional whites, *2 yolks for the sauce base and 5 whites for the soufflé*

½ teaspoon salt

½ teaspoon English dry mustard

⅛ teaspoon cayenne

⅔ cup aged Parmesan cheese, *freshly grated, ½ cup for the sauce base and about 4 teaspoons for the topping*

1½–2 cups poached sole, *coarsely flaked and divided into 4 portions*

In a 2-quart saucepan melt 3 tablespoons of the butter, then, off the heat, stir in the 3 level tablespoons of flour. Mix to a smooth paste, pour over the milk, and beat briefly with a whisk to partially dissolve the flour. Return the pan to the heat and bring the sauce to a boil, whisking constantly. The sauce should be thick and smooth. Simmer it for 1 or 2 minutes, then remove the sauce from the heat and beat into it, one at a time, the 2 egg yolks. Add the salt, mustard, cayenne, and ½ cup of the grated Parmesan and mix thoroughly.

Preheat the oven to 425 degrees. Butter 4 large *coquilles* with the tablespoon of softened butter. A half hour before you plan to serve the soufflés, beat the 5 egg whites (in an unlined copper bowl and with a balloon whisk, if possible) until they are stiff enough to grip the beater firmly and their small white peaks stand upright on the beater when it is lifted out of the bowl. Be careful not to underbeat. Thoroughly mix 2 large spoonfuls of the whites into the warm cheese sauce, then, with the aid of a large rubber spatula, pour the sauce over the remaining egg whites in the bowl. Fold gently but thoroughly together until no streaks of white show through the mixture, but be particularly careful not to overfold.

Working quickly, place a large tablespoon of the soufflé mixture on the bottom of each *coquille,* arrange the flaked fish on top, and spread a thick, slightly mounded layer of the soufflé mixture over it. Make sure the fish is thoroughly covered, but leave ½ inch of the outer circumference of the shell exposed. Sprinkle each soufflé with 1 teaspoon of grated cheese. Place the *coquilles* on a cooky sheet and bake the soufflés for 15 or 20 minutes, turning the oven down to 400 degrees after the first 10 minutes. They should be well puffed and browned when they are done. Serve immediately.

The soufflés may be served alone or with either of the following sauces which, incidentally, would make good use of the 3 egg yolks remaining from the soufflé: the lemon sauce (p. 221) or the hollandaise sauce (p. 220)—with or without mustard.

Scandinavian Fish Cakes

Serves 4

1 cup potatoes, *freshly mashed* (about 4 medium baking potatoes boiled)

1 cup (firmly packed) poached sole, *finely flaked*

5 or 6 anchovy fillets, *drained, washed, dried, and finely chopped* (about 1 tablespoon)

2 eggs (yolks only)

1 tablespoon onion, *finely grated*

1 tablespoon butter, *softened*

1 tablespoon fresh dill, *finely chopped*

½ teaspoon salt

⅛ teaspoon cayenne

1–3 tablespoons fine dry bread crumbs (optional)

½ cup cornstarch or flour, *sifted*

6 tablespoons butter, *melted* ⎫
2 tablespoons vegetable oil ⎭ *combined*

It is imperative, for the success of these little fish cakes, that your freshly boiled potatoes be thoroughly dried over low heat in an ungreased frying pan before you mash them. And to mash them most effectively put the potatoes through a potato ricer immediately after you have cooked and dried them.

In a large mixing bowl combine the mashed potatoes, fish flakes, and chopped anchovies, beating them vigorously with a large spoon until they are thoroughly amalgamated and the mixture is perfectly smooth. Beat in, one at a time, the egg yolks, then the grated onion, softened butter, fresh dill, salt, and cayenne. The mixture should be solid enough at this point to hold its shape in a spoon. If it isn't, beat in up to 3 tablespoons of bread crumbs to give the mixture the proper density. Although the cakes may be made and fried at once, they will be somewhat easier to handle if the mixture is chilled for 1 hour or so. In any event, form the fish mixture into patties* about 3 inches in diameter.

In a large heavy frying pan heat the butter-oil mixture until the fat begins to sizzle. Quickly dip the cakes into the sifted cornstarch or flour (the cornstarch produces a more perceptible crust), shake them free of any excess, and fry the cakes over fairly high heat until they are a crisp, deep brown on both sides. Add a little more fat to the pan, if necessary, when you turn them over. Serve at once.

* *Note:* These fish cakes may, if you like, be formed into small balls instead of patties and then either sautéed (as suggested for the cakes) or deep-fried at 375 degrees until they are golden brown and crisp. They make fine hors d'oeuvres with or without a sauce.

Chilled Sole Alsacienne

Serves 4
DRESSING

1 egg
¼ teaspoon salt
½ teaspoon Dijon or Düsseldorf mustard
⅛ teaspoon cayenne
½ cup olive oil
2 teaspoons lemon juice

1 tablespoon heavy cream
2 tablespoons cucumber, *peeled and shredded*
1½ tablespoons scallions (part of the green stem also), *finely chopped*
2 tablespoons parsley, *finely chopped*

4–6 substantial pieces poached sole, *chilled*
2 medium tomatoes, *peeled and sliced*
8–12 black olives, Mediterranean type if possible

Small bunch crisp watercress

To prepare the dressing, drop the egg into a pan of simmering water and cook it slowly—3½ minutes, if the egg was chilled; 3 minutes, if it was at room temperature. Shell it carefully, drop the yolk into a small mixing bowl, and put the barely set white aside. With a small whisk, or a rotary or electric mixer, beat the yolk for 1 or 2 minutes until it thickens and clings to the beater, then add the salt, mustard, and cayenne, and beat for a few seconds longer. As if making mayonnaise (which, in effect, this sauce is—albeit an unusual version), beat in the olive oil, ½ teaspoon at a time, until ⅛ cup has been used, then increase it to 1 teaspoon at a time for the second ⅛ cupful. By now, the mayonnaise will have thickened to the point where it will be difficult to manage; thin it with 1 teaspoon of the lemon juice. Continue beating, but pour the oil in a thin stream (if you are using an electric mixer), or continue adding it a teaspoon at a time until you have used the whole ½ cup. Thin with the remaining teaspoon of lemon juice and the heavy cream. Stir in the shredded cucumber, the chopped scallions and parsley, and taste for seasoning.*

Arrange the pieces of sole on an attractive small chilled platter and mask them completely with the sauce. Surround with the sliced tomatoes, overlapping them around the fish, intersect with the olives, and ring with sprays of watercress. Serve at once.

* *Note:* You may, if you like, stir into the dressing the cooked egg white you put aside earlier, but chop it finely.

Dilled Fish Salad

Serves 4

1 tablespoon lemon juice
½ teaspoon salt
⅛ teaspoon cayenne
3 tablespoons olive oil
2 tablespoons shallots or scallions, *finely chopped*
2 tablespoons fresh dill, *finely chopped*
2 cups poached sole, *chilled and cut into 1- or 2-inch pieces*

1 cup freshly made mayonnaise (p. 218) or un-sweetened prepared commercial mayonnaise
2–3 cups romaine or Boston lettuce, *thoroughly dried, shredded, and chilled*
2 hard-cooked eggs, *sliced*
4 small tomatoes, *peeled and sliced*
2 tablespoons capers, *drained, washed, and dried*

Mix together in a small mixing bowl the lemon juice, salt, cayenne, olive oil, shallots or scallions, and 1 tablespoon of the dill. Pour it over the cold fish and toss together gently. Let the fish marinate in this mixture for about 1 hour, turning the pieces over every now and then.

Choose a large glass or crystal bowl in which to construct and serve the salad. Combine the marinated fish with its marinade and ½ cup of the mayonnaise. Arrange this mixture on the shredded greens in the salad bowl. Stir a tablespoon of dill into the remaining mayonnaise and spread it over the fish, masking it completely. Alternately overlap the sliced tomatoes and hard-cooked eggs around the edge of the bowl and sprinkle the capers over the masked fish. Serve chilled.

► ◄

A Classic Whole Salmon Simmered

4 quarts water	3 bay leaves
½ cup white wine vinegar	6 sprigs parsley
4 tablespoons salt	2 teaspoons leaf thyme, *crumbled*
3 carrots, *thinly sliced*	1 tablespoon whole black peppercorns
4 medium onions, *thinly sliced*	7- to 8-pound whole fresh salmon, preferably
6 stalks celery with tops and leaves	with head left on

Combine the water, vinegar, salt, carrots, onions, celery, bay leaves, parsley, thyme, and peppercorns in a 6-quart soup kettle or casserole. Bring to a boil, then turn down the heat to barely simmering and cook for about 20 minutes with the pan half covered. Strain the *court-bouillon* and let it cool.

Wash the salmon under cold running water and, without drying it, wrap it securely in a double layer of cheesecloth. Leave about 6 inches of cloth at each end, twist them tightly, and tie them with string. Place the salmon in a large fish poacher or in a deep roasting pan equipped with a cover, and pour the *court-bouillon* over it. If the liquid doesn't quite cover the fish (and that will depend upon the size of the pan), add enough water so that it does by at least 2 inches. Cover the pan and slowly bring the liquid to a boil. Turn the heat down then to the lowest point and simmer the salmon for 30 to 35 minutes, timed from the moment the water comes to a boil. Timing the simmering of a salmon has less to do with the actual weight of the fish than with its thickness. If your salmon seems more than ordinarily heavy-set, simmer it 5 or 10 minutes longer; undercooked salmon has little to recommend it.

To serve the salmon hot, remove it from the broth, using the two ends of the cheesecloth like a sling to help you turn the salmon out onto a heated platter. With a small knife peel off the skin, leaving the head and tail on, and serve the salmon with a bowl of hollandaise sauce (p. 220).

To serve the salmon cold, let it rest in the *court-bouillon* until the broth cools to lukewarm. Then proceed as described above. Peel it, and before chilling in the refrigerator, cover it with plastic wrap. Serve with a bowl of mayonnaise *fines herbes* (p. 219).

► Contrary to what is generally supposed, fresh salmon is not always red. Depending upon where it comes from, it can range from the palest silvery pink of the coho salmon to the deep-red hue of the sockeye. But whatever its color, all salmon may be cooked as described in the classic whole salmon simmered.

► If a whole salmon is difficult to find, poach salmon steaks instead, following the recipe for the classic whole salmon. Have the steaks cut 1 to 1½ inches thick. The weight of each will be determined by the size of the fish; a steak should weigh from about ¾ to 1 pound. The center cuts of salmon are the best. Wrap each steak securely in cheesecloth and poach for about 20 minutes. The steaks are done when they feel firm to the touch and flake when pierced with a fork.

► Canned salmon of the best quality may be used with discretion to supplement an insufficient quantity of freshly cooked salmon for the following salmon improvisations. Drain the canned salmon thoroughly, place it in a colander, and dip it quickly in cold water to wash away the canned salmon oil. Gently pat the salmon dry with paper toweling before combining it with the fresh salmon.

IMPROVISATIONS

Salmon Bisque

Serves 4–6

3 tablespoons butter
4 tablespoons shallots or scallions, *finely chopped*
4 tablespoons flour
2 teaspoons tomato paste
3 cups chicken stock, fresh or canned, *thoroughly degreased*
¾–1 cup cooked salmon, *flaked*
1 cup cooked green peas, fresh or canned

2 eggs (yolks only) ⎫
½ cup heavy cream ⎭ *combined*
½ teaspoon salt
⅛ teaspoon cayenne
¼ teaspoon lemon juice
2 tablespoons butter, *softened* (optional)
1 tablespoon fresh chives, *finely cut,* or parsley, *finely chopped*

Melt the 3 tablespoons of butter over moderate heat in a 2- or 3-quart saucepan. Add the shallots or scallions and cook for about 3 minutes, without letting them brown, however. Off the heat, stir in the 4 level tablespoons of flour and the tomato paste, then pour in the chicken stock. Beat with a whisk to partially dissolve the flour, then return the pan to the heat and bring the stock to a boil, whisking almost constantly. When it is lightly thickened and smooth, turn down the heat to barely simmering, stir in the flaked salmon and the peas, and cook the soup with the pan half covered for about 20 minutes.

Pour the soup through a sieve over a large bowl and press down hard on the salmon and peas with the back of a spoon forcing through as much as you can before throwing the residue away. Stir into the soup the egg-yolk-cream mixture, then return the soup to the saucepan and slowly bring it almost to the boil, whisking constantly. Add the salt, cayenne, and lemon juice and, although this is not absolutely necessary, strain it again. Just before serving, reheat it, beat into it the optional softened butter and sprinkle with the chives or parsley.

Salmon Chive Pâté

Makes 2 cups

¼ pound sweet butter, *softened*
1½ cups (firmly packed) cooked salmon, *cold,* *flaked*
1 teaspoon onion, *finely grated*

1 tablespoon lemon juice
1 teaspoon salt
⅛ teaspoon cayenne
3 tablespoons chives, *cut into ⅛-inch lengths*

Cream the butter by beating it in a large mixing bowl until it is smooth and pale in color. In a large mortar or heavy bowl, mash and pound the salmon with a wooden pestle as energetically as you can. When it is perfectly smooth and pasty, beat it, bit by bit, into the creamed butter. Beat in the onions, lemon juice, salt, cayenne, and chives, and transfer the *pâté* to a 2-cup crock or two 1-cup ones. Chill for at least 3 hours, or overnight. Serve the *pâté* as a spread on crisp French or Italian bread, pumpernickel, or crackers.

Coulibiac

Serves 6–8

PASTRY

¼ pound sweet butter, *chilled and cut into ½-inch pieces*

3 tablespoons lard or vegetable shortening, *chilled*

2 cups flour

1 teaspoon salt

⅓ cup ice water

FILLING

3 tablespoons butter

4 tablespoons shallots or scallions, *finely chopped*

½ teaspoon garlic, *finely chopped*

2 cups mushrooms, *finely chopped* (*about ½ pound*)

4 tablespoons flour

½ cup chicken stock, fresh or canned, *thoroughly degreased*

3 tablespoons fresh dill, *finely chopped*, or 1 tablespoon dried dill

1 tablespoon lemon juice

1 teaspoon salt

⅛ teaspoon cayenne

2 **cups cooked salmon**, *cold, not too finely flaked*

2 cups cooked rice, *cold, well seasoned with salt and pepper* (about ⅔ cup raw rice cooked), or an equivalent amount of cooked buckwheat groats, *cold*

2 hard-cooked eggs, *coarsely chopped*

1 egg (yolk only)

2 tablespoons heavy cream } *combined*

ACCOMPANIMENTS

Melted butter

Sour cream

In a large mixing bowl combine the cut-up butter, lard or shortening, flour, and salt. Quickly rub through the thumb and forefingers of both hands until the fat and flour are well mixed and most of the lumps have disappeared. Don't allow the mixture to become oily, but small bits of unassimilated fat here and there won't affect the final result. Pour the ice water over the flour all at once. Toss together with both hands until all the flour particles are moistened sufficiently to adhere to each other. Quickly and lightly press the dough together into a compact ball and dust it lightly with a small handful of flour. Wrap in waxed paper and chill for 2 hours or longer.

To prepare the filling, melt the butter in an 8-inch frying pan. When the foam subsides, sauté the shallots or scallions and the garlic for about 2 minutes, then add the chopped mushrooms. Cook, stirring almost constantly, over high heat, until the mushrooms begin to release their juices. Then turn down the heat to moderate and continue to cook for about 10 minutes or so, or until the mushrooms are quite dry but not brown. Off the heat, stir in the 4 level tablespoons of flour, and when they are well combined pour in the stock. Beat together with a whisk and return the pan to the heat. Cook, stirring almost constantly, until the sauce becomes very thick. Add ½ tablespoon of the dill, the lemon juice, salt, and cayenne, then scrape the mixture into a bowl. Add the salmon and gently combine with the sauce; if possible, try not to mash the salmon pieces during the process. Have the rice or groats, hard-cooked eggs, and egg-cream mixture on hand before you begin to roll out the pastry.

Preheat the oven to 425 degrees. Remove the pastry from the refrigerator at least 15 minutes before you plan to roll it out; it must not be too hard. Meanwhile butter a heavy cooky sheet. On a floured surface, roll out the pastry into an approximate rectangle shape about ⅛ inch thick. Trim this more precisely into a rectangle 12 inches wide and 17 inches long. Working quickly (should the pastry soften too much, place it in the refrigerator to firm it up a bit), spread 1 cup of the cold rice or groats on the rectangle, leaving a space approximately 4 inches all around it. Sprinkle the rice with half the remaining dill, then spread over half the chopped eggs and all the salmon mixture. Cover the salmon with the remaining chopped eggs, dill, and the other cup of rice or groats. Draw the long edges of the pastry up and over the filling and either pinch them together to seal them or brush the edges with cold water and press firmly to make them adhere. Cut triangles of pastry from each corner of the roll and, like the flaps of a large envelope, bring up the ends and seal with cold water. With the largest spatula you have (use two if they are small) gently, turning the *coulibiac* over, ease it onto the cooky sheet, so that all the pastry seams are concealed. Cut two or three 1-inch slits onto the top and sides and brush with the egg-cream mixture.

Bake the *coulibiac* in the center of the oven for 10 minutes, then turn the heat down to 350 degrees and continue to bake for another 50 minutes or so, or until the pastry is golden brown all over.

To serve, slide the *coulibiac* onto a heated platter, carefully pour the hot melted butter into the slits, and cut into 1½- to 2-inch slices. A small bowl of melted butter and another of sour cream are the traditional accompaniments to this Russian masterpiece.

Salmon Beignets

Serves 6–8

6 tablespoons butter, *cut into ½-inch pieces*
1 cup water
1 cup flour
4 eggs
1 cup cooked salmon, *cold, flaked*
4–6 anchovy fillets, *drained, washed, dried, and finely chopped (about 1 tablespoon)*

3 tablespoons Parmesan cheese, *freshly grated*
1 teaspoon salt
⅛ teaspoon cayenne
Deep fat for frying

Combine the butter and water in a 2-quart saucepan and bring to a rolling boil. When the butter is completely melted, remove the pan from the heat and add the flour all at once. Quickly mix together—to the consistency of mashed potatoes—and cook briefly, stirring constantly until the paste becomes a smooth, doughy mass. Off the heat, make a well in the center of the paste with a spoon and drop in one of the eggs. Beat vigorously until it is completely absorbed. Add the other eggs in a similar fashion, beating vigorously after each addition. When the last egg is in, beat the paste for 3 or 4 minutes until it is smooth and shiny. Stir in the salmon, anchovies, grated cheese, salt, and cayenne. Although the paste will now be somewhat resistant, beat it for 1 or 2 minutes more. All the ingredients should be thoroughly combined. Taste for seasoning and heighten with more salt and cayenne if the mixture seems too bland.

Heat deep fat—at least 3 inches in depth—to a temperature of 375 degrees on the deep-fat frying thermometer and preheat the oven to 250 degrees. A heaping teaspoon at a time, drop the paste into the fat, pushing it off the spoon with your finger or the back of another spoon. Do not fry too many *beignets* at the same time; the temperature of the fat will drop too much and the *beignets* may stick together. Cook them until they double in size and are a deep brown all over. Turn them periodically with a large slotted spoon. When they are done, put them in a paper-towel-lined baking dish to drain and keep warm in the oven until all the *beignets* are done. Serve with cocktails.

Salmon-Filled Spinach Roulade with Hollandaise Sauce

Serves 8

The recipe for this dish is exactly the same as the one for the tongue-filled spinach roulade on page 100, except that the following salmon filling is substituted for the tongue filling.

FILLING

3 tablespoons butter
3 tablespoons shallots or scallions, *finely chopped*
1 cup mushrooms (about ¼ pound), *finely chopped*
3 tablespoons flour
¾ cup chicken stock, fresh or canned, *thoroughly degreased*

1 egg (yolk only)
2 tablespoons heavy cream } *combined*
2 teaspoons lemon juice
¾ teaspoon salt
⅛ teaspoon cayenne
2 tablespoons fresh chives, *finely cut*
2 cups cooked salmon, *flaked*

Prepare and bake the spinach roulade as described on page 101. While the roulade is baking (or earlier, if you like), make the salmon filling. In an 8-inch frying pan melt the butter and sauté the shallots or scallions over moderate heat for about 2 or 3 minutes. Add the mushrooms, raise the heat, and cook until they begin to release some of their juices. Turn the heat down to moderate and continue to cook for about 8 minutes, or until the mushrooms are dry but not brown. Off the heat, stir in the 3 level tablespoons of flour, and when it is well combined pour in the stock. Beat together with a whisk and return the pan to the heat. Cook, stirring constantly, until the sauce is smooth and very thick. Mix 1 tablespoon of the warm sauce into the egg yolk–cream mixture to heat it through; then reverse the process and pour the mixture into the sauce. Still stirring, bring the sauce to a boil, then immediately remove the pan from the heat. Add the lemon juice, salt, cayenne, chives, and salmon. Gently combine, and try, if possible, not to mash the salmon to a paste during the process.

When the roulade is done, turn it out, spread it with the reheated salmon mixture, and roll it up as described on page 102. Serve with either hollandaise sauce (p. 220) or lemon sauce (p. 221).

Salmon Spinach Soufflé

Serves 6

6 tablespoons butter, *1 softened for buttering dish, 4 for the sauce base, and 1 for cooking the spinach*

½ cup Parmesan cheese, *grated*

3 tablespoons shallots or scallions, *finely chopped*

5 tablespoons flour

1½ cups milk

8 eggs, *6 yolks for the sauce base and 8 whites for the salmon and spinach mixtures*

1 teaspoon salt

⅛ teaspoon cayenne

1 package frozen spinach, *thoroughly defrosted and squeezed dry, chopped as finely as possible,* or ½ pound freshly cooked spinach, *finely chopped*

A few gratings of nutmeg

¾ cup cooked salmon, *finely flaked*

2 teaspoons tomato paste

The soufflé should be baked and served in an 8-cup straight-sided soufflé dish or charlotte mold. Thoroughly coat the inside of the dish with the tablespoon of softened butter and toss in 2 tablespoons of the grated Parmesan. Tip the dish from side to side so that the cheese spreads evenly all over the inside surface, then turn the dish over and rap it sharply on the table to dislodge the excess. Preheat the oven to 400 degrees.

Melt 4 tablespoons of the remaining butter in a heavy saucepan and when the foam subsides sauté the shallots or scallions over moderate heat for about 3 minutes, stirring them frequently. Don't let them brown. Off the heat, mix in the 5 level tablespoons of flour, stirring it to a smooth paste. Add, all at once, the 1½ cups of milk and beat vigorously with a whisk to partially dissolve the flour. Return the pan to the heat and, whisking constantly, bring the sauce to a boil. It will be very thick. Turn down the heat and let it simmer for 1 or 2 minutes before removing from the heat. While the sauce is still hot, beat into it, one by one, 6 egg yolks. Divide the sauce (there should be a fraction over 2 cups of it) between two fairly large mixing bowls. In a small frying pan melt the remaining tablespoon of butter and cook the spinach over fairly high heat until any residual moisture has evaporated and the spinach begins to stick lightly to the pan. With a rubber spatula scrape it into the sauce in one of the mixing bowls and mix thoroughly together. Add a few gratings of nutmeg and taste for seasoning. Stir into the sauce in the other mixing bowl the flaked salmon and tomato paste and also taste for seasoning. Both mixtures should be very highly seasoned if they are to hold their own after being combined with the egg whites.

Beat the 8 egg whites (at room temperature and preferably with a large balloon whisk in an unlined copper bowl) until they are stiff enough to cling to the beater solidly without their small peaks wavering when the beater is lifted from the bowl. With a large spatula cut a line approximately across the middle of the mass and scrape half the whites into the spinach mixture and the rest into the salmon mixture. Working quickly, fold the whites thoroughly into each in turn. There should be no streaks of white showing when you finish, but be careful not to over-fold. Pour approximately half the spinach mixture into the soufflé dish, then gently pour all the salmon over it. Top with the remaining spinach; with a spatula spread the spinach mixture out so that it thoroughly masks the salmon.

Sprinkle 2 tablespoons of grated Parmesan over the top of the soufflé and bake it in the lower third of the oven. Five minutes after the soufflé has gone in, reduce the heat to 375 degrees. Depending on whether you prefer your soufflé soft in the center—as the French do—or somewhat firmer, bake it, undisturbed, for anywhere from 30 to 45 minutes. Serve at once, either alone or with hollandaise sauce (p. 220) or lemon sauce (p. 221).

Gratin of Crêpes Stuffed with Salmon and Mushrooms

16–20
crêpes

The recipe for this dish is exactly the same as the one for *gratin* of *crêpes* stuffed with chicken and mushrooms on page 134. Substitute 2 cups of firm cooked salmon for the chicken, and use 1 tablespoon of chopped fresh dill in place of the tarragon if you prefer.

Salmon-Stuffed Eggs in the French Style

Serves 4–6

The recipe for this dish is exactly the same as the one for tongue-stuffed eggs in the French style on page 105. Substitute ½ cup of flaked cooked salmon for the braised tongue and omit the teaspoon of Dijon mustard.

Pickled Salmon

Serves 4–6

2 **cups firm cooked salmon,** *chilled and cut into 2-inch pieces*
1 cup onions, *thinly sliced*
2 bay leaves, *crumbled*
1 teaspoon salt

2 tablespoons fresh dill, *finely cut*
1 cup white wine vinegar
½ cup olive oil
Boston or romaine lettuce, *shredded*

In order to pickle the salmon with any success, it must be firm, cut into fairly large pieces, and not in the slightest degree overcooked or else it will simply disintegrate in the marinade.

One or two days before you plan to use it, place the salmon in one layer in an enamel or glass baking dish, then combine the onions, bay leaves, salt, dill, vinegar, and oil and pour this marinade over the fish, spreading it over the surface carefully. Cover with plastic wrap and marinate (at room temperature, preferably) for one, two, or even three days before using. Turn the fish over from time to time, but refrigerate it if your kitchen tends to get too warm, particularly in the summer.

To serve, remove the salmon from the marinade and place the pieces on a bed of shredded lettuce. Mayonnaise mixed with a little finely cut dill would be a suitable accompaniment.

Cold Salmon Mousse

Serves 4–6

2 teaspoons vegetable oil
1 envelope unflavored gelatin
¼ cup dry white wine
¾ cup chicken stock, fresh or canned, *thoroughly degreased*
2 **cups (firmly packed) cooked salmon,** *chilled*
2 teaspoons tomato paste

1 teaspoon imported Hungarian paprika
1 tablespoon onion, *very finely grated*
1½ teaspoons salt
1 tablespoon lemon juice
⅛ teaspoon Tabasco
½ cup heavy cream

Oil a 2- or 3-cup fish or decorative mold by brushing it with the vegetable oil, then invert the mold onto a double thickness of paper toweling to drain.

Soften the envelope of gelatin in the wine for 5 minutes. Meanwhile bring the chicken stock to a simmer in a small saucepan; stir it into the softened gelatin. Cook for 1 or 2 minutes until the gelatin dissolves, then pour it into the jar of an electric blender. Add the salmon and blend at high speed until the mixture is an absolutely smooth purée. Scrape it out of the jar into a small mixing bowl and stir in the tomato paste, paprika, grated onion, salt, lemon juice, and Tabasco. Taste for seasoning.

Whip the cream in a chilled bowl until it is not quite stiff but firm enough to cling lightly to the beater when it is lifted out of the bowl. Set the bowl of puréed salmon into a larger bowl filled with ice and a little cold water. Stir it with a metal spoon for a few minutes until it begins to stiffen (and this will happen sooner than you think), then gently fold into it the whipped cream. Continue to fold until no streaks of cream remain. Pour at once into the oiled mold, smooth the top, cover with plastic wrap, and refrigerate for at least 2 hours or until firm.

When you are ready to serve it, run a small sharp knife around the inside edge of the mold, dip the bottom of the mold into hot water for a second or two, and wipe it dry with a towel. Place a chilled platter on top of it, invert it, and rap it smartly on the table once or twice to dislodge it. Serve it with plain mayonnaise or curry mayonnaise (p. 219).

Chilled Salmon Alsacienne

Serves 4–6   The recipe for this dish is exactly the same as the one for the chilled sole Alsacienne on page 168. Substitute 4 to 6 pieces cold salmon for the sole.

Dilled Salmon Salad

Serves 4   The recipe for this dish is exactly the same as the one for dilled fish salad on page 169. Substitute 2 cups of cold cooked salmon for the sole.

► ◄

Classic Boiled Lobsters with Clarified Butter

6 live lobsters, 1½ pounds each*
Salt

½ pound sweet butter
Lemon quarters

Bring to a rolling boil a pot of water large enough to hold the 6 lobsters comfortably; an 8-quart soup pot filled with about 6 quarts of water should do admirably, but lacking this, use a large deep roasting pan that has a cover. Add 1 tablespoon of salt for each quart of water. When you are ready to cook them, grasp one lobster at a time directly behind its head, with your hand well away from the claws (which, ideally, should have been pegged or tied by your fishman) and drop it, antennae first, into the boiling water. After the last lobster is in, cover the pot tightly and boil vigorously for exactly 15 minutes, timing from the moment the water begins to boil again. When the lobsters are done, remove them with a pair of large tongs, and immediately plunge any lobsters you plan to save into a pot of cold water to stop their cooking. Refrigerate them as soon as they are cool.

Prepare the hot lobsters for serving by laying each on its back and splitting it down its center with a large sharp knife. Lobsters 1½ pounds or under have comparatively thin shells and can be split without much difficulty; but use a hammer or mallet with the knife to assist you, if you must. Remove the long intestinal vein from each lobster and also the gelatinous sac behind the eyes. The green liver, called the tomalley, and the red coral, if any, are great delicacies and should not, under any circumstance, be discarded. To make the lobster meat in the claws more accessible, split the convex side of each claw with a sharp blow of your knife. Serve the lobsters at once with individual dishes of clarified butter and a plate of lemon quarters.

To prepare the clarified butter, cut the ½ pound of sweet butter into 8 or 10 pieces and, over the lowest heat, melt it without letting it brown. Off the heat, let the butter rest for a couple of minutes, then tilt the pan and with a large spoon remove as much of the clear butter as you can without disturbing the milky solids—or whey, as it is called—at the bottom of the pan. Throw the solids away and reheat the clarified butter before serving.

* *Note:* This recipe is theoretically planned for four, or one lobster per person. It is suggested that you cook six, saving two for future improvisations, but you may cook as many extra as you wish.

▶ If you are of the school which believes that boiled lobsters should be started in cold water (and its culinary advantages have yet to be proven conclusively), instead of plunging them into boiling water by all means do it your way. For this method, cover the lobsters with cold water, bring it to a boil, and let it boil briskly for about 5 minutes. Turn down the heat and simmer the lobsters with the pot half covered for about 10 minutes longer. Proceed then, as described in the preceding recipe for classic boiled lobsters with clarified butter.

▶ Canned lobster of the best quality may be used with discretion to supplement an insufficient amount of boiled lobster for the lobster improvisations. Much to be preferred, of course, would be cooked, picked lobster meat available in many better fish stores. Frozen lobster meat, on the other hand, tends to be tough and rubbery when it is recooked.

IMPROVISATIONS

Lobster Bisque

Serves 4–6

3 tablespoons butter
3 tablespoons flour
1 teaspoon tomato paste
1½ cups dry white wine
4 cups chicken stock, fresh or canned, *completely degreased*
2 lobster carcasses, *broken up as finely as possible*
1 small onion, *thinly sliced*
1 small carrot, *thinly sliced*
A bouquet consisting of 3 sprigs parsley, 3 sprigs dill, 2 celery tops with leaves, and 1 small bay leaf, *tied together with string*

1 egg (yolk only)
¼ cup heavy cream
½ teaspoon lemon juice
The tomalley and coral of the lobsters (optional)
½–¾ cup cooked lobster meat, *cut into small pieces*
Salt
Cayenne

Melt the butter in a 2- or 3-quart enamel saucepan or casserole; off the heat, stir into it the 3 level tablespoons of flour. Stir it to a paste, mix in the tomato paste, then pour over it the white wine and chicken stock. Stir briefly with a whisk to break up the flour particles and, still stirring, bring the soup to a boil. When it is quite smooth and lightly thickened, add the lobster carcasses, the sliced onion and carrot, and the bouquet. Simmer with the pot half covered for about 40 minutes. Strain it through a fine sieve, pressing down hard on the vegetables and lobster shells with the back of a large spoon to extract all their liquid before throwing them away. Return the soup to the casserole, and bring it again to the simmering point. Mix together the egg yolk and heavy cream and, before stirring it into the soup, first add a couple of tablespoons of the hot liquid. Then bring the bisque almost to the boiling point, add the lemon juice, the optional tomalley and coral (first rubbed through a sieve), and the lobster meat. Heat briefly without boiling and salt to taste. Stir in a few specks of cayenne and serve.

Small Lobster Quiches

Makes	8 tablespoons butter, *6 chilled and cut into*	½ teaspoon salt
24 quiches	*½-inch pieces for dough and 2 softened for*	¼ teaspoon sugar
PASTRY	*greasing muffin tins*	1½ cups flour
	2 tablespoons lard or vegetable shortening, *chilled*	3½ tablespoons cold water

FILLING	**1½–2 cups cooked lobster meat,** *cut into ½-inch pieces*	¾ cup heavy cream
	2 tablespoons Parmesan cheese, *grated*	½ teaspoon salt
	1 whole egg plus 1 additional yolk	⅛ teaspoon cayenne
		¼ teaspoon English dry mustard

Combine in a large bowl the 6 tablespoons of cut-up butter, lard or shortening, salt, sugar, and flour. Quickly rub through the thumb and forefingers of both hands until the fat and flour are well mixed and most of the lumps have disappeared. Sprinkle the water over the flour and toss together until the flour particles are moistened sufficiently to adhere to each other. Gently press the dough together into a compact ball and dust it lightly with a small handful of flour. Wrap in waxed paper and chill for 2 hours or more. (On page 134, there is a description of how to make the dough in an electric mixer—if it is one that is equipped with a pastry arm.)

Using a pastry brush heavily grease the cups of 2 small trays of muffin tins (those which come in nests of 12, each cup about 2 inches in diameter across the top) with the 2 tablespoons of softened butter. Remove the pastry from the refrigerator and let it soften for 10 minutes or so before rolling it out. On a floured wood, formica, or marble surface roll the dough out quickly into a sheet about ⅛ inch thick. With a 2½- or 2¾-inch cooky cutter (or the rim of a small glass) cut out as many rounds as you can. If you have less than the required 24, gather together the scraps of remaining dough, quickly knead it into a ball with a little extra flour, and roll it out again. Cut out the necessary number of rounds and carefully fit them into the tins. Don't fuss with them too much, but be sure to press the bottom of the rounds firmly into the bottom and the sides of each cup with a light pressure of the forefinger. Refrigerate until ready to fill.

Preheat the oven to 425 degrees. In each pastry cup place 1 or 2 pieces of lobster meat and ¼ teaspoon of grated Parmesan. Mix together in a small bowl the whole egg and the additional yolk, the heavy cream, salt, cayenne, and mustard. With a small spoon fill each cup to the brim with the mixture; try not to let the cream spill over the sides. Bake in the center of the oven for 10 minutes before turning the heat down to 325 degrees. Continue to bake for another 15 to 20 minutes, or until the *quiches* are well puffed and brown on top. Run a small sharp knife around each *quiche* to free it from the pan and serve at once.

Coquilles of Lobster

Serves 4 as
a main course,
6 as a
first course

8 tablespoons butter, *2 for sautéing shallots or scallions and lobster, 2 for sautéing mushrooms, 3 for the sauce, and 1 softened for topping*
2 tablespoons shallots or scallions, *finely chopped*
1½–2 cups cooked lobster meat, *cut into small chunks*
¼ cup dry white wine
⅓ pound fresh mushrooms, *thinly sliced (about 2 cups)*
4 tablespoons flour

¾ cup chicken stock, fresh or canned, *thoroughly degreased*
½ cup milk
1 egg (yolk only)
2 tablespoons heavy cream
Lobster tomalley and coral, if any (optional)
½ teaspoon salt
⅛ teaspoon cayenne
½ teaspoon lemon juice
3 tablespoons Parmesan cheese, *grated*
2 tablespoons bread crumbs

Over moderate heat melt 2 tablespoons of the butter in an 8-inch enamel or stainless-steel frying pan. When the foam subsides, add the shallots or scallions, cook for 2 or 3 minutes, then add the lobster meat. Stir continuously for about 30 seconds, pour in the wine, and raise the heat. Cook the wine completely away as quickly as possible and scrape the entire contents of the pan into a mixing bowl. Melt 2 more tablespoons of the butter in the same pan and sauté the mushrooms for about 5 minutes, stirring from time to time. Then add them to the lobster mixture in the mixing bowl.

To prepare the sauce, melt 3 tablespoons of the remaining butter over moderate heat in a 2-quart saucepan. Off the heat, stir in the 4 level tablespoons of flour and mix to a smooth paste. Pour over, all at once, the chicken stock and milk, and beat briefly with a whisk to partially dissolve the flour. Return the pan to the heat and, whisking almost continuously, bring the sauce to a boil. It should be smooth and thick. Simmer a moment or two before removing the pan from the heat, then beat in the egg yolk, and the cream. Add the optional tomalley and coral (first rubbed through a sieve) and season the sauce with the salt, cayenne, and lemon juice.

Preheat the oven to 375 degrees. Combine two thirds of the sauce with the lobster-mushroom mixture—for best results don't include any juices which may have collected in the mixing bowl. Lightly butter 4 large or 6 small scallop shells and divide the lobster-mushroom mixture among them. Spoon a little of the remaining sauce over each one, sprinkle with a little Parmesan cheese and bread crumbs, and dot with the tablespoon of softened butter. Bake for about 20 minutes, or until the sauce begins to bubble. Slide briefly under a hot broiler to brown before serving.

Small Filled Egg Rolls in the Chinese Style

Makes 12 egg rolls

Serves 4–6	3 eggs	½ teaspoon salt
BATTER	¾ cup flour	3 tablespoons vegetable oil
	¾ cup water	

FILLING	2 tablespoons vegetable oil	1 teaspoon cornstarch
	½ pound fresh boneless pork, *finely shredded*	½ teaspoon salt
	⅓ cup celery, *finely shredded*	⅛ teaspoon sugar
	¾ **cup cooked lobster**, *finely shredded*	1 tablespoon soy sauce
	¼ cup scallions (part of the green stem also), *coarsely chopped*	1 egg, *lightly beaten with 2 tablespoons cold water*

Deep fat for frying
Bowls of white vinegar and/or soy sauce for
   dipping

So-called egg-roll skins are available in Chinese noodle factories or noodle shops or in Chinese grocery stores. If you live near a Chinese community, it is worth making a special effort to buy them. Making egg-roll skins by hand from scratch in the Chinese fashion is complex and time-consuming, and although the skins have a special texture impossible to achieve in any other than the traditional way, the following simple pancake batter offers a more than tolerable substitute.

Break the eggs into the flour and mix them together thoroughly, adding the water a little at a time to make a fairly fluid batter. Season with the salt and beat for a few minutes until smooth. Use a 6-inch frying pan in which to make the pancakes. Heat the pan until a drop of cold water flicked on its surface evaporates instantly. With a pastry brush lightly grease the pan with the vegetable oil, then lift the pan over the bowl of batter. Ladle 2 tablespoons (more or less) into the pan and rotate the pan until the batter covers the entire surface. The pan should be hot enough so that the batter grips on contact. Immediately tilt the pan over the bowl and pour off the excess batter. Fry the pancakes on one side only, taking care they do not become too brown, and slide each from the pan the moment it is set. You should have about a dozen pancakes when you are through.

To prepare the filling, heat the vegetable oil in a small frying pan and fry the shredded pork over high heat for 2 or 3 minutes until it is lightly brown and tender. Scrape it into a small mixing bowl. Blanch the shredded celery by dropping it into a pan of boiling water. Cook briskly for 2 minutes, then drain, dry, and add it to the pork in the bowl. Stir in the lobster, scallions, cornstarch, salt, sugar, and soy sauce. Mix thoroughly and taste for seasoning. Paint a 1-inch band of egg wash (the egg-water mixture) around the edges of each pancake. Spread about 1 tablespoon of filling on the lower third of each pancake, then roll it up tightly, enclosing the ends as you go along as if you were wrapping a small package. Seal the flaps by lightly brushing them with the egg wash, then refrigerate the rolls, covered with plastic wrap, for at least ½ hour before frying them; otherwise the rolls will unwrap while frying.

Heat the deep fat to 375 degrees on the thermometer and fry the rolls, 2 or 3 at a time, for about 5 minutes, or until they are crisp and brown. Serve with small dishes of white vinegar and/or soy sauce into which the ends of the rolls are dipped as they are eaten.

Paella with Lobster

Serves 4–6 The recipe for this dish is exactly the same as the one for *paella* Sevillana on page 120. Substitute 2–2½ cups of cooked lobster (cut into 1-inch chunks) for the roast chicken, or use a combination of both.

Lobster-Filled Crêpes

16–20 crêpes

Serves 4–6

CRÊPE BATTER	1 cup milk	½ teaspoon salt	
	¼ cup cold water	3 tablespoons butter, *melted and cooled*	
	1¼ cups flour	3 tablespoons butter, *melted* ⎱ *combined*	
	3 eggs	1 tablespoon vegetable oil ⎰	

SAUCE	4 tablespoons butter	¾ teaspoon salt
	6 tablespoons flour	⅛ teaspoon white pepper
	2 cups chicken stock, fresh or canned	¾ teaspoon lemon juice
	2 eggs (yolks only)	
	1 cup heavy cream, *½ cup for filling and ½ cup for masking sauce*	

FILLING	4 tablespoons butter, *2 for sautéing and 2 softened for topping, cut into bits*	1 teaspoon paprika
	3 tablespoons shallots or scallions, *finely chopped*	½ teaspoon lemon juice
	1½–2 cups cooked lobster meat, *cut into small pieces*	1 tablespoon parsley, *finely chopped*
		Salt
	⅓ cup dry white wine	Cayenne
	1 teaspoon tomato paste	4 tablespoons Parmesan cheese, *grated*

To make the *crêpe* batter in a blender, put the milk, water, flour, eggs, salt, and butter in the blender jar. Blend at high speed for a few seconds, then, with the machine off, scrape down the sides of the jar with a rubber scraper. Blend again, this time for about 40 seconds. Ideally, the batter should rest for about 2 hours before being used, but it can be used at once, if you wish, at a slight sacrifice of tenderness.

To make the batter by hand, combine the flour and eggs in a mixing bowl, then slowly mix in the milk and water and salt. Beat with a whisk or beater until the floury lumps disappear, strain it through a fine sieve, and stir in the melted butter.

Use a 6-inch frying pan in which to make the *crêpes.* Heat the pan until a drop of cold water flicked on its surface evaporates instantly. Using a pastry brush, grease the pan with the butter-oil mixture, then lift it over the bowl of batter. Ladle 2 tablespoons (more or less) into the pan and rotate the pan until the batter covers the entire surface. The pan should be hot enough so that the batter grips on contact. Immediately tilt the pan over the bowl and pour off the excess batter. You may have to lose a few *crêpes* until you perfect this technique, but the paper-thin *crêpes* you will finally make are worth it. Cook each *crêpe* over fairly high heat until a faint rim of brown shows around the edge. Turn the *crêpe* over and cook for a few seconds before sliding it onto a plate. Continue with the remaining batter in the same fashion; you should end up with at least 16 perfect *crêpes* and, after a little practice, with about 20. There is no need to trim them into perfect circles; since they are to be rolled, whatever imperfections they have will be concealed.

To prepare the sauce, melt the 4 tablespoons of butter in a 2- or 3-quart saucepan, then, off the heat, stir in the flour. Add, all at once, the 2 cups of chicken stock and mix with a wire whisk; stir to dissolve the *roux*. Cook over moderate heat, stirring constantly, until the sauce is smooth and thick. Combine the 2 egg yolks with ½ cup of the cream and mix into it a few tablespoons of the simmering sauce. Then reverse the process and slowly pour the egg-cream mixture into the saucepan, continuing to stir as you do so. Bring the sauce to a boil and continue to boil it for about 10 seconds. Remove from the heat at once; season with the salt, white pepper, and lemon juice.

To prepare the filling, melt 2 tablespoons of the butter in a 10-inch enamel or stainless-steel pan and sauté the shallots or scallions for about 2 minutes, or just about long enough to soften them without letting them color. Add the lobster meat. Stir it constantly over moderate heat for about 2 minutes, then pour in the wine. Raise the heat and rapidly boil away the wine, then mix in the tomato paste and paprika. Cook for a few seconds longer and scrape the entire contents of the frying pan into a small mixing bowl. Add 1 cup of the previously prepared sauce, the lemon juice, and the chopped parsley. Mix thoroughly and taste for seasoning; it will probably need salt and perhaps a few specks of cayenne.

Lay a scant 2 tablespoons of the lobster mixture on the lower third of each *crêpe* and roll up without tucking in the ends. Place the *crêpes* side by side in a buttered baking dish just about large enough to hold them comfortably. Thin the remaining sauce with the reserved ½ cup of heavy cream. Using a large spoon, carefully mask each *crêpe* with the sauce, pouring any extra around the *crêpes* in the dish. Sprinkle the grated cheese over the top and dot with the bits of softened butter.

Covered with plastic wrap, the *crêpes* may be kept refrigerated, if necessary, for a day before you bake them. When you are ready to serve the *crêpes*, preheat the oven to 375 degrees and bake for about 20 minutes, or until the sauce begins to bubble. Before serving, slide the pan beneath the broiler briefly to brown the cheese.

Linguine with Lobster and Fresh Tomato Sauce

Serves 4

7 tablespoons butter, *3 for sautéing lobster and 4 softened and creamed for buttering pasta*

1½–2 cups cooked lobster meat, *cut into small chunks*

¼ cup olive oil

3 tablespoons shallots or scallions, *finely chopped*

1 teaspoon garlic, *finely chopped*

½ cup dry white wine

2 teaspoons tomato paste

1½ teaspoons dried basil or 1 tablespoon fresh basil, *chopped*

1½ teaspoons oregano

2 pounds fresh ripe tomatoes, *peeled, seeded, and coarsely chopped (about 3 cups tomato pulp)*

2 tablespoons parsley, *finely chopped*

Salt

Freshly ground black pepper

Lobster tomalley and coral, if any (optional)

1 pound *linguine*°

Melt 3 tablespoons of the butter in a 10-inch heavy enamel or stainless-steel frying pan. When the foam subsides, add the lobster meat and cook over fairly high heat for about 1 minute, stirring constantly. Remove the lobster with a slotted spoon and set it aside. In the same pan heat the olive oil and sauté the shallots or scallions and garlic for 5 minutes over moderate heat, without letting them brown, however. Pour in the wine, raise the heat, and boil it away almost completely. Off the heat, stir into the pan the tomato paste, basil, and oregano, and mix the ingredients to a paste. Add the tomatoes, mix thoroughly, and cook briskly for about 10 minutes, or until most of the liquid in the pan has boiled away and the sauce has become thick. Add the reserved cooked lobster and the parsley to the pan, season to taste with salt and a few grindings of black pepper, and stir in the optional tomalley and coral, first rubbed through a sieve. Keep the sauce warm over the lowest possible heat, or in a double boiler set over simmering water, while you cook the *linguine*.

Bring 4 quarts of salted water (use about 2 tablespoons of salt) to a boil in a large pot. Add the *linguine* and boil rapidly for about 10 minutes, or a little longer if you prefer your *pasta* less chewy. Drain at once in a large colander, lifting the strands of *pasta* with a fork to make certain you have rid it of all its cooking water. Transfer the *linguine* to a hot serving bowl and thoroughly mix in the creamed, softened butter, lifting the *pasta* strands up and over each other until they are completely coated with the butter. Pour in the lobster sauce and mix it with the *linguine* in the same fashion. Serve at once on heated plates.

* *Note:* Any thin, tubular *pasta* like *spaghetti* or *spaghettini* may be substituted for the flat *linguine* in this recipe.

Lobster Newburgh

Serves 4–6

4 tablespoons butter	1 cup heavy cream
2 cups cooked lobster, *cut into fairly large chunks*	4 eggs (yolks only)
	½ teaspoon salt
¼ cup cognac	⅛ teaspoon cayenne
¼ cup Madeira	½ teaspoon lemon juice

Melt the butter over moderate heat in a large enamel or stainless-steel frying pan. When it stops foaming, add the lobster meat (dry the pieces first in paper toweling if they seem damp) and, stirring constantly, cook briskly for about 1 minute, then remove from the heat. Warm the cognac either in a ladle or a small pan, set it alight with a match, and pour it over the lobster. Shake the pan back and forth until the flame dies out. Then pour the Madeira and ½ cup of the heavy cream over the lobster. Bring this to a boil, reduce the heat, and cook for about 2 minutes, stirring constantly.

In a small bowl mix the egg yolks and the remaining ½ cup of cream. Add 2 tablespoons of the hot sauce from the frying pan, then reverse the process and slowly pour the egg mixture into the frying pan, stirring constantly. Heat until the sauce thickens, but under no circumstances let it come to a boil or it will most assuredly curdle. Season with the salt, cayenne, and lemon juice, adding more if you think it necessary.

If the lobster Newburgh must wait, keep it hot in the top of a double boiler set over barely simmering water. Should the sauce thicken too much, thin it with a little cream. Serve either in patty shells or with cooked rice or over buttered toast.

Lobster Fritters with Curry Mayonnaise

Serves 4

1 cup flour, *sifted before measuring*
¾ cup warm water
½ teaspoon salt
3 tablespoons vegetable oil
1 egg (white only)

Deep fat for frying
2 cups cooked lobster meat, *cut into approximately 1-inch pieces*
1 tablespoon salt
Curry mayonnaise (p. 219)

Prepare the batter about 2 hours before you plan to use it. In a small mixing bowl mix the flour (sifted before measuring) with the water, salt, and oil, which you have previously combined, stirring the liquid mixture in, little by little, until a fairly smooth paste is formed. Overbeating develops the gluten in the flour and produces a rubbery batter. Let the paste rest for a couple of hours.

Preheat the deep fat to 375 degrees on the deep-fat thermometer. A few minutes before cooking the fritters, beat the egg white until it is stiff, then carefully and lightly fold it into the batter. There should be no white streaks visible when you have finished.

Lightly salt each piece of lobster, then, holding it with a pair of tongs, dip it in the batter and drop it into the fat. Don't fry too many fritters at a time or the temperaure of the fat will drop and will produce soggy rather than crisp fritters. Drain the fritters on paper toweling and serve at once with a bowl of curry mayonnaise (p. 219).

Parmesan Cheese Soufflé with Lobster Sauce

Serves 4

SAUCE

4 tablespoons butter, *2 for sautéing the lobster and 2 for sautéing shallots or scallions*

1½ cups cooked lobster meat, *cut into small dice*

¼ cup cognac

2 tablespoons shallots or scallions, *finely chopped*

2 teaspoons tomato paste

2 tablespoons flour

½ cup chicken stock, fresh or canned, *thoroughly degreased*

¼ cup dry white wine

6 tablespoons heavy cream

Lobster tomalley and coral, if any (optional)

Salt

Cayenne

½ teaspoon lemon juice

SOUFFLÉ

½ cup plus 4 tablespoons Parmesan cheese, grated

4 tablespoons butter, *1 for buttering mold and 3 for the soufflé base*

3 tablespoons flour

¾ cup milk

5 eggs, *4 yolks for the soufflé base and 5 whites for the soufflé*

½ teaspoon salt

⅛ teaspoon cayenne

½ teaspoon mustard, preferably Dijon

½ teaspoon English dry mustard

Prepare the lobster sauce first. In an 8-inch enamel frying pan set over moderate heat, melt 2 tablespoons of the butter. When the foam subsides, add the lobster meat (dry the pieces first in paper toweling if they seem damp) and, stirring constantly, cook briskly for about 1 minute, then remove from the heat. Warm the cognac either in a ladle or a small saucepan, set it alight with a match, and pour it over the lobster. Shake the pan back and forth until the flame dies out. Transfer the lobster and any juices in the pan to a small bowl and reserve. Add the remaining 2 tablespoons of butter to the pan and sauté the chopped shallots or scallions for 1 minute, or until they are soft but not brown. Remove the pan from the heat and stir in the tomato paste and flour. Stir to a paste, then pour in, all at once, the chicken stock and white wine. Mix together briefly with a whisk to break up the flour particles, then bring the sauce to a boil over moderate heat, stirring almost constantly. It will be very thick. Simmer it over low heat for 1 or 2 minutes and thin it with the heavy cream, added a tablespoon at a time. Stir in the optional tomalley and coral, first rubbed through a sieve. Season with salt to taste, a few specks of cayenne, and the lemon juice. Return the cooked lobster to the sauce and set aside to be reheated when the soufflé is ready.

To prepare the soufflé, butter a 6-cup soufflé dish or charlotte mold. Sprinkle 2 tablepoons of the grated Parmesan into the dish, and tip it from side to side to coat its entire surface. Invert the dish and tap it smartly on the table to dislodge the excess cheese. Then preheat the oven to 400 degrees.

In a 2-quart saucepan melt 3 tablespoons of the butter, then, off the heat, stir in the 3 level tablespoons of flour. Mix to a smooth paste, pour over the milk, and beat briefly with a whisk to partially dissolve the flour. Return the pan to the heat and bring the sauce to a boil, stirring constantly, with the whisk. The sauce should be thick and smooth. Simmer for 1 or 2 minutes, then remove the sauce from the heat and beat in, one at a time, the 4 egg yolks. Add the salt, cayenne, the mustards, and ½ cup of the grated Parmesan and mix thoroughly.

Beat the egg whites (preferably with a balloon whisk in an unlined copper bowl) until they are stiff enough to grip the beater firmly and their small white peaks stand upright when the beater is lifted out of the bowl. Thoroughly mix 2 large spoonfuls of the whites into the warm (but not hot) cheese sauce, then, with the aid of a large rubber spatula, reverse the process and pour the sauce over the remaining egg whites in the bowl. Fold gently but thoroughly together until no streaks of white show through the batter; be particularly careful not to overfold or your soufflé will be heavy and lifeless. Pour the mixture into the soufflé dish, smooth the top (not too carefully) with a spatula, and sprinkle with the remaining 2 tablespoons of grated Parmesan. Turn the oven temperature down to 375 degrees and place the dish in the center of the oven. Bake for 30 or 40 minutes, depending upon whether you like your soufflé soft or firm. But always serve the soufflé the moment it is done, accompanied by a bowl of the lobster sauce, which should be reheated, without boiling, before you remove the soufflé from the oven.

Lobster and Celery Salad in Tarragon Mayonnaise

Serves 4–6

2 tablespoons tarragon white wine vinegar

6 tablespoons olive oil

½ teaspoon salt

⅛ teaspoon cayenne

2 cups cooked lobster meat, *cut into small chunks or rounds*

1 cup celery, *chilled and cut into julienne strips ½ inch by 1 inch*

1 cup freshly made mayonnaise (p. **218**) or an unsweetened commercial mayonnaise

1 tablespoon fresh tarragon, *finely chopped,* or 1½ teaspoons dried tarragon, *crumbled*

3–4 cups shredded salad greens: romaine, Boston, escarole, or chicory, *or in any combination of greens, washed, dried, and chilled*

2 hard-cooked eggs, *chilled and sliced*

2 tablespoons capers, *drained, washed, and dried*

In a small glass or stainless-steel bowl, mix together the vinegar, oil, salt, and cayenne. Add the cooked lobster meat, coat thoroughly, and marinate, covered and refrigerated, for about 1 hour.

When ready to serve, line a chilled glass bowl with the washed, thoroughly dried, and chilled salad greens. Drain and discard the marinade from the lobster, and combine the lobster meat, celery strips, and ½ cup of the mayonnaise. Spoon the mixture over the shredded greens. Cover with the remaining mayonnaise into which has been stirred the fresh or crumbled dried tarragon. Garnish with the sliced hard-cooked eggs, overlapping them around the edge of the bowl, and scatter the capers in the center. Serve at once on chilled plates.

▶◀

A Few Notes About Cooking Shrimp

Cook raw shrimp in their shells in boiling salted water to cover. Medium to large shrimp should take 5 minutes or less to cook through. If you remember that they should be firm, not soft, when done, it is unlikely that you will overcook them. Other than salt, dispense with such niceties as *court-bouillon,* commercial shrimp seasonings, herbs, spices, and the rest. However strong these flavorings may be, they will have little, if any, effect upon the shell-encased shrimp for the short time it takes to cook them. Plunge the cooked shrimp into cold water when they are done to stop their cooking, then shell and devein them. An ingenious shrimp sheller and deveiner available in most hardware stores will do the job quickly and easily. But lacking that, gently remove the segments of shrimp shell with your fingers, then make a shallow slit along the back of the shrimp with a small sharp knife and lift out the vein with the point of the knife. Refrigerate the shrimp at once.

Canned shrimp, although they come shelled, deveined, and cooked, have little to recommend them. They are almost always overcooked and have either no flavor at all or a pronounced fishy taste. If you must use them, the small bottled Icelandic or Danish shrimp are the best.

Cooked, shelled shrimp may be substituted successfully for the cooked lobster, sole, or salmon in the following recipes:

Parmesan Cheese Soufflé with Lobster Sauce, page 192

Lobster and Celery Salad in Tarragon Mayonnaise, page 194

Lobster Fritters with Curry Mayonnaise, page 191

Coquilles of Lobster, page 184

Lobster Newburgh, page 190

Small Lobster *Quiches,* page 183

Small Filled Egg Rolls in the Chinese Style, page 185

A *Paella* Sevillana, page 120

Lobster-Filled *Crêpes,* page 187

Chaussons of Sole, page 162

Dilled Fish Salad, page 169

Pickled Salmon, page 179

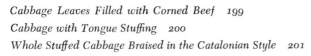

STUFFED VEGETABLES

Stuffed Vegetables

A stuffed vegetable can be only as good as its stuffing. Making a hollow shell of a vegetable in order to stuff it deprives it of much of its bulk and usually some of its character as well. Unless the stuffing can in some measure compensate for the loss, there is little reason to tamper with the vegetable in the first place.

The following recipes offer characteristic and, for the most part, traditional stuffings for those vegetables best suited to being stuffed: tomatoes, peppers, zucchini, potatoes, onions, turnips, mushrooms, eggplants, whole cabbages, individual cabbage leaves and grape leaves.

The essential ingredient of each of these stuffings is derived from one of the classic recipes described earlier in this book. Other ingredients may of course be substituted for the ones suggested and even the stuffing recipes interchanged at will. It is necessary to remember only that vegetable stuffings, to begin with, must be composed of wholly or at least partially cooked ingredients. Most vegetable cases cook through quickly and if forced to cook as long as a raw stuffing requires the vegetables would certainly be overcooked by the time the stuffing was finally done. Ideally, the vegetable and its stuffing should finish cooking at the same time.

Many stuffed vegetables can be served hot or cold with equal success. And to carry this a step further, cold, fully cooked preparations can be stuffed into any number of raw-vegetable cases and served without ever cooking them at all. Raw mushrooms, ripe tomatoes, small tender peppers, and young white turnips lend themselves especially well to this treatment and suitable stuffings for them are listed at the end of this section.

Cabbage Leaves Filled with Corned Beef

Serves 6–8

3-pound green cabbage
9 strips lean bacon
2 tablespoons butter
½ cup onions, *finely chopped*
⅓ cup raw long-grain rice
2 tablespoons parsley, *finely chopped.*

½ teaspoon salt
Freshly ground black pepper
2 cups cooked corned beef, *finely chopped*
1 egg, *lightly beaten*
2–3 cups beef bouillon, fresh or canned
Lemon wedges

Drop the whole cabbage into a large pot of boiling water and let it cook briskly for about 10 minutes. Remove the cabbage (let the water continue to boil) and carefully detach as many of the softened outer leaves as you can until it becomes difficult to separate them. Return the cabbage to the boiling water then and blanch it for a few minutes longer. Remove the cabbage and again detach as many more leaves as you can. Repeat this process until you have separated the whole cabbage into individual leaves. In the same boiling water blanch the 9 strips of bacon by dropping them into the pot and letting them simmer for about 8 minutes before draining them on paper toweling. Chop 5 of the strips finely, and reserve the other 4.

For the stuffing, melt the butter in a small heavy frying pan and sauté the onions over moderate heat for about 5 minutes or so until they are tender but not brown. Add the raw rice and stir it in the butter until the grains become opaque and milky-white. Take care not to let them brown or burn. Scrape the rice and onions into a large mixing bowl. Add the parsley, salt, and a few grindings of black pepper, the chopped bacon, corned beef, and the lightly beaten egg. Taste for seasoning.

Preheat the oven to 350 degrees. Lay the blanched cabbage leaves side by side and with a small knife trim the base of each leaf of its tough rib end. Place 1 teaspoon or more of the stuffing on each leaf (more, naturally, on the larger leaves) and roll them up tightly, tucking in the ends as if you were wrapping a small package. It isn't necessary to tie the rolls.

Choose a shallow baking pan just about large enough to hold the cabbage rolls compactly, and spread the 4 reserved slices of bacon along the bottom. Arrange the rolls on top, seam side down, pressing them as close together as you can. Pour into the pan enough of the beef bouillon to just about cover them (about 2 cups). Place an oven-proof dish on them to weight them down and cover the dish tightly with aluminum foil. Bring to a boil on top of the stove, then place the pan in the oven and bake for about 1½ hours, or until the cabbage leaves are soft to the touch. If, during this period, the bouillon has all cooked away, add 1 tablespoon more every now and then until the rolls are done. Serve hot as a main dish or cold as hors d'oeuvres accompanied by wedges of lemon.

Cabbage with Tongue Stuffing

Serves 6

12 tablespoons butter, 6 *for cooking the cabbage, 2 for the duxelles, and 4 melted for the sauce*

3 tablespoons shallots or scallions, *finely chopped*

¼ pound mushrooms, *finely chopped* (*1 cup*)

3 tablespoons Madeira

2½- or 3-pound firm green cabbage

½ cup onions, *finely chopped*

½ teaspoon garlic, *finely chopped*

1¼ cups cooked tongue, *finely chopped*

5 tablespoons bread crumbs

2–3 tablespoons parsley, *finely chopped*

2 whole eggs plus 1 additional yolk, *lightly beaten together*

1 teaspoon salt

Freshly ground black pepper

To prepare ½ cup of *duxelles*, melt 2 tablespoons of the butter in a small frying pan and add the chopped shallots or scallions. Sauté over moderate heat for about 1 minute without letting them color, then mix in the chopped mushrooms. Stirring every now and then, cook the mixture over low heat for about 10 minutes, or until the mushrooms are dry but not brown. Pour in the Madeira, raise the heat and, stirring constantly, cook the wine away entirely. Remove from the heat and put aside.

Line a 2- or 3-quart mixing bowl with a large linen dinner napkin, leaving the four corners hanging over the edges of the bowl. Carefully remove 5 or 6 large, unblemished leaves from the outside of the cabbage, and arrange them stem ends up in the napkin-lined bowl, their wide leaves overlapping, to form a large symmetrical cup.

Core the remaining whole cabbage and chop it as finely as you can. Melt 6 tablespoons of the butter in a large frying pan and sauté the chopped onions and garlic over moderate heat for about 5 minutes, or until they are soft but not colored. Stir in 3 cups of the chopped cabbage (use any remaining cabbage for another purpose), cover the pan, and cook over moderate heat for 20 minutes, stirring every now and then. The cabbage should be quite soft. Transfer it to a large mixing bowl and add the tongue, *duxelles,* bread crumbs, and 2 tablespoons of the parsley. Mix together gently but thoroughly, then stir in the 2 eggs and the additional yolk. Add the salt and a few grindings of pepper and taste for seasoning. Spoon the stuffing into the prepared cabbage cup. Bring the four corners of the napkin together over the stuffed cabbage and, lifting it up out of the bowl like a pouch, twist the corners and tie securely together with string, enclosing the cabbage in the napkin as tightly as possible.

Drop the cabbage in a pot of rapidly boiling salted water. Half cover the pan and, turning down the heat to its lowest point, let the cabbage simmer for about 1½ hours. Turn it completely over in the water from time to time.

The cabbage may remain in the hot water, off the heat, for at least ½ hour if it is not to be served immediately. To serve, transfer it to a large colander and let it drain for 5 minutes or so. Untie the string and carefully turn the cabbage out of the napkin onto a large heated platter. Let it drain for 1 or 2 minutes again and remove any liquid which accumulates around it. Pour over the cabbage the 4 tablespoons of hot melted butter and, if you wish, sprinkle the top with a little chopped parsley. Cut into wedges.

Whole Stuffed Cabbage Braised in the Catalonian Style

Serves 4

A firm green cabbage, about 2 pounds
Salt
1 tablespoon butter
¼ pound mildly cured salt pork, *finely chopped, as well as four 2-by-4-inch strips, cut about ½ inch thick*
2 tablespoons shallots or scallions, *finely chopped*
½ teaspoon garlic, *finely chopped*
1 small green pepper, *finely chopped (about ½ cup)*
2½ cups cold braised or boiled beef, *finely chopped*

¼ cup black olives (Greek variety, preferably), *finely chopped*
1 tablespoon tomato paste
3 tablespoons parsley, *finely chopped*
1 teaspoon dried oregano
Freshly ground black pepper
2 eggs, *lightly beaten*
1 large bay leaf
3 cups canned beef bouillon

Trim the cabbage of all discolored or coarse outside leaves, then blanch it—that is, drop the cabbage into a large pot of boiling salted water and boil it briskly, uncovered, for about 8 minutes. Lift the cabbage out (let the water in the pot continue to boil) and plunge it into a bowl of cold water. When the cabbage is cool enough to handle, without detaching the leaves from the stem, start carefully separating them one by one. As soon as the tightly packed leaves resist being pulled apart, return the cabbage to the boiling water, this time for about 3 or 4 minutes. Repeat the earlier process; you should now have no difficulty opening the cabbage like a large flower. Cut away the inner core, trim the outside stem down to its base, and the cabbage is now ready to be stuffed and reassembled.

To prepare the stuffing, in a small heavy frying pan slowly fry the finely chopped salt pork in the tablespoon of butter. Don't let the pork brown, but when it has rendered up most of its fat, stir into it the chopped shallots or scallions and the garlic. Cook for a few minutes until they soften without coloring, then add the green pepper. Cook a few minutes longer, then with a rubber spatula scrape the entire contents of the pan into a large mixing bowl. Add the chopped beef, black olives, tomato paste, 2 tablespoons of the chopped parsley (reserving the third for garnish), oregano, 1 teaspoon of salt, a few grindings of black pepper, and the lightly beaten eggs. Carefully but thoroughly stir the mixture together, making sure all the ingredients are well blended. Taste. It will very likely need more salt. Preheat the oven to 325 degrees.

Spread the stuffing in between and on the open leaves of the cabbage, distributing it as evenly as you can. Gently press the cabbage together into a reasonable facsimile of its original shape, and crisscross the 4 strips of salt pork over the top. With thin white cord tie the cabbage securely along its length and around its circumference, using as much cord as you need to keep the stuffing and pork strips in place.

Lay the cabbage gently in a casserole just about large and deep enough to hold it comfortably. Add the bay leaf, then pour around it the 3 cups of stock and quickly bring it to a boil on top of the stove. Remove it from the heat. Drape a buttered sheet of foil loosely around the top of the cabbage, cover the casserole tightly, and place it in the center of the oven. Braise slowly for about 3 hours, basting the cabbage every ½ hour or so with the stock in the casserole, replenishing it if it seems to be cooking away too rapidly. When the cabbage is done, it will be a golden brown with just enough stock left in the casserole for a sauce.

To serve, lift the cabbage from the casserole carefully and cut away the strings. Pour over the remaining braising sauce (reduce it somewhat if it seems excessive or lacking in flavor) and sprinkle the cabbage with the remaining tablespoon of chopped parsley. Cut into quarters.

This cabbage is delicious reheated, either on top of the stove or in the oven.

Stuffed Grape Leaves in the Armenian Style

Dolmades

Makes 26–30 rolls

30–5 grape leaves, preserved in brine, bottled or canned

5 tablespoons olive oil, 3 *for sautéing onions and garlic and 2 for cooking the rolls*

¾ cup onions, *finely chopped*

1 teaspoon garlic, *finely chopped*

½ cup raw long-grain rice

2 cups cooked lamb, *ground or finely chopped*

3 tablespoons pine nuts, *coarsely chopped* (optional)

1½ teaspoons salt

4 tablespoons parsley, *finely chopped*

½ teaspoon allspice

2 tablespoons lemon juice

Freshly ground black pepper

2 cups chicken stock, fresh or canned

2 lemons, *quartered or sliced* (if served cold)

Preserved grape leaves in jars or cans are generally available in fine food stores or in neighborhood Greek grocery stores that carry imported foods. Gently separate the leaves and blanch them by dropping a few at a time into boiling water; cook them vigorously for about 3 minutes. Lay the leaves side by side on paper toweling to drain.

To prepare the filling, sauté the chopped onions and garlic in 3 tablespoons of the olive oil for about 5 minutes, or until they are soft but not brown. Scrape them into a large mixing bowl. Blanch the ½ cup of rice by dropping it into 4 cups of salted boiling water and letting it boil briskly for 5 minutes. Drain through a sieve and plunge the rice into cold water to stop its cooking, then add to the mixing bowl. Stir in the lamb, optional pine nuts, salt, parsley, allspice, lemon juice, and a few grindings of black pepper. Taste for seasoning.

Arrange the vine leaves, glossy side down, on a table. Depending on the size of the leaf, place a teaspoon or more of the filling in the corner of each leaf and roll it up tightly, tucking in the ends as if you were wrapping a small parcel. If a few of the leaves are too small, as frequently happens, overlap another smallish one upon it and roll as before (tying is unnecessary).

To cook them, choose a shallow baking dish which will hold the rolls snugly in one layer. However, if you have no such dish, the rolls may be placed in two layers. Next pour the remaining 2 tablespoons of olive oil into the pan and fill it almost to the top of the rolls with chicken stock (about 2 cups). Preheat the oven to 350 degrees. Place a small platter or a couple of old plates on top of the rolls to keep them in place, then cover with a layer of aluminum foil, tucked in securely to the sides of the pan. Bring the stock to a boil on top of the stove, then place the pan in the center of the oven and bake the rolls for about 1 hour, by which time, all the stock will be absorbed, leaving only the olive oil. Serve the rolls hot, if you wish, with either cucumber-yoghurt sauce (p. 223) or lemon sauce (p. 221), but the *dolmades* are really at their best cold. Let them cool in the pan with the weight still in place. Before serving, brush each roll with a little olive oil and pass them with quarters or slices of lemon.

Stuffed Eggplant in the Italian Style

Serves 4

2 eggplants, about 6 inches long and 3 inches in diameter

4 teaspoons salt

½ cup olive oil, *4–5 tablespoons for sautéing onions, garlic, and eggplant, 4 teaspoons for topping, and the remaining oil for the stuffing mixture*

½ cup onions, *finely chopped*

1 teaspoon garlic, *finely chopped*

1 **cup cooked beef or veal,** *finely chopped*

1 tablespoon tomato paste

1 tablespoon capers, *drained, washed, and dried*

2 tablespoons parsley, *finely chopped*

1 teaspoon oregano

3 anchovy fillets, *drained, washed, dried, and finely chopped*

1 teaspoon salt

1 tablespoon bread crumbs

Freshly ground black pepper

5 tablespoons Parmesan cheese, *freshly grated, 3 for the stuffing and 2 for topping*

½ cup chicken stock, fresh or canned

Lemon quarters

Cut the unpeeled eggplants in half lengthwise and with a small sharp knife cut deep parallel gashes along their lengths about 1 inch apart, being careful not to cut through the skins. Cut similar gashes crosswise. Sprinkle each eggplant half with about 1 teaspoon of salt, turn them over on a double thickness of paper toweling, and let them drain for about ½ hour. Scoop out the soft pulp with a small spoon or sharp knife and be sure not to cut through the shell. Chop the pulp finely.

Heat 4 tablespoons of olive oil in a large heavy frying pan set over moderate heat, then add the chopped onions and garlic and sauté for about 8 minutes, or until they are soft and lightly colored. Add the eggplant pulp (drained of any excess liquid) and cook for a few minutes longer, adding 1 tablespoon or more of the oil if necessary to prevent it from sticking. Scrape the entire contents of the pan into a mixing bowl and add the meat, tomato paste, capers, parsley, oregano, anchovies, salt, bread crumbs, a few grindings of black pepper, and 3 tablespoons of the grated Parmesan. Mix together thoroughly, taste for seasoning (it should be quite sharply flavored), and spoon the stuffing into the eggplant shells, mounding it slightly.

Arrange the stuffed eggplant halves in a baking dish just about large enough to hold them, and sprinkle each half with 1 teaspoon of olive oil and the remaining 2 tablespoons of grated Parmesan. Pour around them the chicken stock and remaining olive oil. Cover the pan with aluminum foil and bake in the center of a preheated 375-degree oven for about 1 hour. Then remove the foil and bake for another 10 minutes to brown the top.

Although the stuffed eggplants are fine served hot, they are even better cold, served either alone or as part of an *antipasto*, but accompany them in either case with lemon quarters.

Baked Chicken-Stuffed Mushrooms

Serves 4

12 mushrooms, each about 2 inches in diameter

6 tablespoons butter, *1 melted and cooled for painting caps, 2 for sautéing, 2 softened for topping, cut into bits, and 1 for buttering pan*

2 tablespoons shallots or scallions, *finely chopped*

2 tablespoons Madeira

1 tablespoon parsley, *finely chopped*

1 tablespoon fresh tarragon, *finely chopped,* or 1 teaspoon dried tarragon

1 **cup cooked chicken or turkey,** *finely chopped*

5 tablespoons dried bread crumbs, *3 for stuffing and 2 for topping*

4 tablespoons heavy cream

Salt

⅛ teaspoon cayenne

2 tablespoons Parmesan cheese, *grated*

Carefully remove the stems from each mushroom by holding the cap securely in one hand and gently bending back the stem with the other until it snaps free. If any part of the stem still adheres to the inside of the cap, cut it away with the point of a sharp knife. Under no circumstances wash the caps or the stems, but if you wish, you may gently wipe the mushrooms with a lightly dampened towel.

Chop the mushroom stems as fine as you can and put them aside. Paint the inside of each cap with about ¼ teaspoon of melted and cooled butter.

Melt 2 tablespoons of the butter in a small frying pan and when the foam subsides add the chopped shallots or scallions. Sauté for 3 minutes or so without letting them brown, then add the chopped mushroom stems. Stir constantly over fairly high heat until the mushroom pieces give off all their moisture and turn lightly brown. Pour in the Madeira and cook it rapidly away. Scrape the entire contents of the pan into a small mixing bowl and combine with the parsley, tarragon, chicken, and 3 tablespoons of the bread crumbs. Moisten with the heavy cream, adding it a little at a time; if it seems dry, add a little more cream (the stuffing should hold its shape yet be pliable). Season with salt to taste and the cayenne.

Stuff the mushroom caps, mounding the tops slightly. Combine the grated Parmesan with the remaining bread crumbs and sprinkle each cap with a little of the mixture and dot with small bits of the softened butter. Arrange the caps side by side in a heavy shallow baking pan, which you have buttered.

When you are ready to serve the caps—they make fine hors d'oeuvres or a light luncheon dish—preheat the oven to 375 degrees. Bake in the center of the oven for about 15 minutes, or until the caps are tender. Slide under the broiler briefly to brown the tops before serving.

Baked Onions Stuffed with Veal and Spinach

Serves 6

6 large onions, preferably the Bermuda or Spanish types, but yellow globes will do

8 tablespoons butter, *4 for sautéing and 4 melted for topping the onions and the stock*

1 teaspoon garlic, *finely chopped*

½ cup (packed down) cooked fresh spinach, *finely chopped,* or 1 package frozen spinach, *thoroughly defrosted and finely chopped*

1 **cup braised veal or beef,** *ground or finely chopped*

¼ cup plus 2 tablespoons dry bread crumbs

4–6 tablespoons heavy cream

Salt

Freshly ground black pepper

2 tablespoons Parmesan cheese, *grated*

½ cup chicken stock, fresh or canned

Drop the unpeeled onions into a pan of boiling water to cover and cook briskly for about 10 minutes. Drain the onions and plunge them into cold water to stop their cooking. Carefully peel them, starting at the root end, and cut away the short stem end, if any, with scissors. Cut a

1-inch slice off the root end of each onion and with a large fork pull out the centers of the onions leaving a hollow cup composed of the last 2 or 3 layers of the onion. Chop the scooped-out onion pulp as fine as you can.

Melt 4 tablespoons of the butter in a large heavy frying pan and cook the onion pulp over moderate heat until all its moisture has evaporated and it has begun to color. Add the garlic. Squeeze the spinach dry—a handful at a time—chop it finely, and mix it into the onion pulp and garlic. Cook over high heat, stirring constantly, until the spinach is as dry as you can get it without letting it burn. Scrape the spinach mixture into a large mixing bowl. Add the veal (or beef) and ¼ cup of the bread crumbs, mixing well with a large fork. Moisten with 4 tablespoons of the cream, and if the mixture seems too dry add 1 or 2 tablespoons more. Season highly with salt and freshly ground pepper and pack tightly into the waiting onion cups. Mound the tops slightly, combine the remaining 2 tablespoons of bread crumbs with the grated Parmesan, and sprinkle the mixture over the onion tops. Arrange the onions in a shallow baking pan just large enough to hold them compactly. Pour around them the chicken stock. Moisten each onion top with ½ teaspoon of melted butter and add the remaining melted butter to the stock. Preheat the oven to 375 degrees.

Cover the pan with either a lid or thick sheet of aluminum foil and bake the onions in the center of the oven for about 30 minutes. Remove the lid or foil and cook uncovered for another 15 minutes, or until the onions are tender and their tops lightly browned. Before serving, slide under the broiler briefly and serve alone or with lemon sauce (p. 221), to which you have added 1 tablespoon of finely chopped parsley.

Stuffed Baked Potatoes Parmentier

Serves 4

4 baking potatoes, 5 or 6 inches long, weighing about ½ pound each

⅜ pound butter, *4 teaspoons softened for buttering potatoes, 1 tablespoon softened for buttering shells, 4 tablespoons softened for mashing pulp, 3 tablespoons for sautéing onions, 1 tablespoon for buttering pan, and 1 tablespoon softened for topping*

3 tablespoons heavy cream

1 teaspoon salt

Freshly ground black pepper

¾ cup onions, *finely chopped*

1½ cups cooked beef or veal, *free of all fat and gristle and cut into ⅛-inch dice*

3 tablespoons white wine vinegar

1 tablespoon parsley, *finely chopped*

2 tablespoons bread crumbs

Preheat the oven to 425 degrees. Wash and dry the potatoes and rub each one with about 1 teaspoon of softened butter so that their skins will remain soft and pliable after they are baked. If possible, bake them on a rack to allow the air to circulate around them in the oven. It should take about 40 minutes to cook the potatoes through, but test by pressing them gently between your thumb and forefinger. When they yield to the pressure quite readily, they are done.

Lay the potatoes flat and with a small sharp knife slice the peel from their tops. Remove all the pulp from the potatoes with a spoon and place it in a mixing bowl. Brush the inside of each potato boat with 1 teaspoon of softened butter and put them aside. While the potato pulp is still hot, force it through a ricer, then beat in 4 tablespoons of softened butter and 3 table-spoons of heavy cream. The mashed potatoes should be creamy and absolutely free of lumps. Season with the salt and freshly ground pepper.

Melt 3 tablespoons of the butter in a small heavy frying pan and sauté the chopped onions over moderate heat for about 10 minutes, or until they are soft and lightly colored. Add the diced beef or veal and, stirring almost constantly, cook it for a few minutes to brown it lightly, then add the vinegar. Raise the heat and, stirring constantly, let the vinegar cook completely away. Scrape the entire contents of the pan into the bowl of mashed potatoes, add the chopped parsley, and mix together gently but thoroughly. Taste for seasoning, then with a small spoon fill each potato boat as fully and as compactly as possible, mounding the top of each one. Arrange them in a shallow buttered baking pan, sprinkle the tops of the potatoes with a few bread crumbs, and dot with the remaining tablespoon of softened butter.

Bake the potatoes in a preheated 400-degree oven for about 15 minutes. They should be lightly browned on top. If they are not, brown them briefly under the broiler before serving.

Stuffed Baked Potatoes Provençale

Serves 6

6 baking potatoes, 5 or 6 inches long

5 tablespoons olive oil, *2 for sautéing vegetables and 3 for greasing potatoes and pan*

3 tablespoons butter, *1 for sautéing vegetables and 2 melted for greasing potatoes and pan*

½ cup onions, *finely chopped*

⅓ cup green peppers, *finely chopped*

½ teaspoon garlic, *finely chopped*

1 pound fresh tomatoes, *peeled, seeded, and coarsely chopped*

½ cup (firmly packed) cooked ham or tongue, *finely chopped*

1 teaspoon paprika
1 tablespoon parsley, *finely chopped*
Salt
Freshly ground black pepper

½ cup fresh bread crumbs
Small dish of melted butter
Fresh chives, *finely cut*

Peel the 6 potatoes with a rotary peeler and slice a thin sliver off the bottom of each so that they will sit solidly without wobbling. With a small sharp knife hollow them out, leaving a boatlike shell about ½ inch thick all around. They should look like small canoes. Blanch them by plunging them into lightly salted boiling water; cook them briskly for about 3 minutes. Drain at once and dry with paper toweling.

Combine 2 tablespoons of the olive oil with 1 tablespoon of the butter in a 6- or 8-inch frying pan. Heat slowly, then add the chopped onions, peppers, and garlic. Sauté for a few moments without letting them brown, then mix in the thoroughly drained chopped tomatoes. Raise the heat and, stirring almost constantly, cook rapidly until all the moisture has evaporated. Take care not to let it burn. Remove the pan from the heat and stir in the ham or tongue, paprika, parsley, and as much salt and freshly ground pepper as you think it needs.

Combine the remaining olive oil and butter. With a soft pastry brush paint the potatoes inside and out with a little of the butter-oil mixture, reserving the rest. Fill the potato boats with the meat and vegetable stuffing and mound the tops slightly. Arrange the potatoes side by side in a baking pan which has been brushed lightly with some of the butter-oil, and pour the remainder of the mixture around them. Bring the pan to a sizzle on top of the stove, cover loosely with either a lid or a sheet of aluminum foil, and place the pan in the lower third of a preheated 425-degree oven. Bake for about ½ hour, then remove the cover and scatter the bread crumbs over the potatoes, allowing the excess to fall around the potatoes and into the pan. Baste periodically with the fat in the baking dish and continue cooking the potatoes, uncovered, until they are tender and brown. When they are done, you should be able to pierce the sides of the potatoes easily with a small knife, but be careful not to overcook them or they will collapse. Serve with a small dish of melted butter mixed with finely cut fresh chives.

Baked Lamb-Stuffed Tomatoes and Peppers

Serves 4

4 medium-sized firm ripe tomatoes
Salt
4 small or 2 large green peppers
6 tablespoons butter, *3 for sautéing, 1 softened for buttering dish, and 2 softened for dotting top of tomatoes and peppers*
½ cup onions, *finely chopped*
½ teaspoon garlic, *finely chopped*
1½ cups cooked rice (½ cup raw rice cooked)

2 cups braised or roast lamb, *finely chopped or ground*
Freshly ground black pepper
4 tablespoons parsley, *finely chopped*
2 teaspoons lemon juice
1 egg, *lightly beaten*
2 tablespoons bread crumbs
½ cup chicken stock, fresh or canned

Prepare the tomatoes for stuffing by cutting a thin slice off their stem ends, then hollowing out each tomato with a small spoon. Sprinkle the inside of each with about ¼ teaspoon of salt (which will draw out its juices) and invert them on paper toweling to drain for about 15 minutes or so. If the peppers are large, cut them in half lengthwise, remove the seeds, and cut away the thick inner white ribs. Smaller peppers can be stuffed whole; cut a thin slice off the stem end of each and remove the seeds and white ribs. However the peppers are cut, blanch them by dropping them into boiling water and letting them cook briskly for 5 to 8 minutes. Then plunge them at once into cold water to stop their cooking.

To prepare the filling, sauté the onions and garlic in 3 tablespoons of the butter for about 5 minutes, or until they are soft but not brown. Then combine them in a small bowl with the cooked rice, the lamb, 1 teaspoon of salt, pepper to taste, the lemon juice, and the lightly beaten egg. Taste for seasoning. Fill the tomatoes and peppers with this mixture and arrange them side by side in a buttered shallow baking dish just about large enough to hold them. Sprinkle the stuffed vegetables with bread crumbs and dot with small bits of the remaining softened butter. Pour the chicken stock into the pan and bake in the center of a preheated 375-degree oven for about 20 minutes, or until the vegetables are tender but not falling apart. Slide briefly under the broiler to brown the tops lightly before serving.

Braised Stuffed Turnips with Duck Risotto

Serves 4

10–12 medium firm white turnips, all approximately the same size

4 cups chicken stock, fresh or canned

5 tablespoons butter, *2 for sautéing onions, 1½ softened for mixing with duck, and 1½ softened for topping*

⅓ cup onions, *finely chopped*

2 tablespoons beef marrow (optional), *chopped*

1 cup raw rice (not the converted type)

¼ cup dry white wine

⅛ teaspoon saffron, *powdered*

¾–1 cup braised duck, *coarsely chopped or shredded*

⅔ cup Parmesan cheese, *freshly grated*

To prepare the turnips for stuffing, peel them with a rotary peeler and remove their root ends. With a small sharp knife cut out their centers, then use a teaspoon to help shape and scrape the insides of the turnips into smooth, hollow bowls about 1 inch thick. Blanch the hollowed-out turnips by dropping them into salted boiling water and letting them cook briskly for about 6 minutes. Don't let them get too soft. Plunge them at once into cold water to stop their cooking and dry them inside and out with paper toweling.

In a small pan bring the stock to a simmer and keep it simmering as slowly as possible while you prepare the *risotto* base. Melt 2 tablespoons of the butter in a 2- or 3-quart heavy baking pan or casserole. Add the chopped onions and sauté them slowly for about 5 minutes without letting them brown. Stir in the optional beef marrow, cook for a moment or two to partially dissolve it, and then add the raw rice. Cook over moderate heat, stirring constantly, for about 2 minutes, or until the rice turns opaque. Pour over the white wine and cook it completely away; this will take only a few seconds. Add 1 cup of the simmering stock and let the rice cook over moderate heat, stirring occasionally, until the liquid is almost completely absorbed. Add another cup of the stock, this time mixed with the powdered saffron. When this has been absorbed, reduce the heat somewhat and add ½ cup more of stock and ½ cup more after that, if necessary, cooking and stirring until the *risotto* is tender and creamy (about 16 to 18 minutes). Add the duck meat and 1½ tablespoons of the softened butter. Stir gently with two forks until the butter is absorbed, then stir in ½ cup of the grated Parmesan. Taste for seasoning.

Preheat the oven to 350 degrees. Stuff the turnips with the *risotto,* mounding the tops slightly and sprinkling each one with a little grated cheese. Dot with the remaining 1½ tablespoons of softened butter and arrange the stuffed turnips side by side in a baking dish just about large enough to hold them. Pour into the dish the remaining cup of simmering stock (there should be enough to come one third of the way up the sides of the turnips—add more stock, if it doesn't), and bring it to a boil on top of the stove. Cover the pan tightly with a lid or aluminum foil and bake the turnips in the center of the oven for about 15 minutes, then remove the cover and cook for 5 or 10 minutes longer, basting the sides of the vegetables every now and then with stock in the pan. Serve the turnips sauced with the braising liquid.

Baked Zucchini Stuffed with Lamb, Rice, and Pine Nuts

Serves 6

6–8 zucchini, about 6 inches long
Salt
4–6 tablespoons olive oil
½ cup onions, *finely chopped*
1 teaspoon garlic, *finely chopped*
1½ cups cooked rice (½ cup raw rice cooked)
2 cups braised or roast lamb, *ground or finely chopped*
3 tablespoons fine nuts

3 tablespoons parsley, *finely chopped*
½ teaspoon oregano
2 teaspoons lemon juice
4 tablespoons bread crumbs, *2 for the stuffing and 2 for the topping*
1 egg, *lightly beaten*
Freshly ground black pepper
2 tablespoons butter, *softened and cut into bits*
½ cup chicken stock, fresh or canned

Scrub the zucchini under warm running water with a stiff brush to remove any wax coating. Cut the zucchini lengthwise and with a small knife cut parallel gashes along their lengths about 1 inch apart, but take care not to cut through the skins. Cut similar gashes crosswise. Sprinkle each zucchini half with about ½ teaspoon of salt, then turn the zucchini over onto a double thickness of paper toweling and let them drain for about ½ hour. Scoop out the zucchini with a small teaspoon and chop the pulp finely and put it aside. With a pastry brush paint the inside of each zucchini shell with a little olive oil (about 1 tablespoon all in all).

Heat 3 tablespoons of the oil in a small heavy frying pan set over moderate heat. Add the chopped onions and garlic and sauté for about 8 minutes, or until they are soft and lightly colored. Add the zucchini pulp, drained of any liquid, and cook a few minutes longer, adding 1 tablespoon or more of the oil if necessary to prevent it from sticking. Scrape the entire contents of the pan into a mixing bowl and add the rice, lamb, pine nuts, parsley, oregano, lemon juice, 2 tablespoons of the bread crumbs, and the lightly beaten egg. Mix together gently but thoroughly and season to taste with salt and freshly ground black pepper. Spoon this into the zucchini shells, mounding the stuffing slightly. Sprinkle the halves with bread crumbs and dot with small bits of the butter. Arrange the zucchini side by side in a shallow baking pan just about large enough to hold them. Pour the chicken stock into the pan. The stock should come up about one third of the way up the side of the vegetables; if it doesn't, add a little more stock.

Preheat the oven to 375 degrees and bake the zucchini in the center of the oven for about 20 minutes, or long enough for the zucchini to become tender without falling apart. Slide briefly under the broiler to brown the tops just before serving. Although the vegetables may be served as they are or with lemon quarters, a fine embellishment would be the lemon sauce on page 221.

Cold Stuffed Raw Vegetables

Mushroom Caps   Prepare the mushrooms for stuffing as described on page 205, then fill with any of the following stuffings, mounding the tops slightly:

Pâté of Pot Roast, page 36

Ham *Mousse*, page 96

Pâté of Corned Beef, page 109

Duck *Pâté*, page 154

Salmon Chive *Pâté*, page 172

Cold Salmon *Mousse*, page 179

Roast Beef *Tartare* (omit garnish), page 26

Tomatoes   Prepare the tomatoes for stuffing as described on page 210. Sprinkle the hollows with salt and let them drain inverted for at least ½ hour before filling with any of the following stuffings:

Pickled Beef in the Italian Style (cubed instead of sliced), page 10

Cold Boiled Beef and *Salsa Verde* (cubed instead of sliced), page 11

A Salad of Celery Root and Roast Beef, page 27

Vitello Tonnato (*pollo* or *lingue*) (cubed instead of sliced), page 67

Veal and Herring Salad in the Scandinavian Style, page 69

Veal, Anchovy, and Watercress Salad, page 70

Chicken, Raw Mushroom, and Rice Salad, page 126

Turkey Mayonnaise and Rice Salad, page 149

Pickled Salmon, page 179

Dilled Fish Salad (sole or salmon), page 169

Lobster and Celery Salad in Tarragon Mayonnaise, page 194

Peppers   Prepare the peppers (preferably small green ones) for stuffing as described on page 210 but don't blanch them. Fill with any of the following stuffings:

Any of the stuffings suggested for stuffed to-matoes

Tongue *Mousse* with Mustard Mayonnaise (pack into peppers instead of into metal mold), page 104

Cold Pork and Fennel Salad, page 81

Ham *Mousse*, page 96

Corned Beef *Mousse*, page 112

French Potato Salad with Julienned Corned Beef, page 112

Duck, Orange, and Red Onion Salad, page 157

Cold Salmon *Mousse*, page 179

Turnips   Prepare the turnips (which should be very young, firm, and white) as described on page 211. Don't blanch them but soak them in ice water for about 15 minutes before drying them thoroughly and filling them with any of the following stuffings:

A Salad of Celery Root and Roast Beef in Mustard Mayonnaise, page 27

Pâté of Pot Roast, page 36

Chicken, Raw Mushroom, and Rice Salad, page 126

Duck *Pâté*, page 154

Notes

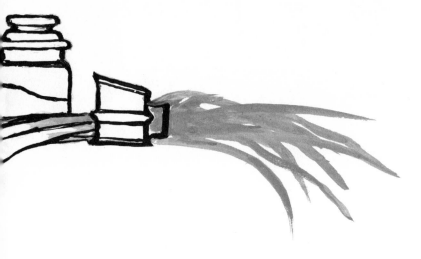

SAUCES

SAUCES

Mayonnaise

Makes 2 cups

3 large eggs (yolks only)
1 teaspoon salt
½ teaspoon English dry mustard or prepared mustard

1 tablespoon white wine vinegar or lemon juice
1½ cups olive oil or vegetable oil or a combination of both in any proportion
2 tablespoons boiling water

To ensure the success of your mayonnaise, the egg yolks should be at room temperature and the bowl in which they are to be beaten rinsed in hot water and dried.

With a whisk, rotary beater, or an electric mixer beat the egg yolks steadily for about 2 minutes until they thicken and cling to the beater. Add the salt, mustard, and vinegar or lemon juice and beat about 1 minute longer. Still beating, add ½ teaspoon of the oil. When it is fully absorbed, add another ½ teaspoon and continue beating and adding oil in this fashion until ½ cup of oil has been used. By now the mixture will have thickened sufficiently to allow you to pour the oil into the mayonnaise in a slow, steady stream. When the last of the oil has been used, beat in the boiling water, 1 tablespoon at a time. Taste for seasoning.

Note: Should the mayonnaise at any point separate, beat an egg yolk with 1 teaspoon of prepared mustard in a clean bowl for 1 minute or so, then beat the separated mayonnaise into it, 1 teaspoon at a time. This procedure never fails.

Mayonnaise Fines Herbes

Makes 2 cups

2 cups mayonnaise, freshly made or a good, un-sweetened commercial brand
2 tablespoons parsley, *finely chopped*

1 teaspoon chives, *finely chopped*
1 tablespoon fresh tarragon, basil, or dill, *finely chopped*

Beat into the mayonnaise the parsley, chives, and choice of other herb. Taste for seasoning.

Curry Mayonnaise

Makes 2 cups

2 tablespoons good curry powder
1 teaspoon lemon juice

2 cups mayonnaise, freshly made or a good, un-sweetened commercial brand

In a small bowl combine the curry powder and lemon juice and stir it to a paste. Little by little beat it into the mayonnaise. If the mayonnaise doesn't seem aromatic enough to your taste (commercial curry powders vary enormously in intensity), add more curry powder mixed with a few drops of lemon juice.

Mustard Mayonnaise

Makes 1½ cups

1 cup mayonnaise, freshly made or a good, un-sweetened commercial brand

½ cup prepared mustard
Lemon juice (optional)

Beat into the mayonnaise the ½ cup of mustard, about 1 tablespoon at a time. Season to taste with a little lemon juice if you think it needs it.

Hollandaise Sauce

Makes
1½ cups

¼ pound sweet butter, *softened and cut into small pieces*
3 eggs (yolks only)
1 tablespoon sweet butter, *cold*

1 tablespoon heavy cream, *cold*
Salt
Freshly ground white pepper
1 tablespoon lemon juice

Melt the ¼ pound of sweet butter in a small pan set over low heat, but do not let it brown. Then keep it warm near the heat. In another small enamel or stainless-steel saucepan beat the 3 egg yolks with a wire whisk for about 2 minutes until they thicken. Place the eggs over moderate heat and add the tablespoon of cold butter. Stir constantly with a whisk until the eggs begin to thicken and the butter is absorbed. Raise the pan from the heat every few seconds to cool it slightly, then whisk over heat again. Be careful not to let the pan get too hot or the eggs will curdle. When the eggs have thickened enough to cling to the whisk, remove the pan from the heat and beat in the tablespoon of cold heavy cream. Now off the heat, start beating in the warm melted butter 1 teaspoon or so at a time, then, as the sauce begins to thicken, pour it in a thin steady stream, constantly beating. When all the butter has been incorporated, the hollandaise should be smooth, shiny, and thick. Season to taste with salt and freshly ground white pepper, then beat in the lemon juice, adding more than the suggested amount if you prefer.

If the hollandaise is not to be used at once, cover the pan tightly with plastic wrap and set it in a bowl of warm, not hot, water. It will keep this way safely for at least an hour. If the water cools too much during this period, replenish it with more warm water from time to time. Lest you worry about the sauce becoming too cool as it rests it is well to remember that hollandaise (and béarnaise, too) should never be served hot, but warm.

Mustard Hollandaise

Makes 1½ cups

1½ cups hollandaise sauce
2 teaspoons prepared mustard

Lemon juice (optional)

Prepare the hollandaise as described in the previous recipe and then beat in the mustard. Taste for seasoning, and add a little lemon juice if you think it needs it.

Béarnaise Sauce

Makes 2 cups

¼ cup tarragon white wine vinegar
¼ cup dry white wine
1 tablespoon shallots or scallions, *finely chopped*
2 tablespoons fresh tarragon, *chopped,* or 2 teaspoons dried tarragon and 1 tablespoon parsley, *finely chopped*

1½ cups hollandaise sauce, omitting the lemon juice
Salt
White pepper
Lemon juice (optional)

In a small enamel or stainless-steel saucepan, combine the vinegar, white wine, shallots or scallions, and 1 tablespoon of the fresh tarragon or 1 teaspoon of the dried. Bring to a boil, then reduce the heat and simmer, uncovered, until the liquid has reduced to 2 tablespoons or a little less. Strain through a fine sieve, pressing down hard on the herbs with a spoon to extract all their liquid before throwing them away.

Make the hollandaise sauce as described in the master recipe, but in place of the lemon juice beat in the warm reduced tarragon-flavored liquid 1 tablespoon at a time. Season to taste with salt, white pepper, and now, add a few drops of lemon juice if you wish. Then gently stir into the finished béarnaise the remaining tablespoon of chopped fresh tarragon or 1 teaspoon of dried tarragon plus 1 tablespoon of chopped parsley. If the béarnaise is not to be used immediately, keep it warm in the same manner as described for the hollandaise sauce.

Lemon Sauce

Avgolemono

Makes 1½ cups

3 eggs (yolks only)
1 tablespoon arrowroot
1 teaspoon salt
⅛ teaspoon cayenne
1 cup chicken stock, fresh or canned, *cold*

1 tablespoon lemon juice
1 tablespoon parsley, fresh dill, or fresh tarragon, *finely chopped*
1–2 tablespoons heavy cream (optional)

In the top of a double boiler combine the egg yolks, the level tablespoon of arrowroot, the salt, and cayenne. Beat together lightly with a whisk and stir in the chicken stock. Beating constantly, cook directly over moderate heat until the sauce begins to thicken. If it forms small lumps—as it often does at this point—beat vigorously with a whisk off the heat, then return the pan to the heat and continue to whisk until the sauce thickens sufficiently to cling heavily to the beater. Don't under any circumstances allow the sauce to come to a boil or it may curdle. Stir in the lemon juice and the chopped herb. If the sauce seems too thick, thin it with a little extra chicken stock or even 1 or 2 tablespoons of heavy cream and add a few more drops of lemon juice.

The sauce may be kept warm, if it must wait, by placing the pan over hot, but not boiling, water. Should the sauce cool too much reheat it over direct heat, stirring constantly and again being careful not to let it come to a boil at any point.

Dill and Caper Sauce

Makes 1½ cups

2 tablespoons butter
2 tablespoons flour
1 cup chicken stock, fresh or canned
1 egg (yolk only)
¼ cup heavy cream
2 tablespoons capers, *drained, washed, dried, and coarsely chopped*

¼ teaspoon lemon juice
1 tablespoon fresh dill, *finely chopped*
Salt
⅛ teaspoon cayenne

In a small saucepan set over moderate heat melt the butter until it has completely dissolved but not browned. Off the heat, stir in the 2 level tablespoons of flour and mix to a paste. Add the chicken stock, hot or cold, and beat briefly together with a whisk before returning the pan to the heat. Continually whisking, cook the sauce over moderate heat until it begins to thicken. When it reaches the boiling point and becomes quite smooth, turn down the heat and simmer the sauce slowly for a moment or two to remove any taste of raw flour. Meanwhile combine the egg yolk with the ¼ cup of cream. Stir into this 3 tablespoons of the hot sauce, then reverse the process and pour the heated cream slowly into the sauce in the pan, stirring constantly. Let it come to a boil, then remove the pan from the heat at once. Stir in the capers, lemon juice, dill, salt, and cayenne. Taste for seasoning and serve.

Cucumber-Yoghurt Sauce

Makes 2½ cups
1 cup cucumber, *peeled, seeded, and coarsely chopped* (about two 6-inch cucumbers)
1 teaspoon salt
2 teaspoons white wine vinegar

2 cups unflavored yoghurt
2 tablespoons fresh dill, *finely chopped*
¼ teaspoon cayenne

Peel the cucumbers and slice them neatly in half lengthwise, then run a small spoon down the center of each half and scoop out the seeds and soft pulp. Chop the cucumbers coarsely and mix them in a small bowl with the salt and vinegar. Let them marinate for at least 1 hour.* Drain them of all their liquid (there will be a surprising amount) and pat them dry with paper toweling.

Combine the cucumbers in a small bowl with the yoghurt and fresh dill and season highly with the cayenne. It is unlikely that the sauce will need any more salt but taste and add some if it does. Chill before serving.

* *Note:* If you plan to mix and serve the sauce immediately after making it, marinating the cucumbers with the salt and vinegar is unnecessary.

Index

A NOTE
ABOUT THE
AUTHOR Michael Field has taught, lectured, demonstrated, and written about cooking for more than ten years now. As a result he has been constantly confronted in his classes and through readers' queries with the problems of women—and men—who cook every day, and it was their needs that sparked the idea for this book. Mr. Field, who was born in New York City, started his career as a concert pianist and became internationally known as a member of the duo piano team of Appleton and Field. Recently the culinary arts have usurped all of his time; he teaches weekly classes at his own school, contributes articles almost every month to *McCall's* magazine and frequently to *Holiday* and *The New York Review of Books,* and is the consulting editor for the Time-Life Foods of the World series. His first book, *Michael Field's Cooking School,* was published in 1965. He and his family—his wife, Frances, and seventeen-year-old son Jonathan—make their home in New York City.

A NOTE ON
THE TYPE The text of this book is set in Caledonia, a typeface designed by W(illiam) A(ddison) Dwiggins for the Mergenthaler Linotype Company in 1939. Dwiggins chose to call his new typeface Caledonia, the Roman name for Scotland, because it was inspired by the Scotch types cast about 1833 by Alexander Wilson & Son, Glasgow type founders. However, there is a calligraphic quality about this face that is totally lacking in the Wilson types. Dwiggins referred to an even earlier typeface for this "liveliness of action" —one cut around 1790 by William Martin for the printer William Bulmer. Caledonia has more weight than the Martin letters, and the bottom finishing strokes (serifs) of the letters are cut straight across, without brackets, to make sharp angles with the upright stems, thus giving a "modern face" appearance.

W. A. DWIGGINS (1880–1956) was born in Martinsville, Ohio, and studied art in Chicago. In 1904 he moved to Hingham, Massachusetts, where he built a solid reputation as a designer of advertisements and as a calligrapher. He began an association with the Mergenthaler Linotype Company in 1929, and over the next twenty-seven years designed a number of book types for that firm. Of especial interest are the Metro series, Electra, Caledonia, Eldorado, and Falcon. In 1930, Dwiggins first became interested in marionettes, and through the years made many important contributions to the art of puppetry and the design of marionettes.